MW01196757

EXPERIMENTS IN EGYPTIAN ARCHAEOLOGY

In this new edition of *Experiments in Egyptian Archaeology*, Denys A. Stocks introduces further experimental research on stoneworking in Ancient Egypt through archaeological and pictorial evidence.

A further 20 years of research has been added to the original publication and the book now includes the results of experiments that test and evaluate over 250 reconstructed and replica tools, bringing alive the methods and practices of Ancient Egyptian craftworking. This practical approach to understanding the fundamentals of Ancient Egyptian stoneworking highlights the evolution of tools and techniques, and how these come together to produce the wonders of Egyptian art and architecture. A new chapter on Predynastic industrial transitions and convergence explores how the surge in technology, particularly in the expanding production of stone vessels and in the production of faience artifacts, drove the expansion of the economy of the Late Predynastic period in Egypt.

Introducing the results of new research to enrich our understanding of the fundamental development of stoneworking, and other supporting technologies in Ancient Egypt, this book remains an important volume for students and researchers wishing to understand Ancient Egyptian technology and development.

Denys A. Stocks is an experimental archaeologist who uses his training in mechanical engineering, together with his experience in teaching high school design and technology, to interpret Ancient Egypt's technical capability. His research interests include the technological similarities between Egypt, Mesopotamia, Minoan Crete and the Indus Valley.

EXPERIMENTS IN EGYPTIAN ARCHAEOLOGY

Stoneworking Technology in Ancient Egypt

Second Edition

Denys A. Stocks

Routledge
Taylor & Francis Group

LONDON AND NEW YORK

Cover image: The northern face of Khufu's Fourth Dynasty Great Pyramid, the only face with a few base casing-blocks still in their original positions. © Denys A. Stocks

Second edition published 2023
by Routledge
4 Park Square, Milton Park, Abingdon, Oxon, OX14 4RN

and by Routledge
605 Third Avenue, New York, NY 10158

Routledge is an imprint of the Taylor & Francis Group, an informa business

© 2023 Denys A. Stocks

First edition published by Routledge 2003

British Library Cataloguing-in-Publication Data
A catalogue record for this book is available from the British Library

Library of Congress Cataloging-in-Publication Data
A catalog record for this book has been requested

ISBN: 978-1-032-21766-6 (hbk)
ISBN: 978-1-032-21757-4 (pbk)
ISBN: 978-1-003-26992-2 (ebk)

DOI: 10.4324/9781003269922

Typeset in Bembo
by Apex CoVantage, LLC

To My Wife, Carol, and Sons, Jeffrey, Ian and Paul

CONTENTS

TABLES

FIGURES

FOREWORD

Progressive demystification is one way I might characterize my 30 years of archaeological inquiry into the culture of Ancient Egypt. Dorothy found that the great and powerful Wizard of Oz, with all his mystery, sound and fury, was really the little man behind the curtain. Similarly the mystery and magic of Ancient Egypt, the mighty monuments built for gods and royalty, veil the lives and labour of real people. The more carefully we look at the details of gigantic pyramids and elegantly poised hundred-ton obelisks, the more they show themselves as very human monuments. At the same time, the deeper is our sense of awe and appreciation for how these real people marshalled labour and resources to create icons with such other-worldly perfection.

'But, in spite of all you have learned', said one of my New Age friends and partisans of alternative archaeology, 'you Egyptologists have never solved how the Ancient Egyptians worked granite'. It is true that how they cut, carved and drilled granite, one of the hardest stones, to produce beautifully polished colossal sculpture, sarcophagi and precisely etched hieroglyphs, has remained one of the more defiant puzzles of their culture.

After he reflected on minute details of Ancient Egyptian granite work, Sir Flinders Petrie concluded that the Ancient Egyptian masons used saws and drills of copper or bronze studded with hard stones like diamonds, beryl and corundum. But these hard cutting materials are scarcely known, or are absent in Egypt. The modern archaeologist has immediately to wonder about foreign sources, procurement and trade networks that such materials would imply, especially given the scale of work in granite and other hard stone at all times in Ancient Egypt. Other scholars suggested sand, all too common in the deserts flanking Egypt, as the cutting agent. Yet others responded that sand could never produce the details we see in ancient saw cuts, and drill holes through the hardest stones that the Egyptian craftsman worked with such aplomb.

In March 1999, I was fortunate to see Denys A. Stocks work granite with tools and techniques that closely approximated those of the ancients. In one of the largest modern quarries of Aswan, Denys demonstrated what he had learned from years of methodical, detailed and technical observation of ancient masonry, and from experiments involving the cutting and drilling of stone. Denys instructed me as I tried to carve a small hieroglyph, an *ankh* ('life') sign, in a chunk of pink granite by using sharp flint flakes like miniature chisels (the flint edges chipped away with each stroke, but powdered away some of granite at the same time). Under Denys's tutelage, after several hours I had a presentable glyph in sunken relief. Perhaps with just a little of the time, training and generations of experience of the ancient masons, I could even have achieved those crisp, sharp edges we see on the Pharaonic monuments.

I saw Aswan quarry workers abandon blowtorches and carbide steel chisels to take up Denys's toothless copper saw blade. With very persistent hard labour and plain desert sand, they sank a cut into a large granite slab. The brightest moment of insight came at the end of the drilling experiment. For 20 hours, three men used a bow drill patterned after ancient representations, with a copper tube and sand as a bit, to sink a circular hole 6 cm deep. A little hammering with chisels popped the core, a tapered cylinder of granite possessing striations very similar to the examples from the Fourth Dynasty Giza pyramids (ca. 2500 BCE) that had so intrigued and puzzled Petrie.

From Denys's hands-on approach and attention to the elementary structures of ancient masonry, we gain more than just solving particular puzzles of ancient techniques. We are given insight into the evolution of the 'interconnected tools and processes' of Ancient Egyptian masonry. And we are informed about how this system fits within the broader, complex adaptive system that is Egyptian civilization. When we glimpse the labour that goes into a single hole drilled through granite, we appreciate the cost of producing tens of thousands of hard-stone vases in Egypt's early formative period (some 40,000 were found under the Step Pyramid of Zoser at Saqqara). When we see what it takes to cast a broad blade of copper or bronze using separate small crucibles, we gain insight into the order of magnitude of mining, smelting and casting saws and chisels to create the colossal statues and obelisks in the age of empire. When we see a loss of copper to stone ranging from 1:4 or 1:1 in sawing and drilling granite, we can better appreciate the cost of a granite sarcophagus, tomb portal, or statue within an ancient economy that used weights (*deben*) of copper or bronze as a standard of value. In seeking to solve the puzzles of Ancient Egyptian stoneworking, Denys A. Stocks offers insights into the society and economy of the Ancient Egyptians.

Mark Lehner

ACKNOWLEDGEMENTS

I would like to express my gratitude to the following organizations and persons for permission to reproduce photographic and line illustrations: Bolton Museum and Art Gallery, the British Museum, the Brooklyn Museum of Art, the Egypt Exploration Society, the Fitzwilliam Museum, the Manchester Museum, the Metropolitan Museum of Art, the Petrie Museum of Egyptian and Sudanese Archaeology, and Terry Dowker, Barry Oswald, J. Stocks and Michael Tite. I sincerely thank Kelly and Chris Godwin, who gave generous help with my research project.

I am especially grateful to NOVA/WGBH Boston, Julia Cort, Mark Lehner, Hamada Rashwan, Hassan Abdel Alim, and the sawing and drilling crews, for their wholehearted assistance with my granite-cutting (drilling and sawing) experiments in Aswan, Upper Egypt. There are many other people who contributed to my research project over the years: collectively, I owe them a great debt of gratitude.

I greatly appreciate the encouragement and support of my wife, Carol, and of my sons Jeffrey, Ian and Paul. Without their constant involvement, this book could never have been written.

I sincerely thank Richard Stoneman and Celia Tedd of Routledge, whose support and care solved many problems on the way to publishing the book's first edition in 2003. I also thank Matthew Gibbons for his assistance and support in the production of the manuscript for this new edition of the book.

I sincerely thank Professor Stuart Campbell, Faculty of Humanities, University of Manchester, for his advice in preparing my 2018/19 Higher Doctorate. Doctor of Letters thesis, which contributed to this new edition.

I especially thank Professor John Healey and Dr Elizabeth Healey for their support over several decades.

Denys A. Stocks
Cheshire
January 2022

ABBREVIATIONS

Publications

AE	*Ancient Egypt* (London)
AEMI	A. Lucas and J. R. Harris, *Ancient Egyptian Materials and Industries*, London: Edward Arnold, 1962
AEMT	P. T. Nicholson and I. Shaw (eds), *Ancient Egyptian Materials and Technology*, Cambridge: Cambridge University Press, 2000
ASAÉ	*Annales du Service des Antiquités de l'Égypte* (Cairo)
Cat. Caire	*Catalogue Général des Antiquités Égyptiennes du Musée du Caire* (Cairo)
CdÉ	*Chronique d'Égypte* (Brussels)
JARCE	*Journal of the American Research Center in Egypt* (New York)
JEA	*Journal of Egyptian Archaeology* (London)
JRAI	*Journal of the Royal Anthropological Institute of Great Britain and Ireland* (London)
RAS	*Revue d'Archéometrie, Supplément, 1981* (Paris)
RdÉ	*Revue d'Égyptologie* (Paris)
ZÄS	*Zeitschrift für Ägyptische Sprache und Altertumskunde* (Berlin)

Museums

BM	British Museum, London
CM	Cairo Museum
MM	Manchester Museum, University of Manchester
MMA	Metropolitan Museum of Art, New York
UC	Petrie Collection, University College London

PREDYNASTIC AND DYNASTIC CHRONOLOGY

Neolithic, northern Egypt: begins ca. 5200 BCE

Predynastic Period

- Ma'adi culture, northern Egypt, ca. 4000–3300/3200 BCE
- Badarian culture, Middle Egypt, ca. 4500–3800 BCE

Naqada culture, southern Egypt

- Naqada I, ca. 4000–3600 BCE
- Naqada II, ca. 3600–3200 BCE
- Naqada III/Dynasty 0, ca. 3200–3050 BCE

Early Dynastic Period

First Dynasty, ca. 3050–2890 BCE

- Aha
- Djer
- Djet
- Den
- Anedjib
- Smerkhet
- Qa'a

Second Dynasty, ca. 2890–2686 BCE

- Hotepsekhemwy
- Reneb
- Nynetjer
- Weneg
- Peribsen
- Khasekhemwy

Old Kingdom

Third Dynasty, ca. 2686–2613 BCE

- Nebka
- Zoser
- Sekhemkhet
- Khaba
- Huni

Fourth Dynasty, ca. 2613–2494 BCE

- Seneferu
- Khufu
- Djedefre
- Khafre
- Nebka
- Menkaure
- Shepseskaf

Fifth Dynasty, ca. 2494–2345 BCE

- Weserkaf
- Sahure
- Neferirkare
- Shepseskare
- Neferefre
- Nyuserre
- Menkauhor
- Djedkare-Isesi
- Unas

Sixth Dynasty, ca. 2345–2181 BCE

- Teti
- Weserkare
- Pepi I
- Merenre
- Pepi II
- Nitocris

First Intermediate Period

- Seventh to Eleventh Dynasties, ca. 2181–2055 BCE

Middle Kingdom

Eleventh Dynasty, unification, ca. 2055–1985 BCE

- Mentuhotep II
- Mentuhotep III
- Mentuhotep IV

Twelfth Dynasty, ca. 1985–1795 BCE

- Amenemhat I
- Senusret I
- Amenemhat II
- Senusret II
- Amenemhat III
- Amenemhat IV
- Queen Sobekneferu

Second Intermediate Period

- Thirteenth to Seventeenth Dynasties, ca. 1795–1550 BCE

New Kingdom

Eighteenth Dynasty, ca. 1550–1295 BCE

- Ahmose
- Amenhotep I
- Tuthmose I
- Tuthmose II
- Tuthmose III
- Hatshepsut
- Amenhotep II

- Tuthmose IV
- Amenhotep III
- Amenhotep IV/Akhenaten (Amarna Period)
- Smenkhkare
- Tutankhamen
- Ay
- Horemheb

Ramesside Period

Nineteenth Dynasty, ca. 1295–1186 BCE

- Ramesses I
- Seti I
- Ramesses II
- Merenptah
- Amenmesses
- Seti II
- Siptah
- Queen Tawosret

Twentieth Dynasty, ca. 1186–1069 BCE

- Sethnakht
- Ramesses III
- Ramesses IV
- Ramesses V
- Ramesses VI
- Ramesses VII
- Ramesses VIII
- Ramesses IX
- Ramesses X
- Ramesses XI

Third Intermediate Period

- Twenty-first to Twenty-fifth Dynasties, ca. 1069–653 BCE

Late Period

Twenty-sixth Dynasty (Saite), ca. 664–525 BCE

- Neko I
- Psamtik I
- Neko II

- Psamtik II
- Apries
- Amasis
- Psamtik III
- Twenty-seventh Dynasty (Persian), ca. 525–404 BCE
- Twenty-eighth Dynasty, ca. 404–399 BCE
- Twenty-ninth Dynasty, ca. 399–380 BCE
- Thirtieth Dynasty, ca. 380–343 BCE
- Thirty-first Dynasty (Persian), ca. 343–332 BCE

This chronology follows K.A. Bard (ed.) *Encyclopedia of the Archaeology of Ancient Egypt*, London: Routledge, 1999.

MAP OF EGYPT

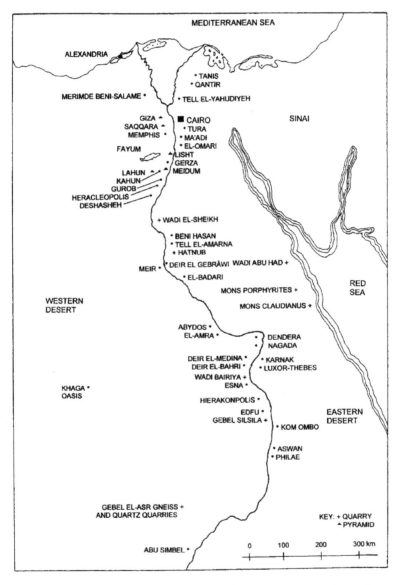

Map of Egypt showing important Predynastic and Dynastic quarry and manufacturing sites

PREFACE TO NEW EDITION

Since this book was first published in 2003, further experimental research by the author indicates that three technological developments *converged* at the beginning of the Naqada II period, ca. 3600 BCE, the first development being the smelting of copper from its ores. Archaeological evidence, and experiments, suggest that following on from the establishment of smelting copper, technical improvements to an important, indicated Late Neolithic drilling tool, and to a previous glazing process, which commenced ca. 4000 BCE, resulted in the tool, and in the process, *transitioning* into more productive forms.

The impetus for these suggested changes is connected with the Late Neolithic site of Merimde Beni-salame (ca. 4750–4250 BCE). Twentieth-century excavations at this site uncovered ceremonial maceheads made of slate, limestone and calcite. These maceheads required straight, narrow, parallel-sided hafting holes drilled completely through the axes of their pear and spherical shapes. However, a part of the new experimental research contained in this new edition demonstrates that experimental replica and reconstructed stone tools are unable safely to create narrow, straight hafting holes in these three stone types. Further experiments were carried out with tubular drills made from common reeds, which grow as completely straight, hollow and woody stems; a drill to suit a particular purpose can be chosen from reeds' variable diameters. When rotated with a bow on dry sand abrasive, a reed drill can make a straight parallel hole through slate and limestone (even hard limestone), and calcite.

Recently analysed and re-evaluated research concerning the experimental manufacture of approximately 250 replica and reconstructed tools, and their associated processes, points towards the introduction of two vital transitions, and the convergence of three separate key industries in the Late Predynastic period, which served to develop and increase Egypt's expanding economy before the foundation of the First Dynasty. These circumstances are explored in this new edition, which also identifies and highlights the most important tools and processes that were responsible for generating Predynastic Egypt's technological expansion, and how this created a strong economy based on manufacturing two particularly valuable artifacts that could be exchanged at regional and interregional levels and, later, for long-distance trade with other countries.

The archaeological and experimental evidence introduces new insights as to how technical developments in the Late Predynastic period increased Egypt's long-term Dynastic wealth production, giving strong leaders in different locations during the Late Predynastic period the ability to support and control an expansion in craftworking. These leaders supplied necessary raw materials, skilled workers, tools and the administrative authority to ensure continued manufacturing growth, concentrating power into the hands of a few people and, eventually, into the establishment of the first king of the First Dynasty, ca. 3050 BCE.

INTRODUCTION

Social and organizational changes are generated in any society that introduces, and absorbs, technical advantages. Recently, the results from experiments with more than 200 replica and reconstructed tools indicate the development of interrelated technology, tools and materials in key areas during the Predynastic period (ca. 4500–3050 BCE) of Ancient Egypt. These experiments also suggest that later evolutionary changes to the designs of particular tools significantly increased the production rates of artifacts, giving impetus to the creation of increasing amounts of material wealth. This book attempts to explain what these technical introductions, tools, materials and relationships were, and how the development of technology and craftworking generated social and organizational changes to Predynastic and Dynastic Egyptian society.

In Predynastic Egypt, the ability to produce progressively complicated artifacts gradually grew from the designing and manufacturing skills of craftworkers, assisted by an intelligent use of an abundance of naturally occurring materials acquired from the local environment. These included stone, wood, minerals, sand and many kinds of vegetation. Predynastic technological developments can be divided into several distinct areas, each with its own specialized tools and techniques, but sometimes sharing other tools, methods and materials. In particular, the establishment of the tools and procedures for the large-scale manufacture of stone vessels during the Naqada II (ca. 3600–3200 BCE) and the Naqada III/Dynasty 0 (ca. 3200–3050 BCE) periods crucially contributed to the growth of other technologies in these periods, and in the following Dynastic era. For example, the carving of the ceremonial schist palette of King Narmer (Dynasty 0), and Dynastic hard-stone statuary, benefited from the skills and tools established for shaping earlier Predynastic hard-stone vessels, stone hand-axes and maceheads. Also, it is possible that the Late Predynastic expansion in faience manufacture can be attributed to an increased availability of copper-contaminated quartz powders, a waste product obtained by

DOI: 10.4324/9781003269922-1

drilling calcite (Egyptian alabaster), hard limestone and igneous stone vessels with copper tubes and sand abrasive.

Rare examples of Badarian (ca. 4500–3800 BCE) black or dark grey basalt vases came from a disturbed cemetery and village rubbish,[1] but in the Naqada I period (ca. 4000–3600 BCE) vessels made of hard and soft stones, such as basalt, granite, calcite, gypsum and limestone, were produced in increasing numbers.[2] The rapid expansion of hard-stone vessel production in the Naqada II period indicates that new, faster and reliable vessel manufacturing methods were introduced during this time. What were these new production techniques, and why did they emerge and affect later industrial developments? In endeavouring to answer these questions, the manufacture of hard- and soft-stone vessels was used as a focal point in investigating Predynastic and Dynastic technical developments. Vessels of stone were the first substantial artifacts in this material, and therefore a stone vase was made with the reconstructed stone vessel manufacturing tools in order to test them. The special problems associated with the successful shaping and hollowing of hard- and soft-stone vessels were relevant to the development of other Egyptian tools, processes and artifacts. For example, the Dynastic sarcophagi made from single blocks of hard stone were drilled out with copper tubes, similar to the initial hollowing techniques in use for the hard-stone Predynastic vessels.

Several important areas of ancient technology remain shrouded in mystery, particularly those concerned with stoneworking: our ability to assess the development of Ancient Egyptian technology, despite finding many tools, artifacts and tomb illustrations of manufacturing processes, is frustrated by an incomplete knowledge of important crafts, and virtually no knowledge at all of significant tools missing from the archaeological record. In trying to understand the technical steps achieved by craftworkers from all periods of Ancient Egypt, a study of the environmental factors, the natural resources, the artifacts and the existing tools in our possession, combined with a review of the archaeological and pictorial evidence, preceded the manufacture and use of the replica and reconstructed tools. All of the tools' characteristics, and their effectiveness for working stone, wood, metal and other indigenous materials under manufacturing and test conditions, were evaluated and recorded. The examination of Predynastic production methods, materials and tools was assisted by additionally focusing on the Dynastic archaeological evidence, using it as a frame of reference for the experiments. Later, by looking forward to the Dynastic era from a newly established Predynastic perspective, the reasons for Dynastic manufacturing developments, and their effects, might more fully be understood.

We do not know, with reasonable certainty, how particular materials were worked in any given situation: tools' cutting and wear rates need to be established for a range of materials. The precise construction and use of the stone vessel drilling and boring tool is only partly perceived, and none of the New Kingdom period mass-production equipment for drilling stone beads, a development of the single bead drill, has survived. Only some illustrations in six New Kingdom tombs[3] at Thebes indicate the existence of an important and systematic drilling procedure.

The constructional methods and tools for making sarcophagi and statuary in hard stone, the close fitting of the stone blocks used for architecture, the source of the frit and the faience core and glaze materials, and the cutting of incised and low reliefs, and of hieroglyphs, in hard and soft stone are also incompletely understood. Certain tomb illustrations show ancillary tools for working wood and metal, and these were made and tested as an integral part of the research project.

The Egyptian craftworker shaped stone, wood, metal and other materials by selecting the relevant casting, hammering, sawing, drilling, boring, chiselling, cutting, chipping, punching, scraping, carving, heavy and light pounding, grinding and polishing processes. Although this book predominantly examines stoneworking technology, the ability of craftworkers to work this material into artifacts depended upon the development of other necessary, supporting technologies; these are also investigated. Many of the technical processes, and their associated terminology, are explained in the Glossary of Technical Terms.

The replica tools followed the designs of tools found at different sites in Egypt by archaeologists; the reconstructed tools conformed with the archaeological evidence and the tomb illustrations, if they existed, but in some cases this was impossible. These tools were manufactured using the physical evidence for their existence as a guide to reconstruction, which was influenced by recognized and accepted ancient techniques and materials in use for making known tools. Naturally, the author's training in mechanical engineering determined the outcome of each tool's exact design, and possibly its function. However, the assessment of a particular tool's design and operation relates to its anticipated development and connection to other tools and processes. Additionally, many of the investigated replica and reconstructed tools are not only placed in context with other tools and manufacturing methods, but are also discussed in relation to their employment in the workers' towns of Kahun, Tell el-Amarna and Deir el-Medina, together with other centres of work, such as Hierakonpolis, Ma'adi and Giza. In the following chapters, there is no intention to examine how every type of Ancient Egyptian artifact was made throughout the Predynastic and Dynastic periods, although some objects' constructional techniques are closely analysed. Rather, the intention is to show how important tools and processes were developed to work the stones, metals, woods and vegetation available to ancient craftworkers into all manner of artifacts.

Notes

1   G. Brunton and G. Caton-Thompson, *Badarian Civilisation and Predynastic Remains Near Badari*, London: British School of Archaeology in Egypt, 1928, p. 28, pl. XXIII, 9–11.
2   E.J. Baumgartel, *The Cultures of Prehistoric Egypt*, Oxford: Oxford University Press, vol. I, 1955, pp. 102–19.
3   The Eighteenth and Nineteenth Dynasty Theban tombs of Puyemre (Th 39), Rekhmire (Th 100), Amenhotpe-si-se (Th 75), Sebekhotep (Th 63), Nebamun and Ipuky (Th 181) and Neferrenpet (Th 178).

PART I
Skills and tools
Fledgling industrialists

1

CRAFTWORKING

Industry's driving force

Craftworking: mind over matter

Extant in papyri, writing boards and ostraca, and originally composed in the Middle Kingdom, is the text of *The Satire on the Trades: The Instruction of Dua-Khety*.[1] The story contains the teaching and advice that Dua-Khety gives to his son Pepy regarding the scribal profession and literature. Dua-Khety emphasizes the attractiveness of the office of scribe by describing the uncomfortable and tiring occupations of the stoneworker, the coppersmith, the carpenter, the jeweller, the reed-cutter, the potter, the bricklayer, the furnace-tender and several other workers. Ironically, craftworkers had already established a comprehensive set of working practices during the Predynastic period, well before the introduction of the office of scribe. In any event, some of the scribe's work depended upon Egypt's industrial output in many areas, which in turn relied upon the skills of different types of craftworker.

What exactly is craftworking? What human abilities are brought into play? The most important is verbal and non-verbal communication, such as a description, a sketch, or a demonstration of an idea or a new skill. In the separate society of the craftworker, there exists, certainly in recent times, a relationship between artisans engaged in similar work. There is support for the fellow worker, expressed in the form of cooperation and admiration for competent handicraft;[2] this relationship must have existed in ancient times. The association between craftworkers and their apprentices is even more remarkable. A worker responsible for training a young person will assume the rôle of a mentor quite willingly. In fact, a keen apprentice will eventually be shown all of the craftworker's skills over an extended period of time.[3]

Jacob Bronowski, the physicist, identified a significant factor affecting the development of craftworking. He stated that although an object and a law of nature

DOI: 10.4324/9781003269922-3

are both concealed in the raw material, a person in one age could never identically copy a creation or a discovery made by someone else in another age.[4]

This fundamental truth faces anyone who attempts to place themselves in the position of an ancient craftworker. Ancient workers lived in a different environment and developed their collective skills over millennia: the last Pharaonic workers died over 2,000 years ago, together with many of their skills. A modern craftworker must take account of these factors. In particular, the creation of a replica artifact by a craftworker in a later age can never be identical to the original made by a craftworker in an earlier age. Also, in order to penetrate the secrets of ancient craftworking, a present-day artisan needs to suffer some of the trials and tribulations experienced in ancient times, and perhaps be exposed to some health risks because of this strategy.

Bronowski also differentiated between the shaping of compliant materials, such as moulding clay with the hand, and the splitting of wood and stone with a tool. He suggests that an intellectual step forward is made when a person splits an intractable material and lays bare nature's structure.[5]

Bronowski's comments usefully illuminate the change from Early Dynastic mud brick architecture to buildings made from stone blocks shaped with cutting tools: the prime example is the construction of the Step Pyramid at Saqqara (Figure 1.1). The much more durable limestone block, which in this pyramid followed the shape of the mud brick (Figure 1.2), albeit a little larger in size, allowed fundamental changes to the architectural construction of this monument. In later times, ancient

FIGURE 1.1   The Third Dynasty Step Pyramid at Saqqara

Source: Image by D. Stocks

FIGURE 1.2   Limestone core-blocks in the Step Pyramid, shaped like the mud brick

Source: Image by D. Stocks

tools and skills became more sophisticated, which permitted the manufacture of more complex artifacts from difficult stones to work, such as granite.

Bronowski also suggested that over an extended period of human evolution, the hand and the brain interacted, each feeding back to the other, which allowed the brain to become particularly adept at manipulating the hand.[6] Although Bronowski is referring to the activities of the human species as a whole, a similar observation can be made with regard to a craftworker learning a trade. Each learned action has to be stored in the brain, and is implemented every time a similar response is required. Some modification to the action may be necessary, because no two circumstances are ever exactly alike. This is called experience. A highly trained and skilled craftworker is able to recall that experience at will, and is able to assess a raw material for a new artifact with confidence. In fact, so strong is the mental picture generated by the brain, a consequence of manipulating hand-operated tools for years, that the finished object can be 'seen' in the 'mind's eye'. The supreme confidence of ancient craftworkers, which was required to begin difficult and intricate stone artifacts, must owe much to this phenomenon.

A craftworker's ability to fashion any material into an artifact depends upon training and the adoption of a pragmatic attitude. In Ancient Egypt, an artisan class slowly grew from small beginnings, benefiting from families protecting and keeping acquired knowledge. While craftworking is sometimes a shared experience, an individual worker develops skills unique to her/himself. In particular, the full development of a worker's skills takes a lifetime, not just the apprenticeship period.

FIGURE 1.3   Carved palm fronds in a stone column capital

Source: Image by D. Stocks

Therefore, *any* artifact produced by a particular craftworker is a consequence of the skills acquired *up to that time*; no two objects can ever be identical.

Ancient craftworkers assiduously probed the natural materials present in the environment. How much inspiration did they obtain from the shapes of vegetation when designing tools? It is known that the structural form of certain vegetation influenced some architectural features in stone buildings. For example, stone columns sometimes imitated bundles of papyri or reeds, while their capitals could follow the form of tree foliage (Figure 1.3) or the lotus bud. The evidence later presented in this book indicates that important tool designs also owed much to nature's architecture.

Traditionally, the city of Memphis, the first administrative capital of Upper and Lower Egypt, was founded ca. 3100 BCE at a site some 25 km south of Cairo. The city's creator-god, Ptah, was the patron of all craftworkers. At this early period, these industrious people may have enjoyed relatively high status as the creators of much of the wealth of the Upper Egyptian Naqada culture, which eventually possessed the power to join Upper and Lower Egypt together. This is quite contrary to the way in which Dua-Khety perceived the craftworker's stature in the Middle Kingdom period.

Important tools, materials and artifacts: a brief overview

The introduction of the Neolithic period in Egypt (ca. 5200 BCE) further freed the workers traditionally responsible for manufacturing artifacts in the community to spend much more time and energy on designing and making new stone tools. The introduction of farming had gradually replaced a hunter-gatherer and fishing culture existing in Egypt prior to this date.[7] Neolithic people began to cultivate crops and to herd goats, cattle, pigs and sheep in settled locations, such as the Fayum (ca. 5200–4500 BCE), Merimde Beni-salame (ca. 4750–4250 BCE) and el-Omari (ca. 4600–4400 BCE) in northern (Lower) Egypt.[8] In the lowest, or earliest, stratum (Phase I) of Merimde, retouched lithic blades and flakes were made into side-scrapers and end-scrapers, as well as arrowheads and small perforators.[9]

In Phases II–V were located carefully chipped, ground and polished hand-axes of quartzite, basalt, granite, chalcedony, schist and crystalline limestone.[10] In particular, the craftworker was able, by eye, to shape hard-stone axes into highly symmetrical, smoothly ground and polished artifacts (Figure 1.4); flaked flint axes were also polished, but not completely smoothed. Axes were often used as adzes for hollowing logs; an axe's cutting edge was fastened at a right angle to its wooden shaft's long axis.[11] Stone was bifacially flaked into concave-based projectile points,

FIGURE 1.4   An early Predynastic basalt hand-axe

Source: Image by J. Stocks

triangular points, long drills or borers, large denticulated (serrated) knife and sickle blades, as well as non-bifacial perforators and endscrapers.[12] Also discovered at Merimde were small vessels of calcite, and perforated maceheads made of slate, calcite and hard limestone.[13]

The working of the hard stones, such as quartzite, basalt, granite, chalcedony and schist, predated the introduction of edged copper tools. However, even if Merimden craftworkers had possessed sharpened copper chisels, the experiments with copper, bronze and even iron chisels demonstrated their total inability to cut certain hard stones, particularly the igneous types. The necessary techniques and stone tools for working the hardest stones continued to be developed throughout the Predynastic period, enabling Dynastic craftworkers not only to shape the hard stones into statuary, obelisks, sarcophagi and a multitude of other artifacts, but to incise hieroglyphs and reliefs into them. At el-Badari, and other Badarian (ca. 4500–3800 BCE) sites in southern (Upper) Egypt, Predynastic craftworkers also created non-bifacial stone end-scrapers and perforators; bifacial lithic tools included concave-base projectile points, denticulated sickles, as well as triangles and ovate axes.[14] Badarian artisans also worked with copper; the earliest Badarian copper objects found in Egypt, four beads, were found by Guy Brunton in grave 596 at Mostagedda, a site just north of el-Badari. Toward the end of the Badarian, and its development into the Naqada I period, small pins, needles, drills and punches were hammered from copper. Badarian ground stone vessels made their appearance ca. 4000 BCE, and the coating of carved steatite beads, and of other stones, with a green alkaline glaze was also invented about this time.[15] The manufacture of the glaze for these beads is associated with the use of malachite, a copper ore, which was then mixed and fired with a finely ground waste sand powder, possibly obtained from grinding out the stone vessels with stone borers and sand abrasive.[16]

The Naqada I (Amratian, ca. 4000–3600 BCE) culture followed, somewhat overlapping the Badarian period. The workers at el-Amra, Upper Egypt, hollowed lug-handled jars from basalt with grinding stones and sand abrasive; the short lugs were probably perforated with flint tools and grinders. Disc- (e.g. Bristol Museum and Art Gallery H 1502) and narrow, biconal-shaped ('hammer') maceheads were chipped, probably with flint tools, and ground from granite and other hard stones. They were perforated in a similar fashion to the vessels' lugs.

The Naqada II period (Gerzean, ca. 3600–3200 BCE) saw the introduction of truly smelted and cast copper tools at Ma'adi, a settlement just south of the Delta,[17] and at Gerza and other sites in southern Egypt. These tools included small chisels, adzes and axes, but saws, knives and hoes were also cast and beaten into shape. By the late Naqada II and III/Dynasty 0 periods (ca. 3300–3050 BCE), the manufacture of stone vessels was established as an important industry, particularly at Hierakonpolis.

Associated with, and probably responsible for, the expansion of stone vessel production at the commencement of the Naqada II period, particularly vessels made from the harder stones, was the introduction of the copper tube force-fitted

FIGURE 1.5   A reconstructed copper tubular drill fitted to a wooden shaft

Source: Image by D. Stocks

to a specialized stone vessel drilling tool. The drill-tube would have been formed around a rod of wood from thinly beaten, cast plate copper.[18] Possibly, larger, Dynastic, diameter tubes were cast directly into vertical tubular moulds.[19]

The copper tubular drill's design is a copy of the common reed's (*Phragmites communis*) tubular shape, which was converted into copper after ca. 3600 BCE for drilling stones harder than slate, calcite and hard limestone (see Chapter 4). The experimental drilling of these stones with reed tubes and necessarily dry sand abrasive indicates that craftworkers could have drilled slate, calcite and hard limestone this way before ca. 3600 BCE, particularly for perforating maceheads made from these three stones. The copper tube, also in use with sand abrasive, was force-fitted to the end of a straight shaft (Figure 1.5) driven with a bow, the shaft's top end rotating in a hollowed, and lubricated, hand-held capstone. The experiments with the copper tubes and sand abrasive suggest that the Naqada II igneous stone maceheads, particularly the spherical- and pear-shaped (e.g. Bristol Museum and Art Gallery H 1936) varieties needing long holes, were undoubtedly perforated with copper drill-tubes, not with inappropriate stone borers. It is possible, therefore, that the capability of relatively long copper tubes deeply to drill into hard stone influenced the designs of Naqada II maceheads.

The establishment of a flourishing stone vessel industry near to the end of the Predynastic period generated abundant quantities of waste, finely ground sand powders suitable for making modelled and moulded faience cores, in addition to faience glazes. The change from glazed carved stone cores had begun in about 4000 BCE.[20] Therefore, did the availability of finely ground quartz-based waste powders containing varying amounts of copper particles worn off the tubular drills replace specially made glazing powders containing malachite for glazing faience cores? This question will be investigated in Chapter 9.

FIGURE 1.6   The huge statues of Ramesses II at Abu Simbel, Upper Egypt, carved from red sandstone

Source: Image by D. Stocks

The Dynastic *bow-driven* copper tube drilled the interiors of stone sarcophagi and the lifting holes in their lids, but it was originally used in this configuration to perforate the long tubular lugs carved on the exteriors of some late Naqada II hard-stone vessels.[21] A cast copper, flat-edged saw, also in use with sand abrasive, possibly cut some of the hard stones to shape (e.g. granite) after they became fashionable for architecture during the First and Second Dynasties, although the first attested use for such a saw occurred in the Third Dynasty with the sawing to shape of Sekhemkhet's calcite sarcophagus.[22] This saw was essential for cutting igneous stone sarcophagi to shape, as well as for removing excess stone from statuary.[23]

Consequent upon the establishment of reliable Predynastic stoneworking techniques, Dynastic stoneworkers became master masons and accomplished manufacturers of other artifacts made of stone, some notable examples being statuary (Figure 1.6), vessels of many shapes, sizes and stone types, as well as stone beads, stelae, sarcophagi and obelisks. Limestone, sandstone and, to a lesser extent, granite, were employed for building (Figure 1.7), with the occasional use of calcite, basalt and quartzite:[24] pyramid building began in the Third Dynasty, after a period constructing mud brick mastabas incorporating some stone.[25] The true pyramid, one with smooth sides, developed later in the Third Dynasty, reaching an apogee in the Fourth Dynasty on the Giza plateau with the construction of the Great Pyramid (Figure 1.8) and others in the Giza group (Figure 1.9).

FIGURE 1.7   Hatshepsut's Eighteenth Dynasty temple at Deir el-Bahri, Upper Egypt

Source: Image by D. Stocks

FIGURE 1.8   Khufu's Fourth Dynasty pyramid on the Giza plateau

Source: Image by D. Stocks

FIGURE 1.9 Khafre's pyramid at Giza

Source: Image by D. Stocks

Some of the research for this book closely examines the abilities of various tools to work different stones. Wherever clarification and emphasis are needed, stones are provided with their Mohs hardness numbers,[26] but there is a summary of a cross-section of the stones in use for buildings, vessels, beads, statuary, obelisks and other artifacts in Table 1.1. The stones are placed into two groups: Mohs 3 and below, and above Mohs 3. This division is indicated by the test use of the replica and reconstructed copper, bronze, iron and stone tools upon a selection of soft and hard stones. (Note: a particular stone favoured by the Egyptians, calcite (calcium carbonate), is usually stated to be hardness Mohs 3, but the tests indicate that Egyptian calcite is probably about Mohs 3.5. Calcite lies near to a boundary dividing what may be referred to as the 'softer' stones – those easily cut with copper and bronze chisels – and the 'harder' stones, which require stone tools effectively to cut them. Calcite, which falls on the harder side of this boundary, definitely needs stone tools to cut and incise it: the marks obtained by experimentally cutting and incising calcite with stone tools are similar to marks on ancient calcite artifacts. This stone is often confused with gypsum (calcium sulphate, Mohs 2), which possesses a similar appearance. However, the subsequent tests will show that calcite and gypsum require completely different tools and methods for cutting, incising and drilling them.)

The tests with metal and stone tools suggest that all Ancient Egyptian stone-working was governed by an intimate knowledge of the subtle differences between all tools' working characteristics and the hardness of the materials being worked.

TABLE 1.1 List of stone types and Mohs hardness

Stone	Mohs 3 and below	Above Mohs 3
agate		6.5
amethyst		7
basalt		7
breccia		5–6
calcite		3–4
carnelian		7
chalcedony		6.5
chert		7
crystalline limestone		6
diorite		7
dolerite		7
feldspar		6–6.5
flint		7
garnet		6.5
granite		7
greywacke (schist)		4–5
gypsum	2	
hard sandstone		5
malachite		4
marble		4–5
mica	2–3	
obsidian		5
porphyry		7
quartz		7
quartzite		6–7
red sandstone	2.5	
serpentine		4
slate		4–5
soft limestone	2.5	
steatite	3	
syenite		7

Ancient workers empirically knew which tool could be used for a particular material, and which could not. With this in mind, the present experiments with flint and chert, a flint-like stone, indicate that with regard to the cutting of certain igneous stones, only true flint possesses the required cutting characteristics. Chert tools are critically softer than flint for this type of work. Confusingly, the word 'flint' has been used in the archaeological literature, and in museum exhibits, to identify and label artifacts made from both flint and chert. The tests with chert tools show that it can cut most of the materials that flint can, but not all of them. Therefore, for simplicity, the word 'flint' will be used to mean both flint and chert. However, for the igneous stone tests in Chapter 3, a differentiation between flint and chert will be mentioned where necessary.

FIGURE 1.10 An Eighteenth Dynasty bead-making workshop at Thebes, Upper Egypt. From the tomb of Sebekhotep (BM 920)

Source: © The British Museum

The production of stone beads commenced in Neolithic times,[27] continuing into the Predynastic and Dynastic periods. Agate, amethyst, carnelian and lapis lazuli represent some of the stones in use for bead manufacture.[28] Throughout all periods of Ancient Egypt the people were passionately fond of beads; consequently, vast numbers were manufactured. It is clear that the creation of such prodigious numbers of beads became highly organized. In particular, a system of mass-production, illustrated in several New Kingdom tombs at Thebes, Upper Egypt (Figure 1.10), dramatically changed the way stone beads were drilled, leading to a significant rise in manufacturing output.

Although the manufacture of stone vessels commenced during the Predynastic period, the first illustrations of the process are to be seen in two Fifth Dynasty tombs at Saqqara;[29] the last illustration occurs in the Twenty-sixth Dynasty tomb of Aba at Thebes.[30] The earliest representation of the stone vessel maker's drilling/boring tool, the ideogram used in words connected with 'art' and 'craft', and in other words, dates to the Third Dynasty at Saqqara.[31] Among the stones worked into vessels were basalt, breccia, calcite, diorite, granite, greywacke, gypsum,[32] limestone, marble, porphyry, serpentine and steatite.[33] Toward the end of the Old Kingdom, the number of stone vessels decreased considerably, with most of the harder stones going out of use.[34] However, the manufacture of stone vessels continued until the end of Egyptian civilization, a large proportion of them being made from calcite, a relatively soft stone compared with granite or diorite.[35]

The early version of the tool enabling ancient craftworkers to produce such a variety of vessel designs was a simple adaptation of a forked tree branch, a copper tube force-fitted to its lower end and two stone weights fastened just under the adapted fork. Later in Dynastic history, a single, hemispherical stone was used as a weight. After drilling with the tube, a second forked branch, inverted this time, was roped to the original shaft, the fork engaging with variously shaped stone borers; boring generally followed the tubular drilling process, with sand acting as an abrasive in both situations. The forked shaft also drove flint and chert crescents, without an abrasive, for boring into soft gypsum.[36] Reconstructed drilling and boring tools were effective in making an experimental limestone vase, which will be discussed in a later chapter.

A number of ancient tools, and their uses, are familiar today. The shapes of the present chisel, adze and axe remain unchanged, but the metals employed to make them have altered. Modern cutting tools are made from carbon steel, but in ancient times copper, followed by bronze and iron, were the metals in use. Although tools of copper increasingly supplemented the use of sharp-edged flint tools as the Neolithic period ended ca. 4000 BCE, the employment of flint for tools continued at least until the Twenty-fifth Dynasty.[37]

A few Predynastic metallic tool designs were probably copies of certain flint tool shapes, particularly the cutting edges. For example, the stone hand-axe and the straight-edged knife were copied in copper without any fundamental changes to their shapes, but it is also likely that the flat copper chisel and the adze blade were inspired by the flint end-scraper (Figure 1.11), or the burin.[38] Experiments[39] demonstrated that these types of flint tool can be struck, like chisels, for removing pieces of wood and stone, or for skimming thin shavings by a glancing blow

FIGURE 1.11   A Predynastic flint end-scraper

Source: Image by J. Stocks

directed toward the worker, just like the hafted metal adze. The denticulated flint knife and sickle[40] probably stimulated the creation of the serrated copper wood-cutting saw. Some tools have been located by archaeologists at different sites in Egypt, but various tool marks on artifacts, together with tomb depictions of working techniques, indicate that key industrial tools are unknown. These include the stone chisels, punches and scrapers used for working the hard stones, the copper tubular drill and its associated bow, the stonecutting saw, the New Kingdom mass-production bead-drilling equipment and the stone vessel hollowing tool, although some flint and chert crescents, and stone borers, used in conjunction with this tool are in our possession.[41]

Tomb artists never recorded certain important techniques, one of them being the manufacture of the sarcophagus from a single block of stone. Furthermore, all of the functions of the tools we do possess may not be known, obscuring our understanding of ancient technology. This lack of information of manufacturing methods also conceals the manner in which ancient workers organized their work. Although much is known of the lives of Ancient Egyptians in general, the craft-worker still remains an indistinct figure on the technological landscape. However, recent experiments with faience manufacture[42] now suggest that several crafts were connected. It is possible that stone vessel and sarcophagus workers supplied the finely ground waste drilling and sawing powders to the faience manufacturers, to the stone bead drillers and to the stone polishers. This indicates that an interrelated and interdependent industrial society existed, where one industry depended upon the waste, or the by-products, of another industry.

By the First Dynasty, most of the major crafts were fully established, particularly stone vessel and faience manufacture. The Egyptian state now played an important part in the expansion of these crafts into other, fully fledged industries. The ceremonial burial of the pharaoh in Early Dynastic tombs incorporating some stone, together with the provision of opulent tomb furnishings, obliged craftworkers to invent new techniques. In the First and Second Dynasties, stone was employed for retaining walls, for roofs, floors and wall linings, and for portcullis blocks and gateways.[43] The commonest stone in use was limestone, but granite was utilized for flooring blocks in the First Dynasty tomb of Den at Abydos,[44] although these blocks were roughly dressed – not sawn – to shape. An important tomb furnishing, the sarcophagus, was made from wood in the First and Second Dynasties,[45] limestone and calcite in the Third Dynasty,[46] followed by granite in the Fourth Dynasty;[47] different tools and techniques were needed to work each material. Similarly, the use of manageable limestone casing-blocks in Zoser's Third Dynasty pyramid at Saqqara led to the employment of the megalithic core- and casing-blocks in the Giza pyramids. However, the accurate fitting of large joint surfaces together required the invention of a tool for testing surface flatness. Although the earliest specimen known, three short wooden rods, two connected with a taut string, originates from Twelfth Dynasty Kahun,[48] the accuracy of the stone block fitting in the Great Pyramid indicates that this surface-testing tool existed in the Fourth Dynasty.

Environmental factors affect inventive progress. The river Nile, the cultivated land and the surrounding deserts must have influenced the course of technological development. For example, craftworkers were aware of the abrasive nature of sand from an early period: sand-contaminated bread caused severe wear to their teeth.[49] The Egyptians would have noticed that sand is normally dry, and that it moves, or flows, like a fluid, either by gravity or from the pressure applied by an object or the force of the wind. Early workers employed clay and mud for pottery and bricks, but these materials were probably exploited in other ways, which will be examined in Chapter 8. Another important resource was wood. Timber, besides being utilized for furniture, provided handles for tools, such as the adze and the axe, and for the bows and the shafts that drove the copper tubular drills. Native Egyptian trees included the acacia, the dom palm, the sycamore fig and the tamarisk. Foreign soft and hard timbers in use included ash, beech, cedar, elm, lime, oak, pine and yew.[50] After ca. 3600 BCE, charcoal was needed in ever-increasing quantities for smelting copper ores, and for melting coppers and bronzes for casting into tools and other objects. Other easily available materials were stone, including flint and chert, and leather, oils, natron (a mixture of alkaline sodium salts), minerals (semi-precious stones), ivory, bone, ash and plant stems. These included the common reed, papyrus, halfa grass, straw and flax.

Experiments and their interpretation

The replica cutting tools were tested for hardness before and after hammering into shape; after test, their life expectancy was calculated. Some experimental specimens of copper and bronze were hardness-tested by J.R. Maréchal.[51] However, replica copper and bronze alloy chisels, forming a *series* containing different constituent metals, or increasing percentages of them, have never been tested for hardness, and used on various materials to establish relationships between chisels' hardnesses and their cutting capabilities. Although it is self-evident what a chisel does, certainty of its precise ancient use upon different materials cannot be stated with complete confidence. Therefore, copper and bronze chisels were thoroughly investigated. Similarly, without using a replica of the surface-testing tool, there is insufficient information from the tomb illustrations to be certain of all its ancient applications. Where tools are known only from tomb illustrations, their construction and uses are even more perplexing.

Three particular craft strategies are still practised today. These are metal casting, the hand grinding of tools and artifacts using abrasive stones and/or a loose abrasive powder, and the scraping of metal by harder metal scrapers. These three important skills originated millennia ago and although some tool materials have changed from the ancient ones, the basic techniques are, in all essentials, similar to those invented by ancient craftworkers. Despite any form of turbulence in human society, many skills are passed on from one generation to the next within families, or small groups of workers. In this way, unbroken chains of artisans may stretch from ancient times to the present day. Some technologies became lost, but others survived or were adapted into new techniques.

There are many questions that require definitive answers. For example, were waste products from one industry supplied to other industries, thus establishing a relationship between them? What were the implications for social change and organization caused by the introduction and development of new technologies? What injuries occurred to workers, and did some industrial processes seriously affect their health? Did interrelated Dynastic technology truly develop into industrial interdependence – a modern concept? Some new perspectives to these, and to other relevant questions, will be discussed in the following chapters.

Notes

1 W.K. Simpson (ed.) *The Literature of Ancient Egypt*, New Haven, CT and London: Yale University Press, 1972, pp. 329–36.
2 This is very noticeable during an apprenticeship in an engineering workshop.
3 Most craftworkers are more than willing to show many of their skills over a period of several years. Sometimes, a retiring craftworker will pass on a large tool collection to a favoured apprentice, anxious to ensure their continued use.
4 J. Bronowski, *The Ascent of Man*, London: British Broadcasting Corporation, 1973, p. 115.
5 Ibid., pp. 94–5.
6 Ibid., pp. 417, 421.
7 M.A. Hoffman, *Egypt Before the Pharaohs: The Prehistoric Foundations of Egyptian Civilization*, London and Henley: Routledge and Kegan Paul, 1980, p. 102.
8 G. Caton-Thompson, 'The Neolithic industry of the northern Fayum desert', *JRAI* LVI, 1926, pp. 309–23; G. Caton-Thompson, 'Recent excavations in the Fayum', *Man* XXVIII, 1928, pp. 109–13; G. Caton-Thompson and E.W. Gardner, *The Desert Fayum*, London: The Royal Anthropological Institute of Great Britain and Ireland, 1934; H. Junker, 'Vorläufiger Bericht über die Grabung der Akademie der Wissenschaften in Wien auf der neolithischen Siedlung von Merimde-Benisalame (Westdelta)', *Anzeiger der Akademie der Wissenschaften in Wien, Philosophische-historische Klasse* XVI–XXVIII, 1929, pp. 156–250; V–XIII, 1930, pp. 21–83; I IV, 1932, pp. 36–97; XVI–XXVII, 1933, pp. 54–97; X, 1934, pp. 118–32; I–V, 1940, pp. 3–25; P. Bovier-Lapierre, 'Une nouvelle station néolithique (El Omari) au nord d'Hélouan (Égypte)', *Compte rendu, Congrès International de Géographie* IV, 1926; F. Debono, 'El Omari (près d'Hélouan), exposé sommaire sur les campagnes des fouilles 1943–1944 et 1948', *ASAÉ* 48, 1948, pp. 561–9; F. Debono and B. Mortensen, *El Omari: A Neolithic Settlement and Other Sites in the Vicinity of Wadi Hof Helwan*, Mainz: Philipp von Zabern, 1990.
9 Junker, 'Vorläufiger Bericht über die Grabung der Akademie der Wissenschaften in Wien auf der neolithischen Siedlung von Merimde-Benisalame (Westdelta)'; J. Boessneck and A. von den Driesch, *Die Tierknochenfunde aus der neolithischen Siedlung von Merimde-Benisalâme am westlichen Nildelta*, Munich: Staatliche Sammlung Ägyptischer Kunst, 1985; J. Eiwanger, *Merimde-Benisalâme*, Mainz: Philipp von Zabern, vols I–III, 1984–1992.
10 Junker, 'Vorläufiger Bericht über die Grabung der Akademie der Wissenschaften in Wien auf der neolithischen Siedlung von Merimde-Benisalame (Westdelta)'.
11 Ibid.
12 Ibid.
13 Ibid.
14 Brunton and Caton-Thompson, *Badarian Civilisation and Predynastic Remains near Badari*, London: British School of Archaeology in Egypt, 1928, pp. 35–7, 61–2.
15 Ibid., pp. 27–8, 41.

16 Before the advent of grinding tubular holes into hard stones with copper tubes and sand abrasive, hard-stone vessels *must* have been internally ground with stone borers and sand. There was no other non-destructive, relatively low-risk method available to craftworkers.

17 M. Amer, 'Annual report of the Maadi excavations, 1930–32', *Bulletin of the Faculty of Arts*, Egyptian University I, 1933, pp. 322–4; M. Amer, 'Annual report of the Maadi excavations, 1935', *CdÉ* XI, 1936, pp. 54–7, 176–8.

18 A length of copper water pipe, 4.7 cm in diameter, was found at the Fifth Dynasty complex of Sahure by L. Borchardt. The pipe must have been formed around a wooden core (L. Borchardt, *Das Grabdenkmal des Königs Saȝhu-re'*, Leipzig: Hinrichs, 1910, vol. I, p. 78).

19 D.A. Stocks, 'Industrial technology at Kahun and Gurob: Experimental manufacture and test of replica and reconstructed tools with indicated uses and effects upon artefact production', unpublished thesis, University of Manchester, 1988, vol. I, p. 59.

20 J.F.S. Stone and L.C. Thomas, 'The use and distribution of faience in the ancient East and prehistoric Europe', *Proceedings of the Prehistoric Society* 22, 1956, pp. 37ff.

21 For example, a Predynastic lugged oblate spheroidal vessel of syenite, MM 1776.

22 W.B. Emery, *Archaic Egypt*, Harmondsworth: Penguin Books, 1984, p. 80; M.Z. Goneim, *The Buried Pyramid*, London: Longmans, Green and Company, 1956, p. 124. The tests show that calcite is hard enough to require sawing to shape with a flat-edged copper saw and sand abrasive. A serrated copper saw is unable to cut this stone (D.A. Stocks, 'Stone sarcophagus manufacture in Ancient Egypt', *Antiquity* 73, 1999, p. 919).

23 For example, Khufu's Fourth Dynasty granite sarcophagus; the schist triad of Menkaure (CM JE46499) is sawn in this way.

24 A. Lucas and J.R. Harris, *Ancient Egyptian Materials and Industries*, London: Edward Arnold, 1962, pp. 52ff. See also, 'Stone', in P.T. Nicholson and I. Shaw (eds) *Ancient Egyptian Materials and Technology*, Cambridge: Cambridge University Press, 2000.

25 Emery, *Archaic Egypt*, pp. 175–91.

26 The German mineralogist Friedrich Mohs devised a scale of hardness for minerals. In the Mohs scale, the softest mineral, talc, is 1; diamond is 10. The number scale is not arithmetic in progression.

27 For example, stone beads were manufactured at the Neolithic site of el-Omari, Egypt.

28 Lucas and Harris, *AEMI*, p. 41. See also 'Stone', in Nicholson and Shaw (eds) *AEMT*.

29 CM JE39866; G. Steindorff, *Das Grab des Ti*, Leipzig: Hinrichs, 1913, pl. 134.

30 N. de G. Davies, *The Rock Tombs of Deir el Gebrâwi*, London: Egypt Exploration Fund, 1902, vol. I, pl. XXIV.

31 C.M. Firth, J.E. Quibell and J.-P. Lauer, *The Step Pyramid*, Cairo: Imprimerie de l'Institut Française d'Archéologie Orientale, 1935–1936, vol. I, pl. 93.

32 Lucas and Harris, *AEMI*, p. 413.

33 Ibid., pp. 420–1.

34 Ibid., p. 422.

35 Ibid., pp. 421–3.

36 Caton-Thompson and Gardner, *The Desert Fayum*, p. 105.

37 A. Tillmann, 'Dynastic stone tools', in K.A. Bard (ed.) *Encyclopedia of the Archaeology of Ancient Egypt*, London and New York: Routledge, 1999, p. 265.

38 D.A. Stocks, 'Technical and material interrelationships: Implications for social change in Ancient Egypt', in W. Wendrich and G. van der Kooij (eds) *Moving Matters: Ethnoarchaeology in the Near East. Proceedings of the International Seminar held at Cairo, 7–10 December 1998*, Leiden: Leiden University, 2002, p. 107.

39 D.A. Stocks, 'The working of wood and stone in Ancient Egypt: The experimental manufacture and use of copper, bronze and stone tools', unpublished dissertation, University of Manchester, 1982, pp. 181–95; Stocks, 'Industrial technology', vol. I, p. 193.

40 Stocks, 'Technical and material interrelationships: Implications for social change in Ancient Egypt', p. 107.

41 For example, two chert crescents from Umm-es-Sawan (MM 8353–4); J.E. Quibell and F.W. Green, *Hierakonpolis II*, London: British School of Archaeology in Egypt, 1902, pls XXXII, LXII.

42 D.A. Stocks, 'Indications of Ancient Egyptian industrial interdependence: A preliminary statement', *The Manchester Archaeological Bulletin* 4, 1989, pp. 21–6; D.A. Stocks, 'Derivation of Ancient Egyptian faience core and glaze materials', *Antiquity* 71, 1997, pp. 179–82.

43 Emery, *Archaic Egypt*, pp. 76, 182.

44 Ibid., p. 80.

45 A.J. Spencer, *Death in Ancient Egypt*, Harmondsworth: Penguin Books, 1982, p. 166.

46 Ibid., p. 167; Goneim, *The Buried Pyramid*, p. 124.

47 W.M.F. Petrie, *The Pyramids and Temples of Gizeh*, London: Field and Tuer, 1883, pp. 84–90.

48 Now MM 28.

49 F.F. Leek, 'Teeth and bread in Ancient Egypt', *JEA* 58, 1972, pp. 126–32; F.F. Leek, 'The dental history of the Manchester mummies', in A.R. David (ed.) *Manchester Museum Mummy Project. Multidisciplinary Research on Ancient Egyptian Mummified Remains*, Manchester: Manchester University Press, 1979, p. 75.

50 Lucas and Harris, *AEMI*, pp. 429–56. See also, 'Stone', in Nicholson and Shaw (eds) *AEMT*.

51 J.R. Maréchal, 'Les outils égyptiens en cuivre', *Métaux, Corrosion, Industries* XXXII, 1957, pp. 132–3.

2

THE CUTTING EDGE

Copper and bronze cutting tools

The introduction of smelted and cast copper at the commencement of the Naqada II period enabled craftworkers to imitate the shapes of certain stone tools in copper, first mentioned by W.M. Flinders Petrie in 1917.[1] Following on from Petrie's suggestion, it is likely that several particular Predynastic stone implements were developed and transformed into five metallic tools. These were the flint end-scraper[2] (the copper chisel and the adze blade), the denticulated, or serrated, flint sickle blade and knife[3] (the serrated copper woodcutting saw, but no Predynastic examples have been found), the flint knife[4] (the copper knife) and the stone hand-axe,[5] manufactured in flint and other hard stones, but sometimes hafted for use as an adze blade (the copper axe). See Figure 2.1 for replica copper adzes, a saw and an axe. Copper tool manufacturing technology shortened previous stone tool manufacturing times, once the infrastructure for making copper tools became fully established. Two stone tools, the hand-axe and the knife, retained their basic shapes and purposes after being cast and beaten in copper, although the copper axe-head, used by carpenters and boat builders (Figure 2.2),[6] was now fitted with a long wooden handle to increase the force of a blow.

The chipping to shape, or the grinding, of stone tools demanded skills that differed enormously from the casting and beating techniques employed for manufacturing metallic copies of their unique configurations. The disparity between the two materials is very marked. While the manufacture of each type of material into tools produced the desired cutting edges, enabling craftworkers to split and shape raw materials, casting a metal tool into an open, horizontal mould in sand, already shaped into a tool's form, immediately caused a reduction in the manufacturing time per tool: this statement disregards the considerable logistical requirements needed to create the molten copper in the first place. The skills for beating a casting

DOI: 10.4324/9781003269922-4

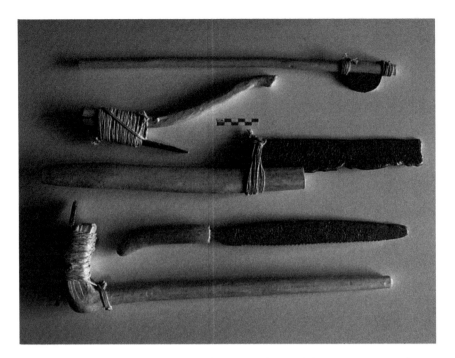

FIGURE 2.1 Two replica copper adzes (bottom and second from top), a serrated copper woodcutting saw (second from bottom) and a round-form copper axe,
with fastening lugs (top). The middle tool is a test, flat-edged copper saw

Source: Image by J. Stocks

FIGURE 2.2 Twelfth Dynasty workers wielding hafted axes. From the tomb of Pepionkh at Meir

Source: D. Stocks after A.M. Blackman and M.R. Apted, *The Rock Tombs of Meir*, London: Egypt
Exploration Society, part V, 1953, pl. XVIII

into a tool, and for grinding its cutting edge, were simpler than those for working flint, although flint tools, including adzes, axes, knives, and possibly chisels and punches[7] outnumbered metal tools at the Twelfth Dynasty workers' town of Kahun, situated in the Fayum district to the west of the Nile. Kahun was constructed by Senusret II to house the workers who built his pyramid at nearby Lahun. The extensive manufacture and use of flint tools there perhaps indicates their continued usefulness and lower production costs.[8] The preponderance of stone tools may also indicate a shortage of metal for making larger tools at this location in the Twelfth Dynasty. However, the knapping by pressure-flaking of flint knives, illustrated in two Middle Kingdom tombs at Beni Hasan, Middle Egypt,[9] suggests that the skills for working the flint were still very much in demand during this period.

Craftworkers often use the same tool for different purposes. For example, the long, slim, flint end-scraper, held in both hands, can be used to pare or scrape materials in a direction *away* from the worker, which craftworkers do today with steel woodcutting chisels. However, by holding the tool in one hand it could be struck as a chisel with a mallet. But by binding a flint end-scraper to a long wooden shaft, its cutting edge fastened at right-angles, or a similarly designed copper tool, it could now be swung *toward* himself for shaving wood (e.g. a ship-building scene in the Fifth Dynasty tomb of Ti at Saqqara) and soft limestone from tomb walls.[10]

Egyptian copper chisels developed into two basic shapes, the 'flat' and the 'crosscut', which are still in use today (Figure 2.3). The flat copper chisel, for working soft stone, was hammered into a wide, double tapering section, ending in

FIGURE 2.3   The shapes of the flat chisel (top) and the crosscut chisel (bottom) tapers

Source: Image by J. Stocks

FIGURE 2.4 A copper crosscut chisel from Kahun (from MM 204)

Source: Courtesy of the Manchester Museum, The University of Manchester

an edge sharpened from both sides; sometimes, like a modern woodcutting chisel, a single slope ended in an edge.[11] The flat chisel was useful for quickly removing large areas of wood and soft stone, where a perfectly flat and smooth surface was not initially important. To make the crosscut chisel,[12] a copper bar was initially hammered into a double taper, but was then turned through 90° and hammered into a second, narrower double taper. This chisel's shorter edge concentrated a blow upon a smaller cutting area; the Egyptian woodworker employed the crosscut chisel's superior strength to cut and lever wood from deep mortises (Figure 2.4). The flat chisel's edge operated on materials in a similar fashion to the adze blade. However, the twin advantages a chisel has over an adze are the craftworker's ability to direct the blade to an exact position on the work piece, *before* a blow is struck, and also to vary the chisel's angle of attack from an acute angle to the work piece through to a vertical position, which enables the tool to split materials like an axe blade.

The axe-head is more robust than the adze blade, having a shorter, but thicker, body in order to resist heavy blows. Egyptian copper and bronze (copper's alloy with tin) axe-heads were lashed to a wooden shaft utilizing single or multiple tying holes pierced into the tool's top edge,[13] or with lugs cast onto the blade (see Figure 2.1, top), the truly socketed axe only making an appearance in iron after the Twenty-sixth Dynasty.[14] The axe is just as good for splitting wood along the grain as well as for chopping it across the grain, as in tree felling. Egyptian adze and axe blades were invariably lashed to their wooden shafts with leather or rawhide thongs.[15]

Copper adze and axe-head blades are quite different to one another in their manner of construction and usage. Axe-head and chisel-edges were equally ground and sharpened from both sides of the blade, but the adze's edge was ground on one side of the blade only, usually on the outer side.[16] The axe was preceded by the chisel and the adze, which were smaller than the Dynastic axe, copper still being scarce in supply after casting of the chisel and adze began in the Predynastic period; the increased volume of copper required for an axe-head delayed its introduction into the craftworker's tool kit.

Slimmer copper chisels for working wood were fitted with wooden handles (Figures 2.5, 2.6).[17] A handle gave the craftworker a better grip on the tool when directing and holding the chisel onto the work piece before striking it with a mallet (Figure 2.7). This type of chisel, when operated with both hands, would also have been used for delicately paring wood, and possibly soft stone in some instances, in addition to scraping awkward corners in these two materials to a fine finish. A wooden handle also afforded some protection to a mallet (Figure 2.8) from the damage caused by impact during use. It is likely that metal chisels were used mainly on relatively soft stone, and, although ancient mallets have been recovered with severe circumferential damage to their surfaces (e.g. MMA 10.130.1013; BM 41187), there may have been another tool causing this damage, which will be

FIGURE 2.5   A copper chisel fitted with a wooden handle from Kahun (from MM 194a)

Source: Courtesy of the Manchester Museum, The University of Manchester

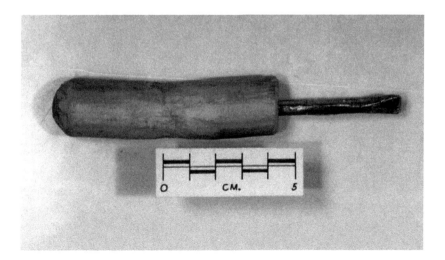

FIGURE 2.6   A replica woodworking chisel

Source: Image by J. Stocks

FIGURE 2.7 A mallet driving a replica woodworking chisel

Source: Image by J. Stocks

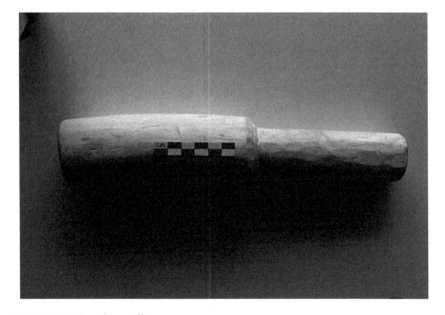

FIGURE 2.8 A replica mallet

Source: Image by J. Stocks

FIGURE 2.9   A necked adze blade, which assisted fastening it to a wooden handle (from MM 203)

Source: Courtesy of the Manchester Museum, The University of Manchester

discussed in the next chapter. Not all mallets were of wood; at least one limestone mallet was located by Petrie at Kahun.[18] The shape of a wooden mallet some-times varied. For example, a shipbuilding scene in the Fifth Dynasty tomb of Ti at Saqqara depicts craftworkers wielding long, club-shaped mallets for driving their woodworking chisels into the ship's timbers. Interestingly, two workers using simi-lar mallets are sat astride a wooden joist supported at each end by sturdy, upright, forked branches, each shaped like a 'Y', which are firmly lodged into the ground for stability.

Copper adze blade widths, necked (Figure 2.9) or straight (Figure 2.10), var-ied considerably,[19] and sometimes were markedly wider than chisels' edges. The wide-bladed adze (Figure 2.11), when accurately swung so that the blade makes a glancing surface blow, is useful for finishing soft limestone surfaces, and this type of work was investigated by Ernest Mackay in tomb chapels at Thebes.[20] It is possible to make a clear distinction between the tools employed in these circumstances. Imagine a right-handed worker using a mallet and chisel on a limestone tomb wall. Slots, the width of the chisel's blade, would traverse the wall in one particular direction. For example, if the chisel started from a top right position, then the slot would travel diagonally downward to the left. The converse would be true for a left-handed craftworker. Also, the chisel's line of travel would deviate here and there from a straight line (chisel shake), and this was observed and commented upon by Mackay.[21] The adze, however, may be swung equally well from either side by left- and right-handed craftworkers; the blade leaves oblique marks, which run from the left or from the right. Interestingly, ancient artists depicted a much lower proportion of left-handed to right-handed craftworkers in tomb scenes. The ratio today is approximately one left-hander to nine right-handers, and a similar ratio probably existed in Ancient Egypt, judging from the tomb representations.[22] The adze was utilized, in conjunction with sandstone rubbers, as a substitute for the

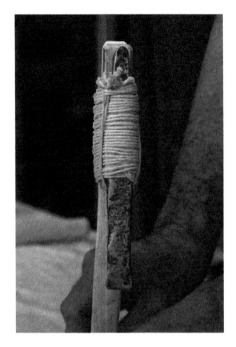

FIGURE 2.10   A replica copper adze

Source: Image by J. Stocks

FIGURE 2.11   A large replica adze blade

Source: Image by J. Stocks

plane to achieve smooth, flat surfaces on wooden objects: Ancient Egyptian artisans never developed the plane for woodworking.

Two other cutting edges deserving a high ranking in the pecking order of craft-workers' implements are serrated and flat-edged copper saws (see Figure 2.1). It is important that a distinction between saws with and without serrations is made at this stage. The earliest located serrated saws for cutting wood, and possibly for cutting soft stone, date to the Third Dynasty;[23] in addition to a model saw from this dynasty, a notched copper saw was found at Meidum.[24] It is likely, however, that the serrated saw originated even earlier than the First Dynasty, when it was employed for sawing wood for coffins. Saws were sometimes hammered with tangs, for fitting curved wooden handles, although in at least one Fifth Dynasty saw the handle was hammered from the same sheet of copper forming the blade.[25] The crudest saw was a blade notched by chopping it on a sharp object.[26] Other serrations may have been produced by sharp-edged sandstone rubbers. The technology for producing thin-bladed saws is linked to the casting of copper plates directly into open sand or pottery moulds and hammering the cooled casting into thinner sheets.

Evidence for the flat-edged copper saw for cutting hard stone is connected, in part, with slots and saw marks found on stone sarcophagi and other stone objects. For example, the Third Dynasty calcite sarcophagus of Sekhemkhet and the Fourth Dynasty rose granite sarcophagus of Khufu were sawn to shape.[27] Some slots have been connected by archaeological evidence to the use of copper,[28] but recent experiments with hard stone[29] have incontrovertibly shown that serrated copper, bronze, or indeed iron and steel saws could not possibly have cut such an unyielding material. A fuller appraisal of the flat-edged saw type, and its working method, will be discussed in Chapter 4, but all that needs to be said at present is that the casting of a plate of copper in an open mould was also utilized for manufacturing flat-edged, stonecutting saws, in addition to serrated woodcutting saws.

Ancient Egyptian craftworkers also employed two types of edged metal tools for drilling materials, and these were the bow-driven copper wood drill for drilling holes in furniture[30] and the bow-driven, and also directly hand-operated, flat-ended copper tubular drill.[31] This tube was employed for drilling not only deep holes in stone, but also shallow, tubular-shaped slots. An example of this practice, thought to be decorative, is a diorite bowl (MM 10959) belonging to Khaba of the Third Dynasty, which was supplied with a truly circular groove cut into the central section of the interior bottom surface.

Hard-stone vessel manufacture accelerated during the Naqada II period, owing its expansion to the increased employment of the copper tubular drill for the initial hollowing of vessels' interiors. The First and Second Dynasties saw the continuation of hard-stone vessel production and, subsequently, in the Third and Fourth Dynasties, the tube was additionally in use for the hollowing of calcite and harder-stone sarcophagi. The use of copper flat-ended tubes and flat-edged

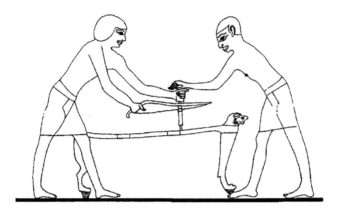

FIGURE 2.12 Two workers drilling a hole in a bed frame. From the tomb of Rekhmire
at Thebes

Source: Drawing by D. Stocks after N. de G. Davies, *The Tomb of Rekh-mi-Rē' at Thebes*, New York,
1943, vol. II, pl. LIII. Courtesy of the Metropolitan Museum of Art

saws upon stone share similar technological origins, and their full investigation
must await a later chapter. However, copper production must have expanded as
the demand for stonecutting tubes increased throughout the Late Predynastic
and Early Dynastic periods, and further increased by the requirement of copper
for stonecutting saws, as the use of stone for architectural and other purposes
came into vogue during, and later than, the First Dynasty. These demands for
the production of copper for tubes and saws were, of course, in addition to the
supply of copper for axes, adzes, chisels, serrated saws, knives, wood drills, awls
and other implements.

The bow-driven copper wood drill, illustrated in several tomb scenes,[32] was in
use for making rows of holes in chairs and beds for anchoring supporting lattices
of leather thong or cord (Figure 2.12). In the tomb of Rekhmire at Thebes,[33]
both uses are illustrated. The wood drill was also used for piercing a woodworking joint to admit dowels (wooden pins) for securing and strengthening it.[34] To
rotate a wood drill, a bow's string was given a single turn around a wooden shaft
into which the drill was tightly fitted. The top of the shaft was rounded to fit
snugly into a lubricated hemispherical-shaped bearing hole, which was chipped
and smoothed into the underside of a capstone. The lubricant was possibly tallow. Ancient wood drills could be shaped like a slim, flat chisel (e.g. BM 6042–3).
However, other drill blades were probably formed by beating the metal into a flat
taper and then shaping it like an arrowhead.[35] Two wood drills were made for test
(Figure 2.13), one with a sharpened, flat chisel-edge, the other supplied with an
arrowhead-shaped cutting point. No Predynastic drills for perforating wood have
ever been discovered.[36]

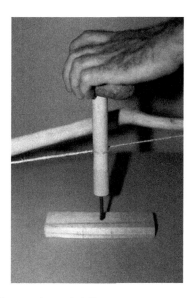

FIGURE 2.13   A replica bow and wood drill

Source: Image by J. Stocks

A cluster of furnaces: the key to manufacturing expansion

Predynastic horizontal open moulds for casting copper[37] were probably pressed into damp sand with angular stones (Figure 2.14): these moulds can only be used once. However, at the Twelfth Dynasty workers' town of Kahun, Petrie[38] found reusable, open pottery moulds lined with a smooth coat of clay and ash, for axe-heads, chisels and knives; fired pottery moulds allowed the mass-production of identically shaped tools, increasing their availability for work. Petrie found unworked cast copper knives, about 1/4 inch (6 mm) thick,[39] which were then hammered down to the thin blades required. The experimental casting of a flat-edged, copper stonecutting saw blade into a shallow, open sand mould revealed that the floor of the mould, when *just* completely covered with molten copper, created a 5 mm thick casting (Figures 2.15, 2.16, 2.17).[40] Therefore, any ancient copper artifact needing a finished thickness of less than 5 mm, such as a serrated saw blade for cutting wood, had to be hammered thinner from its original cast thickness of about 5 mm. However, any artifact requiring a finished thickness of 5 mm, or above, could be left at its cast thickness. This phenomenon will be examined in Chapter 4 in connection with saw slots up to 1/5 inch (5 mm) wide,[41] seen in hard-stone artifacts by Petrie.

Closed pottery and stone moulds (Figure 2.18),[42] in two halves (e.g. CM JE37554), and the lost-wax (*cire perdue*) process created small, solid castings. Many wax figures for the casting process have been found. Good examples are the figure of Isis, a hippopotamus, a falcon and a vulture,[43] but large, lost-wax moulds, with clay cores enveloped within the wax, produced hollow castings that consumed

FIGURE 2.14   A mould pressed into damp sand for casting a flat-edged saw

Source: Image by J. Stocks

FIGURE 2.15   Casting a flat-edged copper saw blade in an open sand mould

Source: Image by J. Stocks

relatively less metal. Cores for closed moulds may have been manufactured from sun-dried clay or pottery, in addition to sand mixed with organic materials.[44]

Ancient Egyptian furnace workers developed two methods for blowing air into their smelting and melting furnaces. These were the blowpipe,[45] and the foot-operated bellows of the Eighteenth Dynasty.[46] Both in the Predynastic and Dynastic periods, the smelting furnace may have been a shallow pit dug into the side of a low hill (Figure 2.19), or in a valley, a technique employed in the Wadi Nasb in the Sinai. Such a furnace-hole would have been connected from its base to the open

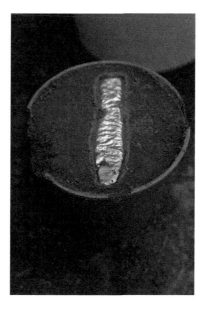

FIGURE 2.16 A cast copper adze blade

Source: Image by J. Stocks

FIGURE 2.17 A cast copper woodcutting saw blade

Source: Image by J. Stocks

FIGURE 2.18 An experimental stone mould for casting a chisel

Source: Image by J. Stocks

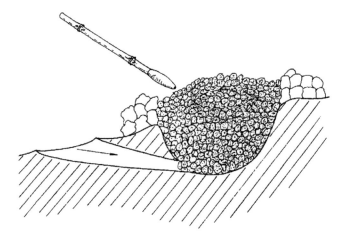

FIGURE 2.19 A possible construction of an ancient smelting furnace

Source: Image by D. Stocks

air by a sloping trench to admit the wind. C.T. Currelly[47] found a smelting furnace in the Sinai, which consisted of a 75 cm-deep hole in the ground surrounded by a stone wall perforated by two wind-admittance holes. However, it is likely that blowpipes were used in conjunction with naturally admitted air, maintaining a higher temperature; the wind is not always reliable. The air for Dynastic melting furnaces was supplied with blowpipes, until the advent of the foot-operated bellows.

Tomb illustrations dating from the Old Kingdom show melting furnaces either upon the ground's surface, or inside some form of fireplace, depicted in side elevation.[48] These furnaces are all supplied with air from blowpipes. An illustration in the Sixth Dynasty tomb of Mereruka at Saqqara shows two rhyton-shaped crucibles placed back to back above the surface of the ground, and it appears unlikely that such furnaces were assisted by the wind. It has been suggested by Alessandra Nibbi[49] that three of these crucibles were stood back to back for support, allowing hot gases freely to circulate; each crucible would have stood at 120° to one another. In the Eighteenth Dynasty tomb of Hapu,[50] two workers are using blowpipes in conjunction with a foot-operated bellows; this may indicate a large crucible full of bronze, which required additional air to melt it.

Ancient smelting furnace-holes were probably lined with stones before filling with charcoal and ore, the finished hole measuring approximately 30 cm in diameter, with a height of about 25 cm. Furnaces of these dimensions have been examined by B. Rothenberg at a chalcolithic copper smelting site at Timna in the Negev desert.[51] Their efficiency was examined by R.F. Tylecote and P.J. Boydell,[52] who constructed experimental furnaces fired with charcoal. The controlled admission of air into a melting furnace is crucial if its interior is to reach the temperature necessary to melt the metal contained in a crucible; copper requires a temperature of 1,083°C. For bronzes containing varying amounts of tin, lower temperatures are sufficient. For example, a bronze containing 10 per cent tin has a melting point some 80°C less than pure copper. Tylecote and Boydell discovered that an air flow of 200 l/minute, delivered through a tuyere, raised the furnace temperature to 1,300°C,[53] more than enough to smelt ore, or melt copper in a crucible. The test furnace, of similar dimensions to the Timna furnaces, enabled an air flow of 200 l/minute to melt 1 kg of copper. This furnace also possessed a maximum melting capacity of 2 kg of bronze, when operated with an air flow of 600 l/minute.

Some experiments were conducted with a reconstructed blowpipe manufactured from a bamboo cane, but in Ancient Egypt blowpipes would have been constructed from the bamboo-like common reed: tomb artists depicted blowpipes with clearly defined leaf joints.[54] Tomb representations also show that two types of blowpipe were in use. In the Eighteenth Dynasty tomb of Rekhmire at Thebes,[55] a jeweller's blowpipe is about 60 cm long, whereas a drawing in the Twelfth Dynasty tomb of Pepionkh depicts furnace blowpipes of approximately 1.5 m in length (Figure 2.20).[56] The experimental cane possessed an average external diameter of just over 2 cm, and a length of 56 cm (Figure 2.21). Workers crucially adapted a reed into a tube by jabbing a slimmer, sharpened reed, or stick, through the leaf-joint partitions and uniting the previously separate hollow sections. The experimental cane was adapted in a similar fashion.

The experimental blowpipe was fitted with a clay nozzle to protect the organic material from the intense heat of the furnace; before the clay dried hard, an 8 mm-diameter nozzle hole was made with a stick. It is likely that ancient nozzle hole diameters varied from pipe to pipe. What volume of air per minute could an ancient furnace worker deliver to the furnace with a blowpipe? An experiment determined that a full breath (approximately 5 litres) could be discharged through the pipe in one second. A sustainable rate of air delivery was found to be about

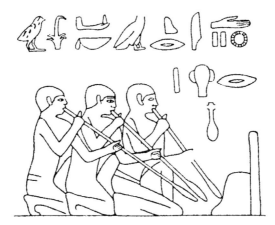

FIGURE 2.20   Ancient furnace blowpipes. From the tomb of Pepionkh at Meir

Source: Drawing by D. Stocks after A.M. Blackman and M.R. Apted, *The Rock Tombs of Meir*, London: Egypt Exploration Society, 1953, part V, pl. XVI

FIGURE 2.21   The reconstructed blowpipe

Source: Image by D. Stocks

50 l/minute: blowing more air than this brought about the unpleasant effects of hyperventilation. This condition causes dizziness which, in extreme cases, can develop into paralysis of the limbs. It is caused by breathing so deeply and quickly that the carbon dioxide in the blood falls to dangerously low levels. Carbon dioxide is essential for the correct operation of the central nervous system.

The main limitation to a furnace's ability to melt metal is the volume of air that constantly can be maintained during the melting process. Tomb illustrations in the Fifth Dynasty tomb of Ti, the Sixth Dynasty tomb of Mereruka, the Twelfth Dynasty tomb of Pepionkh and the Eighteenth Dynasty tomb of Hapu depict furnace workers blowing air by pipes into furnaces.[57] Without the benefit of wind assistance, and before the foot-operated bellows was employed in the Eighteenth Dynasty, melting capacity must have been directly connected to the numbers of workers employed for blowpipe duty. In the tomb of Mereruka at Saqqara, six men are equipped with blowpipes. This number of workers could supply enough air, if blowing it at the experimental rate of 50 l/minute (a total of 300 l/minute), to melt more than 1 kg of copper in a single crucible. Illustrations in the tomb of Asa at Deir el Gebrâwi,[58] in the Twelfth Dynasty tomb of Pepionkh[59] and in the Eighteenth Dynasty tomb of Hapu, respectively depict four, three and two workers blowing through pipes. Although the tomb of Rekhmire depicts a single jeweller using a blowpipe at a small brazier, set upon a low support, this worker is not melting metal, but probably heating it before soldering (Figure 2.22).

The foot-operated bellows was an interesting development of furnace technology; good examples are shown in the Eighteenth Dynasty Theban tombs of (Figure 2.23), Puyemre and Nebamun and Ipuky.[60] These consist of two adjacently placed, flat-bottomed circular pottery bowls, each fitted with a loose leather diaphragm tightly fastened at the rim; a long string is attached to the centre of each diaphragm. Projecting toward the furnace, from the side of each bowl, is a reed tube fitted with a clay nozzle. (An example of a Late Period pottery bowl is BM 22367, from Tell Defenna. The bowl is 19.5 cm high and 56 cm in diameter.

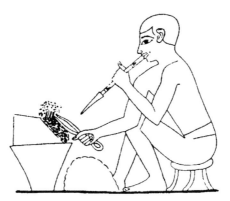

FIGURE 2.22   An Eighteenth Dynasty jeweler at work. From the tomb of Rekhmire at Thebes

Source: Drawing by D. Stocks after N. de G. Davies, *The Tomb of Rekh-mi-Rē' at Thebes*, New York, 1943, vol. II, pl. LIV. Courtesy of the Metropolitan Museum of Art

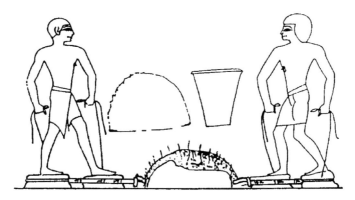

FIGURE 2.23   Eighteenth Dynasty foot-bellows in operation. From the tomb of Rekhmire at Thebes

Source: Drawing by D. Stocks after N. de G. Davies, *The Tomb of Rekh-mi-Rē' at Thebes*, New York, 1943, vol. II, pl. LIV. Courtesy of the Metropolitan Museum of Art

A reed tube was probably sealed into position with mud into the hole pierced through the bowl's side near to its base.) To work the bellows, a worker alternately trod on one diaphragm and simultaneously pulled up the other with the attached string, raising the foot at the same time. A natural 'walking' rhythm ensured a steady supply of air through the reed tubes. Possibly, a small gap in the mud sealing the reed pipe into the bowl's air exit hole, or through the clay nozzle, allowed fresh air to be drawn in when the worker pulled up the diaphragm. Alternatively, an air admission hole cut into the diaphragm, situated under the worker's heel, became sealed during the downward compression cycle.

In an Eighteenth Dynasty scene in the tomb of Rekhmire,[61] the manufacture of a large bronze door is depicted, which must have required the use of several furnaces in order to melt sufficient bronze for the casting operation (Figure 2.24). Even if two or three crucibles of metal were melted in one furnace in the Eighteenth Dynasty, and this is not supported by the scenes of furnaces in the tomb of Rekhmire, no single crucible could have held much more than approximately 1.3 kg of metal. This estimate of a crucible's capacity is recorded by Christopher Davey[62] in his study of six crucibles from the Petrie Collection at University College London. A crucible of this volume is considered to be large by Egyptian standards, and this amount was just sufficient to cast large axe-heads; examples are a 1.2 kg copper axe-head (Figure 2.25) from Kahun (MM 201) and a 1.1 kg bronze axe-head from Gurob (MM 616), an Eighteenth Dynasty town situated close to Kahun.

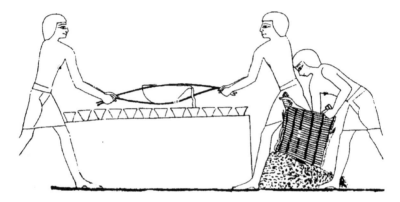

FIGURE 2.24   Casting an Eighteenth Dynasty bronze door. From the tomb of Rekhmire at Thebes

Source: Drawing by D. Stocks after N. de G. Davies, *The Tomb of Rekh-mi-Rē' at Thebes*, New York, 1943, vol. II, pl. LII. Courtesy of the Metropolitan Museum of Art

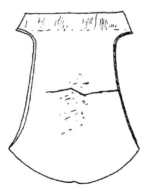

FIGURE 2.25   A copper axe-head from Kahun (from MM 201)

Source: Drawing by D. Stocks after the Manchester Museum, The University of Manchester

FIGURE 2.26   Experimental withies holding a clay crucible

Source: Image by J. Stocks

The crucible possessing a capacity of 1.3 kg came from Qau, and is attributed to the Seventh or Eighth Dynasty. It was constructed from fine clay mixed with straw and shaped like a deep bowl, with a hole in the side. This type of crucible could be rocked forwards, on the ground, to discharge molten metal from a lip, but other types of crucible were carried with flat stones or pottery pads (tomb of Mereruka),[63] and long, slim, green sticks or withies (tomb of Rekhmire, see Figure 2.24).[64] Newly cut sticks (Figure 2.26) have been tested on red-hot crucibles and found adequately to resist burning for a short period. Crucibles came in varying sizes and shapes. These included oval, globular, shallow broad-shaped (tomb of Rekhmire),[65] bowl-shaped and a curved crucible shown in the tomb of Mereruka. This crucible shape (rhyton), when shown back to back in Mereruka's tomb, has been suggested by Davey to be the basis of an Old Kingdom ideogram, which either indicates the use of copper or identifies the person as a metalworker.[66] The crucible is shown releasing molten copper through a hole near to the base, but in the tomb of Rekhmire two workers are engaged in pouring molten bronze into a mould from the lip of a shallow, broad-shaped crucible.[67]

In the Twelfth Dynasty, four large copper boxes were cast in closed moulds. They were excavated at Tôd in Upper Egypt by F. Bisson de la Roque.[68] One of the boxes weighs 37.5 kg, and its walls are 1 cm thick. It is likely that between 25 and 30 large crucibles of copper were needed to cast this box in a single operation, and it is abundantly clear that the use of multiple numbers of furnaces was normal in the Middle and New Kingdom periods. The archaeological evidence for the employment of large diameter copper tubular drills and long copper saws, from the Third Dynasty onward, for the drilling and sawing of calcite and granite sarcophagi indicates that ancient stonecutting tubes and saws, particularly the saws, required a considerable amount of copper to make a single tool.

Before the need for large diameter copper tubes, commencing with the hollowing of calcite sarcophagi in the Third Dynasty at Saqqara, a smaller diameter copper tube, for drilling the hard-stone vessels, required much less copper to make it, only needing a single furnace for its successful manufacture. However, at Old Kingdom stoneworking sites, where large saws and tubes were in demand, a cluster of furnaces, situated to the south of work sites (the wind normally blows from the north in Egypt), must have been concurrently operated for the casting of these two substantial tools. The longest saws probably required up to 20 kg of copper (e.g. for cutting Khufu's granite sarcophagus to shape), the largest known diameter tube for sarcophagus manufacture (Khufu's 11 cm-diameter tube – see Chapter 4) possibly needing between 2–4 kg of copper, depending upon the tube's wall thickness, which, for Khufu's sarcophagus drill-tube, will always remain unknown.

The implications for the sustained production of copper, and its use, are immense. As the demand for larger copper artifacts grew, so the numbers of furnaces must have expanded until a foundry became sufficiently organized for sizeable objects to be cast by the coordinated use of many crucibles. The industrial infrastructure necessary to recover and smelt the copper ores, to distribute metal ingots to foundry sites, to melt and cast the copper and subsequent bronze into large and small tools, and other artifacts, must have taken considerable administration. By the Third Dynasty, Egypt's ability to provide its craftworkers with sufficient tools – chisels, axes, adzes, stonecutting saws and tubular drills, and many other metallic tools – was sufficiently developed to tackle increasingly larger projects, commencing with the Step Pyramid at Saqqara and progressing into the building and furbishing of the Fourth Dynasty pyramids at Giza and later Dynastic undertakings. At Giza, Mark Lehner and his Giza Plateau Mapping Project team are uncovering a large, complex community, including bakeries, copper workshops and workers' houses, which supported the builders of Egypt's greatest monuments – the pyramids of Khufu, Khafre and Menkaure.[69]

Hammering: the art of forceful shaping

The hammering of copper and bronze for both shaping and hardening these metals became an established craft after the introduction of copper casting at the commencement of the Naqada II period. In particular, copper, and later bronze, cutting tools were necessarily hammered in the cold state to achieve maximum hardness.[70] Tongs are not depicted in tomb scenes until the Eighteenth Dynasty tomb of Rekhmire,[71] but it is unlikely that these were ever used for holding hot copper and bronze tools during the hammering process. To illustrate that tongs were unnecessary for this purpose, a bronze bar (95 per cent copper, 5 per cent tin) was raised to a bright red heat and immediately hammered. Within several seconds, the metal fractured into several pieces. Red-hot copper and bronze become brittle because of changes in their crystal structures, which occur at elevated temperatures.[72] However, after a period of cold hammering, copper alloys need to be annealed (softened) by reheating to a dull red colour and allowing them to cool slowly. This restores a metal's malleability and delays cracks in the metal caused by excessive hammering.

In Dynastic tomb scenes, workers are depicted using hand-held stone hammers (Figure 2.27).[73] (Normally, wooden handles were never fitted to stone tools, except for picks, mauls and large pounders – see Chapter 3.) The craftworker must have possessed an extensive collection of hard-stone hammers, which were of different sizes and shapes, to cope with differing metal types, such as copper, bronze, gold and silver. The illustrations in the tomb of Rekhmire show stone hammers to be spherical or hemispherical. Sometimes, the craftworker is using the flat side of the stone hemisphere, sometimes the curved surface. It might be expected that a worker's hand and wrist were jolted with each blow of the hammer, which, after many blows, would cause injury and pain. Experimentally beating copper and bronze artifacts into shape (Figure 2.28), particularly chisels, demonstrated that ancient coppersmiths probably suffered some form of repetitive strain injury.

An illustration in the tomb of Rekhmire[74] depicts a cast plate being thinned upon a smooth stone anvil mounted upon a wooden block, its base buried in the earth (Figure 2.29). A spherical stone hammer is shown for the initial beating of

FIGURE 2.27 Pounding a limestone sphinx and an offering table with spherical stone hammers. From the tomb of Rekhmire at Thebes

Source: Drawing by D. Stocks after N. de G. Davies, *The Tomb of Rekh-mi-Rēʿ at Thebes*, New York, 1943, vol. II, pl. LX. Courtesy of the Metropolitan Museum of Art

FIGURE 2.28   Beating a reconstructed copper saw casting to shape on a stone anvil with a stone hammer

Source: Image by J. Stocks

FIGURE 2.29   Beating copper on a stone anvil mounted upon a wooden block. From the tomb of Rekhmire at Thebes

Source: Drawing by D. Stocks after N. de G. Davies, *The Tomb of Rekh-mi-Rē' at Thebes*, New York, 1943, vol. II, pl. LV. Courtesy of the Metropolitan Museum of Art

the metal, although gold and silver are actually being worked in the tomb scene, not copper. Metalworkers also used spherical and hemispherical hand-held stone hammers for beating metal vessels to shape, which were placed upside down on a tripod anvil, seen in illustrations in the Eighteenth Dynasty tomb of Rekhmire at Thebes (Figure 2.30).[75] (Possibly, stone vessels were also mounted upon the anvil for smoothing their exteriors with stone rubbers.) Craftworkers are depicted beating metal vases with the flat side of a hemispherical hammer, as well as its curved surface. Using the illustration in the tomb of Rekhmire as a guide, a reconstructed New Kingdom anvil consists of a forked branch, the forked end being placed on the ground at an acute angle. A long wooden rod passes easily through an upward

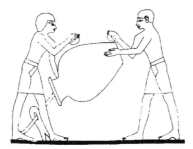

FIGURE 2.30 Beating a metal vase to shape using a tripod anvil. From the tomb of Rekhmire at Thebes

Source: Drawing by D. Stocks after N. de G. Davies, *The Tomb of Rekh-mi-Rēʿ at Thebes*, New York, 1943, vol. II, pl. LIII. Courtesy of the Metropolitan Museum of Art

FIGURE 2.31 The reconstructed tripod anvil

Source: Image by J. Stocks

slanting hole, drilled into the upper, single stem. The rod not only acts as the anvil's third leg, but can be adjusted for work on both small and large vessels by sliding the rod through the hole (Figures 2.31, 2.32, 2.33). The weight of a vessel on the rod and branch interlocks them into a stable tripod during the work. Stability is assured, as any three-legged object is quite steady on uneven ground. It is likely that the end of the rod, when in use for silver and gold vases, could be fitted with interchangeable padded heads, possibly made of leather, which were either curved or angular in shape.

We are so used to modern hammers being fitted with wooden handles that it is perhaps difficult for us to understand why Egyptian stone hammers were not fitted with them. However, the Egyptian craftworker's ability to execute delicate and

FIGURE 2.32 Demonstrating the tripod anvil, adjusted for use with a large vessel

Source: Image by J. Stocks

FIGURE 2.33 Demonstrating the tripod anvil, adjusted for use with a small vessel

Source: Image by J. Stocks

heavy hammering operations on different metals must have been enhanced by a varied and large stone hammer collection. (It is normal practice for craftworkers to keep tools used for present work in case they are needed for future use.) Supplying such a large number of hammers with handles would have been counterproductive. However, a handle existed which could be adapted to almost any weight or shape of stone hammer – the human hand and arm: there was no compulsion on the worker to change a strategy that had already served for many generations prior to the introduction of copper. The elbow, in conjunction with the lower

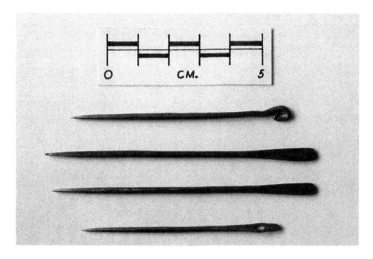

FIGURE 2.34 Three replica Dynastic copper needles and a replica Predynastic copper pin

Source: Image by J. Stocks

arm's ability to twist through nearly 180°, while the upper arm remains stationary, allows humans consistently to apply downward blows that instantly can be varied in weight, frequency and direction; both the lightest, and the heaviest, blows necessary for delicate work on gold vessels, jewellery and leaf, and for fashioning metal tools, can be monitored closely by the eye and the brain, whereas a hammer's head fitted with a handle can easily be misdirected.

These assumptions were tested by making replicas (Figure 2.34)[76] of three Dynastic copper needles (the originals came from Kahun),[77] a Predynastic copper loop-headed pin (the example came from Naqada),[78] a pointed bronze borer (Figure 2.35) and two copper awls, all fitted with handles, and two experimentally cast and hammered bronze punches. After hammering one particular needle to shape, full annealing was carried out. Scraping small, shallow depressions in opposite sides of the soft copper with a flint microlith started the eyehole (Figure 2.36). A hammer-hardened copper punch was used to penetrate through the weakened section (Figure 2.37). Finally, the body of the needle was hammer-hardened, and a sharp point achieved by rubbing on a smooth piece of sandstone (Figure 2.38). H.H. Coghlan,[79] a metallurgist, used a hardened *bronze* punch to make a 4 mm-diameter hole through an annealed copper sheet, 0.75 mm thick. However, the tests demonstrated that a fully hardened *copper* punch was capable of making a hole in annealed sheet copper. Similarly, a hammer-hardened bronze punch can make holes in annealed sheet bronze. The pin's annealed, looped head was formed over the borer which, when firmly forced into its wooden handle, acted as a small anvil.

In the tomb of Rekhmire,[80] craftworkers are depicted piercing leather sandals with awls fitted with wooden handles (Figure 2.39), and experiments with the hammer-hardened awls showed they quickly made holes in leather, and the borer did likewise in leather and wood. Painted scenes in this tomb show craftworkers

FIGURE 2.35 A pointed bronze borer

Source: Image by J. Stocks

FIGURE 2.36 Scraping a depression into an annealed copper needle with a flint tool

Source: Image by J. Stocks

FIGURE 2.37 A hole punched through the head of an annealed copper needle

Source: Image by J. Stocks

FIGURE 2.38 Sharpening the point of a hammer-hardened needle on a smooth piece of sandstone

Source: Image by J. Stocks

FIGURE 2.39 A leather-worker pierces a sandal with an awl. From the tomb of Rekhmire at Thebes

Source: Drawing by D. Stocks after N. de G. Davies, *The Tomb of Rekh-mi-Rē' at Thebes*, New York, 1943, vol. II, pl. LII. Courtesy of the Metropolitan Museum of Art

FIGURE 2.40 Cutting a long thong from a hide. From the tomb of Rekhmire at Thebes

Source: Drawing by D. Stocks after N. de G. Davies, *The Tomb of Rekh-mi-Rē' at Thebes*, New York, 1943, vol. II, pl. LII. Courtesy of the Metropolitan Museum of Art

cutting leather with a curved bronze blade (Figure 2.40). One worker is removing a long thong, by cutting around the circumference of a circular sheet of leather, and another is cutting out a sandal part. Thongs were used in sandal manufacture, for fastening metal tools to their handles and for leather rope (e.g. a plaited leather rope CM JE56282B). A test curved bronze blade cut leather perfectly well.

Enter the bow: a power transmission device

It is thought that bow drilling in Egypt originated from the bow and arrow, which developed into the fire drill.[81] The bow's other uses as a rotational power transmission device included the turning of Predynastic and Dynastic tubular drills of reed, copper and bronze for making small and large holes in stone; the rotation of the Dynastic waisted wooden drill-stock for holding metallic wood drills, short fire drills and possibly flint or other stone borers; the Predynastic and Dynastic single copper and bronze drills for perforating stone beads; the New Kingdom simultaneous multiple bead–drilling apparatus from Thebes, Upper Egypt. Good examples of single bronze bead drills, which were force-fitted into waisted, wooden shafts, were discovered by G.A. Reisner, who excavated them at Kerma in the Sudan.[82]

In order for a bow to rotate any drill – for making fire, for drilling stone beads, for drilling stone with a small-diameter tube – its bow-string had to be adjusted to a correct length, enabling a single twist to be made around the drill-shaft, which automatically placed tension upon the string by inducing a bending force in the seasoned, rigid bow-shaft. The motion associated with the bow drill, a push and pull movement, or a reciprocating motion, is directly turned into alternate clockwise and anticlockwise rotary motion by the string's grip on the drill-shaft. The Egyptian bow for driving the fire drill and the wood drill could sometimes be shaped like a human arm, partly bent at an obtuse angle at the 'elbow'. An example of such a bow, of New Kingdom date (BM 6040), has slots cut into each end with which to secure the bow-string; this shape is also represented in the tomb of Rekhmire at Thebes (Figures 2.41, 2.42).[83] A different bow-shaft is curved at one end, where the driller held it (see Figure 2.44).[84] To make an ancient angled

FIGURE 2.41   An 'elbow'-shaped bow driving a wood drill. From the tomb of Rekhmire at Thebes

Source: Drawing by D. Stocks after N. de G. Davies, *The Tomb of Rekh-mi-Rē' at Thebes*, New York, 1943, vol. II, pl. LII. Courtesy of the Metropolitan Museum of Art

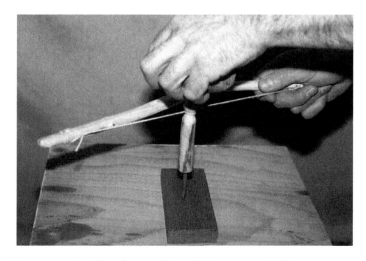

FIGURE 2.42   A replica 'elbow'-shaped bow driving a wood drill

Source: Image by J. Stocks

or curved bow-shaft, a main stem above a forked branch of the correct thickness could be cut away and the slightly raised stump smoothed away. In use, the bow was gripped at the shorter of the two angled parts of the shaft. After seasoning, the replica bow-shafts assumed considerable rigidity, unlike a hunting bow, which must possess flexibility and strength.

String and rope were made from a variety of natural materials, and these included camel hair, halfa grass (*Desmostachya bipinnata*), flax and date palm fibres, as well as linen, papyrus and leather.[85] Ancient string and rope manufacture must have been extensive, and the industry is recorded in nine different tombs. Emily Teeter[86] has summarized manufacturing methods. The first step involved the making of yarns from fibres, which were all twisted in the same direction. Second, several yarns were twisted around each other in the opposite direction. The first yarn twisting, and possibly the twisting of the yarns together into the final product, was achieved by a worker securing them at one end, while the opposite ends of the yarns were either twisted by hand in earlier times or, later, by another worker using a device for this purpose. This artifact, illustrated in the tomb of Rekhmire (Figure 2.43),[87] appears to show two yarns separately tied to a position near each end of a wooden bar, which was given the impetus to revolve by swinging a single, suspended spherical weight from one end of the bar. Rapidly propelling the weighted bar in a circular movement imparted a twist to the yarns.

The scene from the tomb of Rekhmire shows a belt around the worker's waist, possibly of leather, which is fastened to part of the equipment; the worker leans backwards to exert tension on the yarns. This part of the equipment may have consisted of a wooden bearing rod, or peg, which loosely fitted into a hole drilled into the centre of the bar, similar to the principle of the peg carved at the top of

FIGURE 2.43   An Eighteenth Dynasty yarn-twisting device. From the tomb of Rekhmire at Thebes

Source: Drawing by D. Stocks after N. de G. Davies, *The Tomb of Rekh-mi-Rē' at Thebes*, New York, 1943, vol. II, pl. LII. Courtesy of the Metropolitan Museum of Art

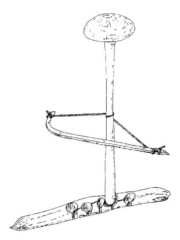

FIGURE 2.44 Twelfth Dynasty fire-making equipment (from MM 63–6)

Source: Courtesy of the Manchester Museum, The University of Manchester

a Twelfth Dynasty bow-driven drill-stock from Kahun. (This peg revolved in a clearance hole drilled into a wooden bearing cap held in the driller's hand – see note 91 and Figure 2.46.) Otherwise, the belt around the worker's waist would gradually have tightened as the revolving bar twisted the yarns together. It is likely, therefore, that a cord fastened to the belt was secured through a hole drilled into the end of the bearing rod nearest the worker's waist. A working reconstruction revealed that a single weight suspended at one end of the bar kept it rapidly rotating upon the bearing rod, clockwise or anticlockwise, according to the required direction of twist. To achieve this, a tight grip of the rod was necessary to rotate it energetically in small circular movements, which transmitted a turning motion to the bar, causing the two yarns to twist together.

Fire-making equipment was found at Twelfth Dynasty Kahun by Petrie.[88] These implements, now exhibited at The Manchester Museum (Figure 2.44), consist of a capstone (MM 63), a wooden block (MM 64), a bow (MM 65) and a fire drill (MM 66). The block was prepared for fire-making by the drilling of several deep holes, probably made with a wood drill. These holes were broken through, or notched, at the block's edges in order to allow smouldering wood powder to fall onto the tinder. It is likely that the bow's original string measured 2 mm in diameter; an example of this diameter string was found at Deir el Bahri (BM 43226).

The Kahun fire drill measures 40 cm in length, gradually tapering from a central narrow waist, 16 mm in diameter, toward the 18 mm-diameter bulbous-shaped ends. In use, the top end rotated in a capstone, the lower end spinning in an unused hole drilled into the block. Effectively, the drill rotated in two bearings. The lubricated stone bearing allowed the operator to apply pressure to the drill, while vigorously turning it with the bow. The experiments with replica Kahun

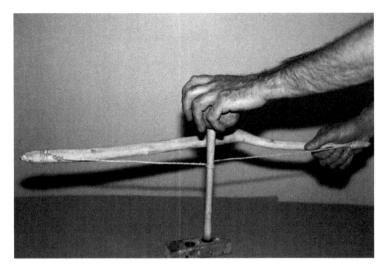

FIGURE 2.45 Experimental fire-making with a reconstructed fire drill

Source: Image by J. Stocks

equipment (Figure 2.45)[89] demonstrated that ancient fire drills were probably made from a hardwood, whereas the blocks needed to be made from a soft wood. The manufacture of a specially carved fire drill was a time-consuming business, and the experiments revealed that a hardwood drill wore slowly during use. Conversely, the block's softer wood is turned into a relatively large amount of charcoal powder.

Fire-making materials were discovered by Howard Carter in the Eighteenth Dynasty tomb of Tutankhamen at Thebes.[90] This equipment consisted of a waisted wooden drill-stock. The bottom end was flat and drilled upward with a centrally placed hole. The stock was found with a short fire drill force-fitted into this hole. Also discovered in the tomb was a block possessing 12 holes, some having been used for fire-making. Flinders Petrie discovered a similar drill-stock at Twelfth Dynasty Kahun,[91] and one at Eighteenth Dynasty Gurob.[92] The Kahun drill-stock's upper end was carved into a central peg, upon which was fitted a wooden bearing cap; the arrangement allowed the stock freely to turn when rotated with a bow, whilst the cap was held steady (Figure 2.46). This stock also has a short, vertical hole drilled into its body, commencing from the centre of the bottom flat end; its purpose was to hold copper and bronze wood drills, as well as small fire drills and, possibly, flint borers. These tools could be released by pushing them out of the vertical hole with a slim stick poked down an inclined hole, which connected the drill-stock's circumference to the blind end of the vertical hole.

The stock has flat faces carved around its tapering circumference, and these extend for the whole length of the tool. Tutankhamen's drill-stock had also been carved in a similar fashion. The Gurob stock is similar in all respects to the Kahun and Theban drill-stocks, but had not been carved with flat faces. Petrie also located a short, Eighteenth Dynasty fire drill at Kahun,[93] which was found associated with

FIGURE 2.46   The Kahun drill-stock with its wooden bearing cap (from MM 23)

Source: Courtesy of the Manchester Museum, The University of Manchester

a scarab belonging to Amenhotep III, and it is likely that the drill was in use with a drill-stock; its pointed upper end made it unsuitable for a bearing cap.

The experiments with the replica Kahun fire drill demonstrated that 20 cm-long push and pull strokes of the bow, delivered at the high frequency rate of 180 strokes/minute, caused a rapid increase in heat production, induced by high frictional forces at the point of contact between the drill and the wooden block. This stroke length and frequency were achieved with a replica bow of similar length to the Kahun bow. Calculations involving the diameter of the fire drill at the point where the bow-string operated, and the suggested stroke length and frequency, indicate that the ancient drill spun at approximately 700 revolutions/minute. A load of 2 kg was applied to the replica drill; the string slipped around the drill at a higher load. Large volumes of smoke accompanied the production of charred wood powder, after an initial 'bedding in' of the drill for about three seconds; the hot powder easily ignited a ball of tinder. The reason for the tapered design of ancient fire drills and drill-stocks becomes apparent during their use. As the bow-string stretches, due to the vigorous movement of the bow, it slackens its grip upon the shaft. However, by allowing the bow-string to engage on a larger diameter of the fire drill, up or down and, therefore, on a greater circumference, it automatically tightens as drilling continues.

After a period of approximately 10 seconds, and this time varied with the rotational speed of the drill and the pressure applied to it, heat production declined

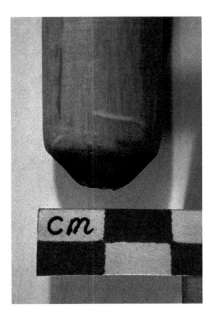

FIGURE 2.47   The charred end of the experimental fire drill

Source: Image by J. Stocks

rapidly, and this was due to the forming of a hard, smooth, carbonized surface on both the fire drill (Figure 2.47) and the hole in the block. Carbon has good lubricating qualities, and it is clear that the blocks were drilled with several holes to enable a fresh hole to be used each time the equipment was required. The drill's carbon layer needed removing before the next fire-making operation commenced.

The Twelfth Dynasty Kahun fire drill was superseded by the employment of a short drill engaged in a drill-stock. The drill-stock hardly suffered damage in use, and the fire drill was easy to replace after becoming too short for further operation. The provision of flat faces around the stock's circumference was found to increase the string's grip, and it is thought that this modification served this practical purpose, rather than being purely decorative.

The technological change to a drill-stock from a directly rotated fire drill established the practice that interchanging parts that suffered wear during fire-making was necessary to conserve the main tool in which a considerable amount of time and energy had been invested. However, the idea of the drill-stock as a permanent part of an interchangeable tool system was not new in Ancient Egypt. The stone vessel drilling and boring tool had already claimed this distinction.

Copper and bronze cutting tools: experimental manufacture and hardness tests[94]

The project furnace for casting coppers and bronzes into open sand moulds was constructed from sheet metal riveted together to form a hood, a flue and a base, which contained a lining of firebricks (Figure 2.48). This lining formed a space for the fuel equal in volume to the average capacity of the ancient furnaces examined by Rothenberg at Timna in the Negev desert. When fully filled with fuel, a bowl-shaped furnace measuring 30 cm in height and 25 cm in diameter was created. An electric blower supplied air through a steel pipe connected to the furnace. The air flow rate could be adjusted from a minimum of 200 l/minute to a maximum of 600 l/minute (Figure 2.49). The maximum flow rate allowed the furnace to reach an

FIGURE 2.48 The author's furnace for melting copper and bronze

Source: Image by J. Stocks

FIGURE 2.49 The furnace in operation

Source: Image by J. Stocks

operating temperature of approximately 1,500°C, the minimum flow rate producing a temperature somewhat in excess of 1,200°C. Three modern silicon carbide crucibles were available for use.

The experimental copper and bronze edged tools were cast in open sand moulds (see Figures 2.16, 2.17). The tools included saw blades, chisels, adze blades, an axe blade, experimental punches, a wood drill, bead drills, tubular drills and a wedge. Some of the sand moulds were created by impressing the required shapes into damp sand with wooden patterns, others with angular stones. Dependent upon the tool, a crucible was charged with its constituent metals after weighing them with electronic scales. Tools designated as 'copper' also contained varying small amounts of tin and iron. Ancient copper implements varied considerably in their percentage contents, and recent analyses of the Kahun copper tools by G.R. Gilmore[95] have shown that the proportions of copper, tin, iron, arsenic and antimony differed significantly from tool to tool.

Test tools designated as bronze were made from commercially produced copper and tin. Eleven chisels were cast in bronze, eight of them containing regularly increasing amounts of tin beginning with 1 per cent tin content to 15 per cent tin content, in 2 per cent increases;[96] three other bronze chisels contained 8 per cent, 10 per cent and 12 per cent tin content respectively. (Two New Kingdom bronze chisels were analysed by J. Sebelian and M.A. Colson[97] and found to contain a tin content of 12 per cent and 13.3 per cent respectively.) Four leaded bronze chisels were cast, each containing significant amounts of tin and lead, plus small amounts of iron and antimony, but in ancient times leaded bronze is thought to have been exclusively in use for bowls, vases, dishes, rings and other domestic objects.[98] In all, 25 chisels for working stone, and one for working wood, were manufactured for test. Tables 2.1, 2.2 and 2.3 give data on the cast and fabricated copper and bronze chisels, flat-edged and serrated saws, adzes, experimental punches, tubular and bead drills, awls, needles, an axe, a point, a wedge, a wood drill and a pin.

In ancient times, as now, the process of melting metal and pouring it into moulds was a dirty and dangerous occupation, considerably increased by the concurrent use of several furnaces in close proximity to one another. For ancient furnace workers, life constantly would have been fraught with ever-present dangers from molten metal spills on their legs and feet, from dust and fumes, and from the possibility of an explosion if water found its way into a crucible, or a mould, full of molten metal.

All of the test chisels were cast into rectangular bars, enabling their tapers and edges to be cold hammered into shape. Maximum deformation and hardness of a casting can be achieved with this method. No annealing interrupted this process, although in ancient times some annealing for certain castings would have been in use, and this is confirmed by two metal-beaters in an illustration in the Fifth Dynasty mastaba tomb of Wepemnofret at Giza, who make these statements about the copper on their anvil. The first worker on the right says: *ps nn iw wšr* (Heat this: it is dried up). Clearly, the meaning is that the copper has become work-hardened and must be annealed. The other worker says: *n wnt šd ps.t(w).f mnh*

TABLE 2.1 Cast chisels in copper and bronze

Test no.	Metal type	Chisel taper	Percentage contents					Cast weight (g)
			Cu	Sn	Fe	Pb	Sb	
1	copper	flat	98	[2]				70
2	copper	flat	96	[4]				73
3	copper	flat	96	[4]				60
4	copper	crosscut	96	[4]				60
6	copper	flat	96	[4]				70
9	bronze	crosscut	97	3				45
10	bronze	crosscut	95	5				55
11	bronze	flat	93	7				73
12	bronze	crosscut	91	9				72
13	bronze	flat	89	11				72
14	bronze	flat	87	13				74
15	bronze	flat	85	15				62
18	bronze	flat	92	8				196
19	bronze	flat	91	9				73
21	bronze	flat	[unknown]					196
22	bronze	flat	88	12				196
25	bronze	flat	90	10				375
26	copper	flat	98	0.6	0.5	0.7	0.2	180
27	*l/bronze	flat	91	4.4	0.5	3.4	0.7	197
28	l/bronze	flat	90	5	0.5	3.7	0.8	192
29	l/bronze	flat	89	5.6	0.5	4	0.8	180
30	l/bronze	flat	88	6.1	0.5	4.5	0.9	188
33	bronze	flat	90	10				970
34	bronze	crosscut	99	1				10
35	bronze	flat	99	1				8
45	bronze	flat	93	7				16

*l/bronze = leaded bronze
Cu = copper, Sn = tin, Fe = iron, Pb = lead, Sb = antimony

TABLE 2.2 Cast tubes, drills, saws, adzes, axe, point, wedge, wood drill and punches in copper and bronze

Test no.	Metal type	Tool type	Percentage contents					Cast weight (g)
			Cu	Sn	Fe	Pb	Sb	
17	bronze	*ts/tube	90	10				169
23	bronze	tube	90	10				179
31	*l/bronze	tube	90	5	0.5	3.7	0.7	182
36	copper	tube	[commercially pure]					830
37	bronze	tube	90	10				90
38	copper	tube	[commercially pure]					110
39	copper	tube	[commercially pure]					175
40	bronze	*Tb/drill	95	5				23

(continued)

TABLE 2.2 *Continued*

Test no.	Metal type	Tool type	Percentage contents					Cast weight (g)
			Cu	*Sn*	*Fe*	*Pb*	*Sb*	
41	bronze	Tb/drill	95	5				26
42	bronze	Tb/drill	95	5				26
43	bronze	★Kb/drill	90	10				11
44	bronze	Kb/drill	98	2				10
5	copper	★s/saw	96	[4]				45
48	copper	s/saw	[commercially pure]					360
24	bronze	★f-e/saw	90	10				158
32	l/bronze	f-e/saw	90	5	0.5	3.8	0.7	178
47	copper	f-e/saw	[commercially pure]					495
49	copper	adze	[commercially pure]					95
50	copper	adze	[commercially pure]					148
51	bronze	axe	96	4				29
46	bronze	point	93	7				12
62	bronze	wedge	99	1				73
63	bronze	wood drill	96	4				12
52	bronze	punch	98	2				4
53	bronze	punch	90	10				4

★ts/tube = test serrated tube
★l/bronze = leaded bronze
★Tb/drill = Theban bead drill
★Kb/drill = Kerma bead drill
★s/saw = serrated saw
★f-e/saw = flat-edged saw
Cu = copper, Sn = tin, Fe = iron, Pb = lead, Sb = antimony

TABLE 2.3 Fabricated artifacts made from commercially produced copper

Test no.	Tool type	Length (mm)	Diameter (mm)	Wall thickness	Weight (g)
64	needle	87	2	–	–
65	needle	85	2	–	–
66	needle	65	1.5	–	–
67	pin	71	2	–	–
68	awl	172	2.5	–	–
69	awl	130	2	–	–
70	★s/saw	210	–	–	22
71	s/saw	200	–	–	30
72	★t/drill	55	10	0.6	–
73	t/drill	76	15	0.8	–
74	t/drill	82	22	0.8	–
75	t/drill	80	29	0.8	–
76	t/drill	63	33	1	–
77	t/drill	112	40	1.25	–
78	t/drill	294	80	1.2	–

★s/saw = serrated saw
★t/drill = tubular drill

FIGURE 2.50 Hammering a bronze casting into a chisel

Source: Image by J. Stocks

(There is no cracking [?] if it is heated excellently).[99] However, metallurgical studies have revealed that ancient tools were sometimes heavily cold-worked without any annealing.[100] The test tools' tapers were shaped by beating the metal with hand-held spherical stone hammers; the lightest stone weighed approximately 1/2 kg, the heaviest about 1 kg (Figure 2.50). The tools' cutting edges were achieved by sharpening the ends of the tapers on coarse and smooth sandstone blocks, and this may follow ancient practices. Each artifact was heavily hammered at first, but as the metal deformation became more difficult softer hammer blows were applied. All of the copper chisels deformed easily, and no cracking appeared. It was a different story with regard to the bronze chisels. Slim-sectioned chisels up to, and includ-ing, 5 per cent tin deformed relatively well without any sign of cracking. However, resistance to deformation in the chisel containing 7 per cent tin became marked, and in the chisels containing 9 per cent and 11 per cent tin considerable hammer-ing was required properly to deform the metal, but no cracking occurred. Cracks appeared in the 12 per cent, 13 per cent and 15 per cent tin in bronze chisels. This last chisel fractured in two places.

Hammering tests were made upon some copper and bronze plates, and it was determined that the copper plate, containing small amounts of additional metals, deformed easily, but that the bronze plate containing higher than 5 per cent tin content required a significant amount of annealing to prevent damaging cracks. A test to destruction was carried out on a thick-sectioned bronze specimen con-taining 10 per cent tin. Hammer blows of extreme force soon caused it to fracture (Figure 2.51), and the highest hardness, Vickers Pyramid Number (VPN) 256, was recorded for this casting.

FIGURE 2.51   A fractured bronze casting caused by extreme hammering

Source: Image by J. Stocks

It is evident from the hardness tests that the bronze chisels containing 8 per cent tin, and over, may be cold hammered to a hardness exceeding that of cold rolled mild steel (see Table 2.4), as did the leaded bronze chisels containing not less than approximately 4.5 per cent tin and 3.5 per cent lead. Leaded bronzes may never have been employed for tool manufacture, but metalworkers must have valued its ability to deform easily in sheet form with little necessity for annealing. Bronze chisels containing 10 per cent tin and over were harder than modern unworked chisel steel. Copper chisels containing small proportions of other substances can be cold hammered to the hardness of cold rolled mild steel, but no harder. The tests on the pure bronzes revealed that the tools made from 90 per cent copper and 10 per cent tin make the best cutting tools with regard to the twin advantages of toughness and hardness. However, ancient bronze tools containing more than 10 per cent tin content were in use, and the test chisel of 12 per cent tin content made a fine tool. Annealing during its shaping would have created a perfect tool devoid of cracks, and the hardness result supports the ancient craftworker's choice of a bronze containing a high tin content. The tests also indicate that an experienced ancient craftworker could easily have detected a metal reaching its limit of deformation.

TABLE 2.4 Some annealed and hammer-hardened copper, bronze, leaded bronze and steel chisels – Vickers Pyramid hardness test

Test no.	Metal type	Annealed hardness no.	Hammered hardness no.	Percentage contents				
				Cu	Sn	Fe	Pb	Sb
26	copper	57	140	98	0.6	0.5	0.7	0.2
9	bronze	75	161	97	3			
10	bronze	94	180	95	5			
11	bronze	99	188	93	7			
12	bronze	101	219	91	9			
25	bronze	–	239	90	10			
20	+bronze	–	256	90	10			
22	bronze	–	247	88	12			
28	*l/bronze	–	195	90	5	0.5	3.7	0.8
30	l/bronze	–	200	88	6.1	0.5	4.5	0.9
–	mild steel	131	192					
–	chisel steel	235	800					

+ bronze = hammered to destruction
*l/bronze = leaded bronze
Cu = copper, Sn = tin, Fe = iron, Pb = lead, Sb = antimony

The hardness tests upon the copper and bronze castings fell into several defined groups. The large and small copper and bronze chisels, the leaded bronze chisels, a saw, and a test bronze casting were hammered and hardness-tested, whereas the adzes, the axe-blade, the experimental punches, the single bead drills (Kerma-type),[101] the wood drill and the wedge were hammered, but not hardness-tested. The tubular drills, the simultaneous multiple bead drills (Theban-type)[102] and the flat-edged stonecutting saws were not hammered at all.

Hardness testing was carried out with a Vickers Pyramid Hardness testing machine. Hardness is determined by the use of a diamond indenter, under a known load for a known time, which leaves an indentation (Figures 2.52, 2.53) whose area, when divided into the load, gives a quotient known as the Vickers Pyramid Number. The hardness number enabled a relationship between different tools to be established, which could then be compared with the tools' character-istics when performing work on wood and stone. Cutting tools' characteristics were especially analysed from a craftworker's point of view, rather than just from a purely metallurgical one; in the absence of a copper alloy tool's performance on materials being known, knowledge of its exact metallic content and hardness number would be of little value. After hardness testing, tools requiring handles were fitted with ones manufactured from seasoned beech – a hardwood. Flint knives, chisels and scrapers were employed for removing the bark from the wood and carving it to shape.

FIGURE 2.52   Hardness testing marks on the taper of a bronze chisel

Source: Image by J. Stocks

FIGURE 2.53   Hardness testing marks on a copper chisel's taper

Source: Image by J. Stocks

To cut, or not to cut – that is the problem

The stonecutting tests[103] were performed with copper, leaded bronze and bronze crosscut and flat-tapered chisels, a modern flat-tapered steel chisel and a steel punch, copper adze blades and the serrated copper saw blades. The stones utilized for test included two sedimentary types (red sandstone and soft limestone), a close-grained hard sandstone, together with hard limestone, calcite, rose granite and diorite. Red sandstone was carved at Abu Simbel for the temples of Ramesses II and his chief wife Nefertari, while soft limestone was shaped into blocks for the Giza pyramids, and other buildings. All of the test chisels were driven with a wooden mallet. A light mallet, made of beech, replicated a mallet from Kahun;[104] a heavier mahogany mallet drove the large chisels. The wooden mallet was not always in use for driving chisels. In the tomb of Rekhmire,[105] a craftworker is depicted engraving a gold or silver vessel with a bronze chisel driven with a small stone hammer. Woodcutting chisels, fitted with handles, were probably always driven with mallets.

Several copper, bronze and leaded bronze chisels were tested upon rose granite and diorite. Each chisel suffered severe damage to its cutting edge. The damage inflicted upon ancient iron chisels by using them to cut igneous stones was considered. To test this proposition, a hardened and tempered engineer's steel chisel (VPN 800), together with a hardened steel punch (VPN 800), was employed to cut a groove 0.5 mm deep into a smoothed surface on a block of diorite. The tools suffered severe damage, similar to the non-ferrous chisels. However, the punch was capable of chipping away small pieces protruding from the rough surface of this igneous stone (see Chapter 3).

No worker would tolerate such a state of affairs, where a valuable tool received severe damage without a commensurate return in work performance. In any event, Ancient Egyptian masons had easy access to cheap and plentiful supplies of a material suitable for the working of hard stones, namely flint.

The cutting tests upon the close-grained hard sandstone, hard limestone and calcite demonstrated that the copper chisels suffered immediate blunting and jagged dents to their edges, and may be discounted as cutting tools for these stones. The leaded bronze chisels were ineffective on the hard sandstone and the hard limestone, but were able to cut the calcite. However, frequent sharpening was expensive in lost metal. Only the bronze chisels exceeding a VPN of 229 cut calcite well, but required sharpening at intervals not consistent with the efficient use of the tools. Consequently, even the hardest ancient bronze chisels must have lost metal at a rate that could not have been acceptable to ancient workers. All of the chisels cut red sandstone and soft limestone with ease, although the softer chisels suffered slight wear over time. Tests with the steel chisel upon close-grained hard sandstone indicated that this stone type, quarried at Gebel Silsila for making blocks, particularly for the Graeco-Roman temples at Philae, Kom Ombo, Edfu, Esna and Dendera, could have been cut with ancient iron chisels. In order to test some realistic working procedures, a bas-relief of the *uas*-sceptre and one of the *ankh* symbol were carved into a soft limestone (Figures 2.54, 2.55), similar to that used to face

FIGURE 2.54 A bas-relief of the *uas*-sceptre and of the *ankh* symbol carved into soft limestone using a copper chisel

Source: Image by J. Stocks

FIGURE 2.55 The finished bas-relief in limestone

Source: Image by J. Stocks

the Great Pyramid, with copper and bronze chisels. Low, or bas, relief means that figures and hieroglyphs were carved so as to stand up from the background. Incised, or sunken relief (en-Creux), involved the cutting of figures and hieroglyphs into a stone's surface. Incised reliefs were often cut into outside walls, where oblique morning and evening sunshine illuminated the carvings; bas-relief was popular for the inside decoration of tombs, but this type of realistic carving took more time to accomplish. The experimental copper and bronze chisels were utilized as scrapers, in addition to flint ones, for executing sharp corners, and the combined use of metal and flint tools would have been common in ancient times. The test bas-relief was smoothed with coarse and smooth sandstone rubbers. The tests revealed that the only other stones indigenous to Egypt that metal chisels were effectively able to cut were gypsum and steatite. All other stones caused varying degrees of unacceptable damage and loss of metal to the copper and bronze chisels.

The replica adzes were employed to shape a soft limestone vase, which was later used to test Ancient Egyptian drilling and boring methods. The adze is an excellent tool for making glancing blows on limestone, and this soft stonecutting capability complements adzes' ancient woodcutting roles in shipbuilding and other works. Petrie made a useful observation with regard to marks left by metallic and flint-cutting tools. He remarked that the adze was used in the chamber of Kho-sekhemui (Second Dynasty), but that the blade was of flint, this revealed by the chips on the tool's edge leaving raised ridges on the stone, whereas a metal tool has jagged dents on the edge which leaves score marks on the stone facing.[106] The tests on limestone with copper, bronze and flint tools fully support these observations.

A close examination of ancient saws revealed that many were supplied with serrations that had been randomly notched into their edges; a saw's serrations were normally set toward the handle, and this evidence has led to the assumption that this type of saw was a pull-saw.[107] Modern saw blades, with one or two exceptions, like the coping saw, are manufactured with serrations that are set away from the handle (a push-saw). It is likely that a simple flint tool was utilized for notching a saw blade. The experimental notching of hammer-hardened replica saws was achieved in the following manner. A flint nodule was broken, so that a long sharp edge could be pointed upwards. The cupped left hand supported the tool under the nodule's smooth exterior surface, or cortex, with the tool's edge parallel to the body. In this position, the blade's edge was brought forcibly down upon the flint tool's edge. This hacking, or chopping motion, which commenced at the handle end, continued without pause while steadily moving the blade toward the operator. The naturally held positions of each arm during the chopping motions automatically ensured that the serrations became set toward the handle. Further, this chopping action caused the copper to bulge sideways at each serration, thereby giving the tool the ability to cut the kerf, or slot, wider than the blade's thickness. This prevents a saw jamming in the slot.

The thin replica saws proved to be efficient when tested on red sandstone and soft limestone, and it is known that ancient sawyers discovered this use for serrated copper saws.[108] Flat-edged, stonecutting saws can cut both soft and hard stone, but serrated saws are able only to cut red sandstone, soft limestone, gypsum and steatite;

FIGURE 2.56   The face of Ramesses II at the temple of Abu Simbel, Upper Egypt

Source: Image by D. Stocks

the rate of cutting is remarkably swift. In this context, serrated saws were employed by modern engineers upon the faces of the red sandstone statues of Ramesses II at Abu Simbel (Figure 2.56), which were sawn into pieces during the removal of the monument to a higher site out of the reach of the rising Lake Nasser, created by the building of the Aswan High Dam in the 1960s.[109] The engineers discovered that little damage occurred to the stone, the pieces being fitted together again with a minimum of repair to the joints.

An interesting piece of technology in use with serrated copper saws is depicted in several tombs, notably in tombs at Meir and Deshasheh (Figure 2.57);[110] reconstructing and testing the device has indicated that the Egyptian saw was neither a pull- nor a push-saw, but a combination of both actions. The equipment consisted of a vertical post, buried in the ground, to which a vertical piece of timber was lashed with a rope. Inserted into this lashing was a short wooden rod, with a stone counterweight hanging by a rope on its free end (Figure 2.58). Standing sawyers are shown holding their saws with both hands and the blades are either horizontal, or with their tips pointing upward. It is likely that a wedge was used to keep a saw-cut open as it deepened. Experiments with a reconstructed rod, weight, rope and cast copper wedge demonstrated that, by sliding the weight along the rod, the equipment could be made to adjust the tension on the rope lashed around the post and the timber. In this way,

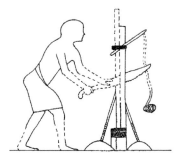

FIGURE 2.57 A counterweighted tourniquet lever illustrated in a tomb at Deshasheh

Source: Drawing by D. Stocks after W.M.F. Petrie, *Deshasheh*, London: Egypt Exploration Fund, 1898, pl. XXI

FIGURE 2.58 The reconstructed counterweighted tourniquet lever

Source: Image by J. Stocks

the lashing could be made to act as a quick-release mechanism, when timber needed sliding up the post as sawing continued; both hands, therefore, were free to hold the saw's handle (Figure 2.59). In one scene, though,[111] the wood is lashed at an angle of 45° to the ground (Figure 2.60), and a scene in the tomb of Rekhmire[112] shows two sitting workers holding small pieces of wood with one hand, set at angles of 55° and 65° respectively to the ground, with the saw cutting in the horizontal plane (Figure 2.61); this facilitated the sawing process in some way. Why?

FIGURE 2.59   Using a saw with both hands while the wood remains firmly lashed to a post buried in the ground

Source: Image by J. Stocks

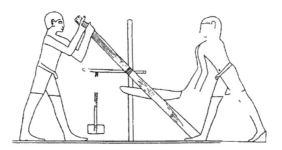

FIGURE 2.60   The counterweighted tourniquet lever holding a plank lashed at 45° to the vertical. From the tomb of Pepionkh at Meir

Source: Drawing by D. Stocks after A.M. Blackman and M.R Apted, *The Rock Tombs of Meir*, London: Egypt Exploration Society, part V, 1953, pl. XVIII

Many ancient saws were supplied with curved wooden handles,[113] and these were useful for pushing as well as for pulling a saw. The sawing tests upon wood clearly demonstrated that a blade's hacked serrations, set toward the worker, needed no particular pulling or pushing emphasis in order to cut the wood efficiently. In fact, a deliberate pull-stroke is quite tiring to perform. Some modern craftworkers might admit to a push-saw, possessing serrations set away from the sawyer, being

FIGURE 2.61   A craftworker sawing a piece of wood angled away from him. From the tomb of Rekhmire at Thebes

Source: Drawing by D. Stocks after N. de G. Davies, *The Tomb of Rekh-mi-Rē' at Thebes*, New York, 1943, vol. II, pl. LIII. Courtesy of the Metropolitan Museum of Art

allowed to cut on the backwards or pulling stroke. Conversely, a replica copper saw, possessing serrations cut toward the operator, cut well enough on the forwards or pushing stroke.

Tomb representations depicting saws with their tips pointing upward do not prove that they were pull-saws. Today, craftworkers fasten wood vertically in a vice and are obliged to tilt their push-saws upward because of their standing position and the height of the wood at the point of sawing. Further, the initial act of sawing, with the saw tilted in this way, reduces the width of the wood to be sawn, and therefore diminishes the effort required by the sawyer. (This method was used to saw the lid off the bottom of the Fourth Dynasty granite sarcophagus of Hordjedef – see Chapter 6.) After a short time, the saw is moved to a horizontal position and the wood sawn down to the lowest level achieved by the first operation. The process can be repeated again and again. The tomb scenes probably show sawyers in positions noticed at that time by the artist. For example, a sawyer depicted with the legs widely spaced apart is in the classic position for ensuring body stability when using a high degree of effort. All of the tests show that ancient sawyers would have adopted stances and sawing techniques individual to the worker and the type and dimensions of the wood being sawn.

The test cutting of hard and soft wood with copper and bronze chisels, saws, adzes, an axe and a bow-driven wood drill indicates that ancient copper and bronze tools possessed such superior hardness over all woods that only infrequent sharpening was necessary. The replica bow-driven wood drills, when rapidly revolved, both achieved cutting rates in softwood of 66 cm^3/hour, whereas holes in hardwood, such as oak and mahogany, were drilled at the rates of 20 and 30 cm^3/hour respectively.

In conclusion, the tests proved that no copper, bronze or leaded bronze tool, except for the tubes and the flat-edged saws with sand abrasive, could effectively cut stone other than red sandstone, soft limestone, gypsum and steatite, and that all of the tools used for cutting woods of all hardnesses were practical for this purpose. Only stones of hardness Mohs 3 and below can effectively be cut with any copper, bronze or leaded bronze edged tool. The tests with the modern steel chisel and punch indicate that Late Period craftworkers did not employ their softer iron chisels for cutting hieroglyphs and reliefs into granite, diorite, porphyry and other stones of similar hardness.

Notes

1 W.M.F. Petrie, *Tools and Weapons*, London: British School of Archaeology in Egypt, 1917, p. 1.
2 B. Adams, *Predynastic Egypt*, Princes Risborough: Shire Publications, 1988, p. 40, Fig. 21, b.
3 Ibid. Fig. 21, d; serrated flint knife BM 29288.
4 Examples are Bristol Museum and Art Gallery H 1920 and BM 29285.
5 M.A. Hoffman, *Egypt before the Pharaohs: The Prehistoric Foundations of Egyptian Civilization*, London and Henley: Routledge and Kegan Paul, 1980, Fig. 49.
6 Petrie, *Tools and Weapons*, pp. 5–8, pl. II, A57, 60–1, 64, 67–9, 76–9.
7 F.C.J. Spurrell, 'The stone implements of Kahun', in W.M.F. Petrie (ed.) *Illahun, Kahun and Gurob*, London: David Nutt, 1891, pp. 51–3; eight chipped flint tools from Kahun (MM 198) may be chisels, although the pointed ones in the group may be punches; Petrie, *Illahun*, pl. VII, 3 (flint axe), pl. VII, 1 (flint adze); W.M.F. Petrie, *Kahun, Gurob and Hawara*, London: Kegan Paul, Trench, Trübner, and Co., 1890, pl. XVI (flint axe, now MM 242), pl. XVI, top left and right (flint adzes, now MM 245, 246), pl. XVI (two flint knives, now MM 239A, 240).
8 A. Tillmann, 'Dynastic stone tools', in K.A. Bard (ed.) *Encyclopedia of the Archaeology of Ancient Egypt*, London and New York: Routledge, 1999, p. 265.
9 F.Ll. Griffith, *Beni Hasan III*, London: Egypt Exploration Fund, 1896, pp. 33–8, pls VII, VIII, IX, X; S.R. Snape and J.A. Tyldesley, 'Two Egyptian flint knapping scenes', *Lithics* 4, 1983, pp. 46–7.
10 E. Mackay, 'The cutting and preparation of tomb chapels in the Theban necropolis', *JEA* VII, 1921, pp. 163–4.
11 For example, First Dynasty chisels were given a single taper (Petrie, *Tools and Weapons*, p. 19, pl. XXI, C1–3). For examples of double tapered flat and crosscut chisels, see ibid., pls XXI, C19–20, 23, XXII, C49, 81.
12 Petrie, *Kahun*, pl. XVII, 4 (now MM 204); Petrie, *Tools and Weapons*, pl. XXI, C23.
13 Petrie, *Tools and Weapons*, pls II, A58, III, A112, LXXIII, A62.
14 Ibid., p. 11, pl. IX, O20.
15 Ibid., pl. V, A133.
16 Ibid., pl. XVI, Z62.
17 Petrie, *Illahun*, pl. XIII, 16 (now MM 194b); Petrie, *Tools and Weapons*, pl. XXII, C73, 86. See also New Kingdom bronze chisels fitted with wooden handles (BM 6045, 6053).
18 Petrie, *Tools and Weapons*, p. 40, pl. XLVI, M62. For further examples of circumferential wear to wooden mallets, see ibid., pl. XLIV, M64–5, 70; MM 55.
19 Petrie, *Kahun*, pl. XVII, 5 (now necked adze MM 203); Petrie, *Tools and Weapons*, pls XVI, Z60–5, XVII, Z76–93.
20 Mackay, 'The cutting and preparation of tomb chapels in the Theban necropolis', pp. 163–4; W.M.F. Petrie, *Egyptian Architecture*, London: British School of Archaeology in Egypt, 1938, p. 30.
21 Mackay, 'The cutting and preparation of tomb chapels in the Theban necropolis', pp. 154–68.
22 An example of depicted left-handed workers can be seen in a representation of a stone vessel craftworker from a Fifth Dynasty tomb at Saqqara (CM JE39866), and a similar worker is shown in the Sixth Dynasty tomb of Mereruka at Saqqara (P. Duell (ed.) *The Tomb of Mereruka*, Chicago, IL: The Oriental Institute, University of Chicago, 1938, vol. I, pl. 30).

23 Petrie, *Tools and Weapons*, p. 43.
24 Ibid., pls XLVIII, S2, L, S1.
25 Ibid., pl. L, S3.
26 Ibid., pls XLVIII, S10, L, S11.
27 M.Z. Goneim, *The Buried Pyramid*, London: Longmans, Green and Co., 1956, p. 108; W.M.F. Petrie, *The Pyramids and Temples of Gizeh*, London: Field and Tuer, 1883, pl. XIV, 1.
28 Petrie, *Pyramids*, p. 174.
29 D.A. Stocks, 'Industrial technology at Kahun and Gurob: Experimental manufacture and test of replica and reconstructed tools with indicated uses and effects upon artefact production', unpublished thesis, University of Manchester, 1988, vol. I, pp. 83–99.
30 N. de G. Davies, *The Tomb of Rekh-mi-Rēʿ at Thebes*, New York: Metropolitan Museum of Art, 1943, vol. II, pls LII, LIII.
31 Petrie, *Pyramids*, p. 175, pl. XIV, 8; A. Lucas and J.R. Harris, *Ancient Egyptian Materials and Industries*, London: Edward Arnold, 1962, p. 74; G.A. Reisner, *Mycerinus, the Temples of the Third Pyramid at Giza*, Cambridge, MA: Harvard University Press, 1931, p. 180.
32 Davies, *Rekhmire*, vol. II, pls LII, LIII.
33 Ibid. A chair is depicted in pl. LII, a bed in pl. LIII.
34 Particularly wooden coffin joints. For coffins, and their construction, see A.J. Spencer, *Death in Ancient Egypt*, Harmondsworth: Penguin Books, 1982, p. 166.
35 Petrie, *Tools and Weapons*, pl. LI, M15. The point was possibly arrowhead-shaped, when new.
36 Adams, *Predynastic Egypt*, p. 43.
37 Petrie, *Tools and Weapons*, p. 6.
38 Petrie, *Kahun*, p. 29; Petrie, *Tools and Weapons*, pl. LXXVII, W249.
39 Ibid., p. 61, pl. LXXVII, W250.
40 Stocks, 'Industrial technology', vol. I, p. 57, vol. II, pl. II, a.
41 Petrie, *Pyramids*, p. 174.
42 Petrie, *Tools and Weapons*, p. 62, pl. LXXVII, W265.
43 Ibid., p. 61, pl. LXXVII, W252–5.
44 Petrie, *Tools and Weapons*, p. 61; W.M.F. Petrie, *The Arts and Crafts of Ancient Egypt*, Edinburgh and London: T.N. Foulis, 1909, p. 101; Lucas and Harris, *AEMI*, p. 222.
45 For example, A.M. Blackman and M.R. Apted, *The Rock Tombs of Meir*, London: Egypt Exploration Society, part V, 1953, pl. XVI.
46 Davies, *Rekhmire*, vol. II, pl. LII.
47 C.T. Currelly, 'Stone Implements', in *Catalogue Général des Antiquités Égyptiennes du Musée du Caire*, Cairo: Imprimerie de l'Institut Française d'Archéologie Orientale, 1913, p. 237; R.L. Mond and O.H. Myers, *The Cemeteries of Armant*, London: Egypt Exploration Society, 1937, vol. I, p. 167.
48 For example, Duell, *Mereruka*, vol. I, pl. 30.
49 A. Nibbi, 'Some remarks on copper', *JARCE* XIV, 1977, pp. 59–66.
50 H.H. Coghlan, *Notes on the Prehistoric Metallurgy of Copper and Bronze in the Old World*, Oxford: Oxford University Press, 1951, Fig. 10.
51 B. Rothenberg, 'Excavations at Timna Site 39. A chalcolithic copper smelting site and furnace and its metallurgy', *Archaeo Metallurgy* Monograph Number 1, 1978, p. 11, Fig. 11.
52 R.F. Tylecote and P.J. Boydell, 'Experiments on copper smelting based on early furnaces found at Timna', *Archaeo Metallurgy* Monograph Number 1, 1978, pp. 27–51.
53 Ibid.
54 Davies, *Rekhmire*, vol. II, pls LII, LIII.
55 Ibid., pl. LIII.
56 Blackman and Apted, *The Rock Tombs of Meir*, pl. XVI.
57 G. Steindorff, *Das Grab des Ti*, Leipzig: Hinrichs, 1913, pl. 134; Duell, *Mereruka*, vol. I, pl. 30; Blackman and Apted, *The Rock Tombs of Meir*, pl. XVII; Coghlan, *Prehistoric Metallurgy*, Fig. 10.

58 N. de G. Davies, *The Rock Tombs of Deir el Gebrâwi*, London: Egypt Exploration Fund, 1902, vol. I, pl. XIV.

59 Blackman and Apted, *The Rock Tombs of Meir*, p. 25, pl. XVI, register 4. One of the three workers, each with a blowpipe, is saying: 'Make a great effort, behold it's molten (?)'.

60 Davies, *Rekhmire*, vol. II, pl. LII; N. de G. Davies, *The Tomb of Puyemrê at Thebes*, New York: Metropolitan Museum of Art, 1922, vol. I, pls XXIII, XXV; N. de G. Davies, *The Tomb of Two Sculptors at Thebes*, New York: Metropolitan Museum of Art, 1925, pl. XI.

61 Davies, *Rekhmire*, vol. II, pl. LII.

62 C.J. Davey, 'Crucibles in the Petrie Collection and hieroglyphic ideograms for metal', *JEA* 71, 1985, pp. 142–8; Petrie, *Tools and Weapons*, p. 61, pl. LXXVII, W245–8.

63 Duell, *Mereruka*, vol. I, pl. 30.

64 Davies, *Rekhmire*, vol. II, pl. LII.

65 Ibid.

66 Davey, 'Crucibles in the Petrie Collection and hieroglyphic ideograms for metal', p. 148; Duell, *Mereruka*, vol. I, pl. 30; S. Hassan, *Excavations at Giza 1930–1931*, Cairo: Government Press, 1936, pp. 192–3, Fig. 219.

67 Davies, *Rekhmire*, vol. II, pl. LII. Three crucibles are depicted, all broad-shaped.

68 F. Bisson de la Roque, 'Trésor de Tôd', in *Catalogue Général des Antiquités Égyptiennes du Musée du Caire*, Cairo: Imprimerie de l'Institut Française d'Archéologie Orientale, 1950, pp. iii, 1–2, pl. I.

69 M. Lehner, 'Lost city of the pyramids', *Egypt Revealed*, Fall, 2000, pp. 42–57.

70 R. Maddin, T. Stech, J.D. Muhly and E. Brovarski, 'Old Kingdom models from the tomb of Impy: Metallurgical studies', *JEA* 70, 1984, pp. 33–41; Stocks, 'Industrial technology', vol. I, pp. 64–82.

71 Davies, *Rekhmire*, vol. II, pl. LIII.

72 T.A. Rickard, *Man and Metals*, New York: Arno Press, vol. I, 1932, p. 116.

73 For example, Davies, *Rekhmire*, vol. II, pl. LV, second register.

74 Ibid., pl. LV, bottom register.

75 Ibid., pl. LIII, bottom register.

76 Stocks, 'Industrial technology', vol. II, pp. 269–70.

77 For examples, see Petrie, *Tools and Weapons*, pl. LXV, N70–4; MM 233W copper needle from Kahun was analysed by G.R. Gilmore. The needle contained 95 per cent copper (G.R. Gilmore, 'The composition of the Kahun metals', in A.R. David (ed.) *Science in Egyptology*, Manchester: Manchester University Press, 1986, p. 458).

78 Petrie, *Tools and Weapons*, pl. LXV, N109.

79 Coghlan, *Prehistoric Metallurgy*, p. 85.

80 Davies, *Rekhmire*, vol. II, pl. LIII. See pl. LII, for leather-cutting. See Petrie, *Tools and Weapons*, p. 50, pls LIII, L49, LXII, L1–2, for examples of the cutting knife.

81 Petrie, *Tools and Weapons*, p. 59.

82 G.A. Reisner, *Excavations at Kerma*, Cambridge, MA: Peabody Museum of Harvard University, 1923, parts IV–V, pp. 93–4.

83 Davies, *Rekhmire*, vol. II, pls LII and LIII.

84 A bow from Kahun for driving a fire drill, now MM 65.

85 Lucas and Harris, *AEMI*, pp. 134–5.

86 E. Teeter, 'Techniques and terminology of rope-making in Ancient Egypt', *JEA* 73, 1987, pp. 71–7, pls VII, 3, VIII, 1, 2, IX.

87 Davies, *Rekhmire*, vol. II, pl. LII.

88 Petrie, *Illahun*, p. 29, pl. IX, 6.

89 Stocks, 'Industrial technology', vol. I, pp. 23–33.

90 H. Carter, *The Tomb of Tut-Ankh-Amen*, London: Cassell, 1933, vol. III, pl. XXXVIII.

91 Petrie, *Kahun*, pl. IX, p. 28. Now MM 23.

92 Petrie, *Kahun*, pl. XVIII, 14; Petrie, *Tools and Weapons*, pl. XLIII, M7.

93 Petrie, *Illahun*, pl. VII, 24.

FIGURE 3.1   The deeply incised rose granite obelisk of Tuthmose I at Karnak temple

Source: Image by D. Stocks

the mention of chert is vital to the understanding of the experimental cutting of particular stones, the chert tools will be distinguished from the tools made of flint.

At Twelfth Dynasty Kahun, there is good evidence that tools of stone were still being produced. For example, a flint axe (MM 242), flint adzes (MM 245, 246), flint knives (MM 239A, 240) and flint chisels and punches (MM 198) were in use alongside metallic tools. Although Middle Kingdom flint tools outnumbered metal ones at Kahun, there is evidence that at the nearby Eighteenth Dynasty town of Gurob metal tools predominated over flint.[3] The archaeological evidence for Dynastic flint tools – large blades, knives, sickles, scrapers, borers, burins and hafted blades used for cutting meat[4] – may be giving an incomplete picture of the true extent to which flint and chert were utilized during the Dynastic period.

Stone tools were employed for various stoneworking applications in Dynastic times. For example, hard-stone mauls dating to the Old and Middle Kingdom times were used as a form of sledge-hammer, and these have been discovered at various sites, including Meidum, Giza and Beni Hasan, and at quarry sites in the Sinai, in Aswan and at Hatnub, where calcite was extracted.[5] The use of mauls for quarrying and bruising stone into shape was widespread throughout Egypt, and must quickly have increased as stone first became employed for architecture in the First Dynasty. Some heavy mauls were hand-held, but a maul for dressing a statue in the tomb of Ti at Saqqara was fitted with a wooden handle.[6] In order that a handle could be fitted, a groove was carved around the middle of the maul, or

FIGURE 3.2   A trench pounded out of the granite on one of the sides of the Unfinished
Obelisk at Aswan

Source: Image by D. Stocks

toward one end. A handle consisted of two short sticks twisted together with thong
lashed around the groove, which made the union between the maul and the handle
extremely secure. A good example is a quartzite maul, with its original handle still
in position (MMA 20.3.190), from the tomb of Mektira. Grooved mauls have been
located at Meidum, Giza and Lisht.[7]

Hand-held stone pounders or mauls are sometimes depicted in tomb illustrations;
examples of recovered dolerite pounders are MMA 11.151.733–5, and an earlier
pounder was found on the basalt floor of the mortuary temple to the east of Khufu's pyramid (Bristol Museum and Art Gallery H 5237). In 1943, The Metropolitan
Museum of Art, New York, published scenes from the tomb of Rekhmire, drawn from
the originals by Norman de Garis Davies. Workers are shown using mauls on a white
limestone sphinx and an offering table (see Figure 2.27).[8] Dolerite balls, whether hand-
held or fitted with handles is not known, were used to pound trenches (Figure 3.2)
around the 1,160-tonne Unfinished Obelisk (Figure 3.3) at Aswan, Upper Egypt: the
pounders were located in the rose granite quarry. The initial working of the stone by
pounding, especially on curved surfaces, can be identified by whitish spots of crushed
stone, particularly on hard stone, left as a result of this type of work.[9] Although the
favoured stone for pounders was dolerite, they were also made from chert and flint
nodules in the Twelfth Dynasty,[10] and probably during other periods.

Flint scrapers were in use for finishing limestone surfaces. For example, they
were employed near to the end of the Third Dynasty in the tomb of Ra-nefer.[11]

FIGURE 3.3   The Unfinished Obelisk at Aswan

Source: Image by D. Stocks

The fine finishing of bas-relief hieroglyphs, in order to create sharp outlines, was aided by the skilled use of flint scrapers.[12] The craftworker must have possessed different scrapers for awkward parts of the work. Equally, the finished surfaces of incised hieroglyphs in softer stones must also have been assisted by the employment of flint scrapers.

In the twentieth century, and probably stretching back two centuries before, engineering craftworkers used hardened steel scrapers upon brass, cast iron and steel. During a mechanical engineering apprenticeship, apprentices were taught to use a flat steel scraper, which had a slight lateral curve to its cutting edge. This scraper was utilized to finish the machined steel surfaces of sliding steam engine valves, which opened and closed the inlet and exhaust ports (holes) to and from the steam cylinder. These steam valves, in order to work efficiently, had to be steam-tight under considerable pressure, and this method of scraping them ensured their integrity against the loss of high-pressure steam during the opening and closing cycles. Similarly, the fitting of large brass bearing shells to engine crankshaft main bearings, and to the big-ends of piston rod bearings, was achieved with hardened steel spear-point scrapers that curved toward a point in two planes – laterally and vertically. These specially designed scrapers are precisely suited for scraping curved metal surfaces. Flint tools, possessing similar curved edges,[13] are also ideal for this type of work on stone. Fundamentally, modern scraping skills closely resemble those used in Ancient Egypt; it is only the materials from which the modern scrapers are made that have changed. Experiments have shown that the scraping of stone much harder than soft limestone is possible, and this aspect will be mentioned later in the chapter.

The use of Late Period iron chisels to cut hieroglyphs and reliefs into igneous stones has been discussed and rejected in the previous chapter. In support of this, there is written evidence from an ancient source that iron was not in use for cutting very hard stones. The classical writer Theophrastus (fourth to third century BCE) provides a valuable insight as to whether iron or stone tools were used for cutting the hard stones. In Books LXXII and LXXV of *History of Stones*,[14] Theophrastus says:

> As that some of the Stones before named are of so firm a Texture, that they are not subject to Injuries, and are not to be cut by Instruments of Iron, but only by other stones . . . and others yet, which may be cut with Iron, but the Instruments must be dull and blunt: which is much as if they were not cut by Iron.[15]

Were flint and chert the 'other stones' that Theophrastus referred to? Early in the twentieth century, Reginald Engelbach[16] confirmed Theophrastus' statement by trying to cut granite with an iron chisel, but became convinced that the Ancient Egyptians used a much harder tool upon this stone. The iron tools available in Theophrastus' time were probably inferior in hardness and toughness to the steel tools[17] likely to have been available to the Roman masons working the porphyry and the grey granite at Gebel Dokhan (Mons Porphyrites) and Mons Claudianus respectively in the Eastern Desert of Egypt during the first to the fourth centuries. This is suggested by the hardness tests conducted on a second-century Roman high carbon steel stonemason's chisel from Chesterholm, UK, which revealed a variable edge hardness of VPN 579 down to 464, with the body of the chisel at VPN 136.[18]

It is likely that the Roman masons in the Eastern Desert were supplied with steel tools capable of being forged and hardened to at least the hardness of the second-century Chesterholm chisel. The constituents of the edge of this chisel – work-hardened ferrite and some martensite and other materials – prove an intention to harden the tool by heating and quenching but, more importantly, they prove that the smith deliberately increased the carbon content, albeit unequally, by placing the semi-forged tool into a reducing area of the hearth.[19]

Although a Roman flat-tapered steel chisel of VPN 579 might have been capable of chipping away small pieces of the fine-grained porphyry from a block's rough surface, a slightly easier stone to cut than the Aswan rose granite, its edge would rapidly have become blunted, necessitating unacceptably frequent re-forging and hardening. Tests with a modern steel punch (VPN 800) on diorite suggest that the type of Roman tool in use for roughly shaping the porphyry and granite in the Eastern Desert was probably a punch, not a chisel.

This method is in use today in Hamada Rashwan's rose granite quarry situated in Aswan, Upper Egypt. Here, a mason creates sculptures by gradually chipping away the coarse-grained granite with a hardened steel punch (probably around VPN 800, but not tested for hardness – see Table 2.4). The original point gradually becomes flattened as the chipping proceeds, making a small square at the end of the four-sided taper. This square forms edges at the four sides of the taper, each possessing an angle of approximately 95°. These can be made to act as chisel-edges, as well as using the tool as a straightforward punch. A flat-tapered chisel's edge forms an angle of approximately 60°, which is likely to become blunted more quickly than a punch's four obtuse edges. Modern flat-ended steel punches are quite effective on rough igneous stone surfaces for a time, but still need fairly frequent re-forging and hardening.

Driving the hardened steel punch into a flattened and smoothed diorite surface thoroughly tested it. The four obtuse chisel-edges were rapidly blunted, small bits of metal being torn from them. The punch caused some limited damage to the stone, but the necessarily frequent re-forging and hardening of the tool was counter-productive to its efficient use for this purpose. The Aswan quarry smith quenched the last few millimetres of a re-forged point by placing the tool vertically in shallow cold water contained in a metal tray. He could be observed busily hammering and hardening dozens of punches at a time. However, the total number of punches in circulation was sufficiently high to keep all the masons working without interruption. Did the Romans practise this method in the Eastern Desert?

With regard to the *cutting* of the inscriptions into the porphyry and granite at Gebel Dokhan and Mons Claudianus, did the Roman masons use flint chisels and punches, rather than risk rapid and unnecessary serious damage to their steel tools? In support of this hypothesis, Roman quarry workers and masons certainly had relatively easy access to the grey flint at the Wadi Abu Had, some 50 km to the north of Gebel Dokhan, and there is evidence for a fourth-century Roman installation there.[20] This installation (WAH 30) is contemporaneous with the late Roman extraction of porphyry at Mons Porphyrites, but there may be earlier, as yet unknown, Roman association with the Wadi Abu Had during the first to the third centuries: several small, late Roman installations were found by Bomann[21] in the Wadi Dib, which is adjacent to the Wadi Abu Had.

It is possible that the Wadi Abu Had fourth-century Roman installation was connected with the collection of flint nodules contained in the limestone hills of Gebel Safr Abu Had, situated within the Wadi Abu Had.[22] The nodules could have been knapped into chisels and punches near to the point of collection, reducing weight to a minimum for transportation, or taken back to Gebel Dokhan and Mons Claudianus for knapping there. The knapping of flint nodules into tools creates a considerable number of noticeable flakes, but it is unlikely that the small fragments broken from any flint chisels and punches used for cutting the inscriptions into the porphyry and granite blocks would immediately be visible in the heavily sanded quarry sites today.

The position and nature of the marks left in the stone of certain monuments persuaded Engelbach[23] to conclude that Ancient Egyptian sculptors used a tool similar to a modern mason's metal pick, a hammer pointed at both ends fitted with a wooden haft, although no such tool has ever been located in Egypt. Dieter Arnold refers to quarry marks, also made by 'picks'.[24] In fact, many unfinished ancient artifacts, made from hard stone, show marks which indicate that hand-held pointed mauls, or stone punches and chisels driven with hammers, were used in their manufacture. In some objects, the marks (pits) progressively become smaller as the work moves toward completion. A collection of Late Period unfinished dolerite, schist and granite sculptures and other works contained in the Cairo Museum (JE33301–33313, 33321, 33388, 33473, 33476), and examined by C.C. Edgar and Alfred Lucas,[25] clearly show these interesting production features, although they were manufactured when iron tools existed in Egypt. However, the experimental work suggests that, even in the Late Period, tools for working the igneous stones, and for quarrying them, must have been manufactured from stone, and that the chief designs of tools made from stone were spherical and pointed mauls, as well as chisels and punches. Iron chisels would have been in use for the softer stones, as copper and bronze tools were in earlier times, but the experimental use of ferrous chisels and punches on the hard stones demonstrated the tools' severe limitations for this type of work.[26]

At Kahun, several Twelfth Dynasty flint artifacts (MM 248) were discovered, which could have been driven with a hammer or a mallet for punching into hard and soft stone. The flints are pointed at one end, while the opposite ends have been dressed to a flat surface. Ancient tools of such size and shape are indicated both by the experimental working of hard and soft stone and by the examination of tomb illustrations. For example, in the tomb of Rekhmire at Thebes,[27] the head of a seated red granite colossus (Figure 3.4), constructed to nearly twice life-size, is being carved to its final shape with a stone hammer driving a chisel or a punch. This seems to be an important piece of evidence with regard to two aspects of working the hard stones: the employment of a stone hammer for this work and the use of a tool which is, in association with granite, most unlikely to have been made from copper or bronze. Iron must be discounted because of the Dynastic period. The chisel or punch must, therefore, have been manufactured from stone, and this stone was probably flint. The craftworker shown chiselling the sphinx in the tomb of Rekhmire,[28] may have been using a flint tool, even though the sphinx is made of white limestone. The ancient concurrent use of both metal and stone chisels on soft stone cannot be ruled out, and the archaeological and the later experimental evidence in this chapter support the use of stone chisels and punches on soft stone. In any event, it has already been shown that flint adzes and scrapers were used on soft stone.

In association with large-scale limestone working at Giza, Petrie[29] found flints in rubbish tips near to the Great Pyramid. He noted that the masons' waste chippings were disposed of by throwing them over the cliffs situated to the north and to the south of the Great Pyramid. These rubbish tips were made up of layers of large

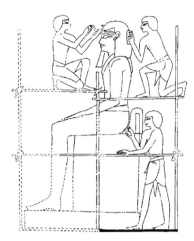

FIGURE 3.4   A granite colossus, as depicted in the tomb of Rekhmire at Thebes

Source: Drawing by D. Stocks after N. de G. Davies, *The Tomb of Rekh-mi-Rē' at Thebes*, New York, 1943, vol. II, pl. LX. Courtesy of the Metropolitan Museum of Art

chippings, fine dust and sweepings, and layers of flints and sand, indicating that a piece of desert ground had been cleared in order to increase the space for working. It is possible that these flints were produced by knapping the tools from nodules at the building site, the tools having been required for preliminary rough work on the pyramid's limestone and interior granite blocks. If indeed this was the case, the gradual destruction of the flint tools would also have contributed to the density of sharp flints scattered over the working area. Periodic clearing of the flints would have been necessary for safety reasons. Near to the pyramid of Senusret I, Dieter Arnold[30] found layers of builders' debris containing granite dust, indicating that the material was worked there. There were no detectable traces of greenish discoloration from copper tools, but the large amounts of flint flakes suggest that flint tools were used for dressing the granite.

Often, pitting of a stone's surface may be seen in the bottoms of hieroglyphs incised into various types of stone. This pitting, caused by a pointed punch, is normally scraped to a flat finish. However, two sarcophagi in the Musée du Louvre, Paris, illustrate the difficulties inherent in this procedure. Both sarcophagi have hundreds of small, incised hieroglyphs on their inside surfaces. In sarcophagus N345 D9, made from greywacke, the bottoms and sides of the incised signs have been scraped to a flat finish. In the other sarcophagus (N346 D10), made from black granite, which is considerably harder than the greywacke, no attempt was made to scrape the pitted stone in a similar manner to the greywacke sarcophagus. The effort to accomplish such a task would have been enormous, due to the length of time required for each sign. Good examples of similar pitting of unfinished incised hieroglyphs and figures in calcite are shown in a broken Fourth Dynasty calcite statue of Menkaure in the Boston Museum of Fine Arts (11.3146), and the Nineteenth Dynasty canopic jars of Thenry in the Brooklyn Museum of Art (48.30.1–4), from Saqqara. A basalt stela in The Manchester Museum (8134) displays a similar pitted surface on the representations incised into the stone.

Also in the Musée du Louvre is a good example of a chisel-worked granite statue (D31) of a group of four baboons. Grooves chipped to represent the animals' fur have not been smoothed, but appear to have been left rough, just as the craftworker chiselled them. Variations to the width and to the depth of the chisel marks indicate that several stone chisels were in use and that the strength of the hammer or mallet blows altered as each groove was cut. In some places, the chisel has penetrated to a greater depth than normal, chipping away a larger piece of stone.

Flint and chert: a brief description

Although copper began to supplement flint tools as the Neolithic period ended, ca. 4000 BCE, flint remained in use as a tool-manufacturing material throughout the Predynastic period, and most of the Dynastic era. However, flint and chert sharp-edged tools gradually declined in numbers and quality during the Dynastic period, more or less ending as the technological processes for making wrought iron into quenched and tempered steel became established in the seventh century BCE.[31] Even after this date, though, flint and chert chisels and punches must have been produced for working the very hard stones.

Certain hard stones have been considered as candidates for ancient tool manufacture. These are obsidian, dolerite and diorite. However, obsidian was an imported volcanic glass-like stone. Its scarcity and extremely brittle nature excludes it from further consideration. Although dolerite, a coarse-grained basalt, was useful for pounding other hard stones, fragments of dolerite, and chisels of diorite, have been tested by Antoine Zuber[32] and by Reginald Engelbach[33] to cut granite. However, as tool materials, they both suffer from an inability effectively and decisively to cut into the hard stones. Extensive tests of diorite, dolerite, silicified, or crystalline, limestone tools, and of flint and chert chisels and punches[34] show that only *flint* tools can truly cut into *all* igneous stones, particularly the coarse-grained variety, such as rose granite. The March 1999 experiments with some *chert* chisels and punches on the rose granite in a quarry at Aswan demonstrated that the tools were not quite hard enough to cut this stone.[35]

The availability of large deposits of flint and chert as a resource for manufacturing sharp-edged tools ensured that Dynastic craftworkers were equipped to make most artifacts, even if metal tools were temporarily in short supply. Flint, as a manufacturing material, is cheaper to obtain than copper smelted from ore, but takes longer to shape into an individual tool than casting a similar tool in metal. For many millennia before the establishment of Egyptian civilization, and the introduction of copper tools, flint had been chipped into arrowheads and spear points for hunting, and into tools of many designs, which were used for the splitting, cutting, scraping, carving, sawing and boring of materials, such as plants, animal skins, ivory, wood and stone. The Predynastic craftworker employed flint tools to perforate hard, semi-precious stone beads, to shape hard- and soft-stone vessel exteriors and to hollow soft-stone vessel interiors with flint or chert crescents.[36] The concurrent use of comparably designed flint and metal tools in the Predynastic and Dynastic periods would not have been considered unusual, nor the substitution of flint tools in place of similarly designed, but unavailable, copper tools. In the Dynastic period, the carving of wood probably still involved the use of flint tools, particularly for removing the bark from newly cut stems. Flint tools continued in use for many other tasks, including the cutting of vegetable materials, such as those in use for rope-making, and linen and papyrus manufacture.

Flint is a dense form of silica, being dark grey or black in colour (see Figure 3.6).[37] Although flint's hardness is classed as Mohs 7, tests[38] show that it is slightly harder than quartz, also Mohs 7. Flint occurs as nodules and layers in the Eocene limestone, and also can freely be picked off the ground where weathering has released them. Flint nodules assume quite convoluted shapes, being originally formed from the silica skeletons of dead sponges that lived in the shallow sea covering part of Egypt some 50 million years ago.[39] These skeletons were deposited on the sea's embryonic limestone floor, among the millions of small marine creatures from which this sedimentary rock is composed. The silica skeletons dissolved, and this material was later deposited as flint nodules, which individually occupied spaces in the limestone. The most southerly source of flint is in the mountains of Thebes West, but excellent quality flint was mined at the Wadi el-Sheikh and the Wadi Sojoor, both about 130 km south of Cairo, and in the eastern environs of the Nile valley.

When struck with a hammer (percussion-flaking), which in ancient times may have been made from bone, antler, stone or wood, flint breaks with a conchoidal (shell-shaped) fracture; newly fractured flint possesses extremely sharp edges, and these may be refined by pressure-flaking, a technique employing the skilled use of a pointed tool. In particular, providing a flint tool with denticulations increased the total length of an edge operating upon a material. Any two adjacent denticulations meet at a point, which protrudes beyond them. Therefore, the denticulated edge is a forerunner of the serrated metal saw. So important is this efficient cutting capability that many modern steel knives are given denticulated cutting edges. The process of hollow-grinding denticulations into a steel knife is only applied to one side of the blade's edge. Some curved denticulations in modern hollow-ground knives are remarkably similar to those seen in Ancient Egyptian flint sickles and knives.

Chert nodules are also to be found in the limestone, and ancient craftworkers sometimes used them for making tools. For example, chert mauls and chisels were found at Eighteenth Dynasty Thebes by Howard Carter,[40] the chert nodules probably coming from the Wadi Bairiya, opposite Armant, just south of Thebes. The tools used for roughly hacking out the limestone during tomb construction were made at the work sites, judging from the heaps of flakes found there. Chert has a light grey or a light brown colour and, although composed almost entirely of silica, breaks with a flat fracture, rather than with the shell-shaped depressions and elevations of fractured flint. The reconstructed chert tools were adequate for working most stones. However, the experiments with both the flint and the chert tools upon particular igneous stones demonstrated a critical disparity in hardness between them.

The experiments with the flint tools

The main tool types investigated were rudimentarily manufactured knives, chisels, punches, scrapers, gravers, adzes and pounders (mauls), each tool type being made from flint and chert. Assessments of the flint tools were carried out by the test cutting of rose granite, close-grained blue granite, diorite, hard and soft limestones and sandstones, in addition to calcite, copper, bronze and wood in Manchester, England, during 1981–1982. Chert chisels, punches, scrapers and gravers were tried on rose granite at Aswan, Upper Egypt, in March 1999, and later in the year upon hard and soft limestones and sandstones, calcite, copper, bronze and wood in Manchester.

Although flint and chert knapping is a highly skilled art, and worth the investment of time to make tools only in use upon softer materials, the roughly made flint chisels and punches manufactured for use upon the granites and the diorite proved adequate for the experiments. The simplicity of sharpening a flint tool makes it attractive to a mason. Percussion of the stone, further back along the blade, causes a fresh, sharp edge to be created. The test use of such flint and chert tools upon the soft stones, for example limestone, produced little damage to the blades' edges, and the rate of removal in soft limestone was considerable. No doubt, a chisel fashioned for use upon soft stone would retain its original form for a protracted period, and this is suggested by a skilfully made flint chisel found at the bottom of the pit containing Khufu's boat at Giza. The 15 cm-long chisel was probably used alongside copper chisels for fitting the limestone roofing blocks over the pit.[41] The struck end comprises the nodule's smooth, rounded exterior cortex, which was ideal for striking with a wooden mallet, or with a stone hammer. It is likely that the mason knocked the tool through a gap in the limestone roofing slabs while fitting them, being unable to descend to recover it.

Dynastic flint adzes, which were so effective for working the soft limestone, would not have been utilized upon the harder stones. These tools' edges splinter and quickly become useless. Numerous experiments indicate that ancient flint adzes could only have been effective for working wood and soft stones, that is, soft limestone, soft sandstones, such as red sandstone, and gypsum. While the glancing blows of an adze were very effective on soft stone and wood, tests demonstrated that the hardness of calcite, and of harder stones, proved too much for this technique to be of any real use, and it is likely that flint chisels and punches, their cutting edges and points positioned vertically upon hard-stone surfaces, were driven by a sudden blow delivered with a mallet or a stone hammer.

In museums in Adelaide (Australia), Boston and Philadelphia (United States of America) and in Bolton, London and Manchester (United Kingdom) there each stands a rose granite column: they all came from the Nineteenth Dynasty Temple

FIGURE 3.5 An unfinished hieroglyph, *nb*, in the granite column, Bolton Museum and Art Gallery 1891.14

Source: Image by J. Stocks from Bolton Museum and Art Gallery

of Herishef, a ram-headed god, at Heracleopolis. The temple site, near to the Fayum, was excavated by Edouard Naville in the late nineteenth century.[42] Palm fronds were carved into each column's capital, but some of the capitals are now missing. All the columns have been incised with finished signs into their polished, curved surfaces, attributable to Ramesses II, with other unfinished signs ascribed to the following pharaoh, Merenptah.

The tool marks visible around, and sometimes in, the unfinished signs incised into several of these columns were closely examined and measured. The finished signs are incised to a maximum depth of 2.5 cm; the bottom of each sign gradually curves from a minimum depth at its centre to a maximum depth at the edges. On this column, and the others, all the signs in the alternate panels adjacent to Ramesses II's signs are unfinished. Upon close examination, these signs are, at this stage of the work, crudely hacked out of the stone; the edges are extremely uneven. The hacked-out surfaces are very rough and quartz crystals protrude from them. However, chisel marks of different sizes, and at random angles to the signs' edges, may be seen Figure 3.5). Within the finished panels of Ramesses II, the surface has been grooved in places. This grooving has been smoothed, unlike the group of four baboons at the Musée du Louvre. The unincised surfaces of the column are polished, but there are small pits left in them.

One of the finished column symbols is the wickerwork basket-shaped biliteral sign, *nb*. The sign measures 14 cm in length, 5 cm in width and 2.5 cm in depth, having an approximate volume of 120 cm³. A similar, though smaller, test sign was marked upon a block of rose granite, after it had been prepared flat. The sign was marked out

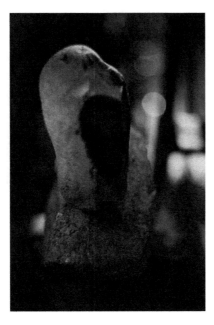

FIGURE 3.6   Pounding a granite surface flat with a flint nodule

Source: Image by J. Stocks

to be 9 cm long and 2.2 cm at its widest point. The total area of the sign was 13 cm². The initial stone flattening process was achieved by using a hand-held flint nodule (Figure 3.6); the high points of the granite's surface were abraded and crushed until an area of 120 cm² became acceptably flat. The time taken for this operation was 45 minutes. It was noticed that the flint pounder became damaged at its point of contact with the granite. This damage consisted of small pieces of flint chipped out of the maul's surface. However, the sharp points left in the flint's surface struck the high spots on the granite with good effect. The granite was further prepared with coarse and smooth sandstone rubbers. These were employed for 15 minutes. A smooth surface resulted, which was an average of all the highest and lowest places on the stone. The small pits left in the surface would have taken much work to eradicate and they were left, just as the ancient craftworkers did with the granite columns.

The possible ancient use of wooden mallets and stone hammers, for driving flint tools, now needs to be investigated. A stone hammer eventually shatters the struck end of a brittle flint tool, especially if the hammered end is not formed from the flint's exterior cortex; injury from flying fragments is likely. The experimental striking of flint tools with a stone hammer demonstrated that small cuts could be caused to the operator's face and arms by the steady destruction of the flint as work progressed. It is likely that some eye damage could also have been caused by flying flints in ancient times. A flint punch, or chisel, knapped to a flat striking surface, like the Kahun punches, could have been driven with a stone hammer into soft

FIGURE 3.7 A wooden mallet, Bolton Museum and Art Gallery 1904.48.67 from Deir el-Bahri, Upper Egypt, has wedge-shaped slots impacted into its striking surface

Source: Courtesy of Bolton Museum and Art Gallery

and hard stones, especially for fine carving purposes. But awkwardly shaped flint tools invite the use of a wooden mallet for driving them. Wood absorbs some of the impact, and any flint splinters penetrate the wood and, later, fall harmlessly to the ground as the mallet's surface becomes eroded.

Some ancient mallets show severe circumferential wear. A New Kingdom mallet (Bolton Museum and Art Gallery, 1904.48.67) from Deir el Bahri, Upper Egypt, has wedge-shaped slots impacted into its striking surfaces (Figure 3.7). Although it is likely that they were caused with a metal tool, the wedge-shaped slots suggest the characteristic cross-sectional shape of a thin flint tool. Petrie has stated that the mallet used for striking the chisel was always wood. No doubt, Petrie was referring to metal chisels. However, it is possible that circumferential wear to wooden mallets was caused by flint tools, in addition to metal ones. The experimental use of flint punches and chisels on hard and soft stones demonstrated that, by and large, stone hammers were more favourable for driving flint chisels and punches into the harder stones, such as the igneous varieties, whereas mallets were better for driving flint tools into the softer stones (Figures 3.8, 3.9).[43]

The chipping of hard stone for the cutting of hieroglyphs demonstrates a great need to direct the edges and the points of chisels and punches in order to control the shape of the sign. Therefore, a stone's surface must be struck with a tool *after*

FIGURE 3.8   Chipping out pieces of hard sandstone with a mallet-driven flint chisel

Source: Image by J. Stocks

FIGURE 3.9   An incised *ankh* sign carved into hard sandstone with flint chisels and punches

Source: Image by J. Stocks

FIGURE 3.10   The crystal structure of rose granite

Source: Image by J. Stocks

placing its cutting edge, or point, in the correct position. The cutting tool transmits the blow of the hammer through its body. (It is most unlikely that small hieroglyphs were ever hacked out with hand-held stone chisels or punches, although large hieroglyphs may have been achieved by this method.) This is a fundamental change from pounding an object to shape. The concept of causing a change to the surface of a material by striking a chisel, or a pointed punch, with a hammer or a mallet is an important technical change in tool use, whenever it occurred.

Rose granite is a coarse-grained stone, mainly composed of quartz, mica and feldspar, the latter mineral being slightly softer than the quartz (Figure 3.10). The pinkish feldspar, widely distributed within the stone's matrix, and larger in size than the quartz and mica crystals, made this granite particularly attractive to the Ancient Egyptians. The chiselling action on the rose granite is improved if the chisel's edge is twisted to a new angle of attack, after a preceding blow. In this way, account may be taken of the different quartz crystal positions within the stone. After roughing out the test sign, pointed punches were employed to reduce the chiselled surface to a flatter finish. The characteristic pitted appearance of ancient artifacts was in evidence at the bottom of the sign. These findings were confirmed by experimentally chipping smoothed and polished hard limestone and diorite with flint punches (Figure 3.11). Examination of the tools' marks showed that these, too, closely resembled ancient tool marks.[44] Flint punches were also used to make the hemispherical-shaped holes in capstones for use with the reconstructed bow-driven tubular drills.

Four cubic centimetres of rose granite were removed in 45 minutes' work, equal to a rate of 5.3 cm^3/hour (Figure 3.12). By way of comparison, Antoine Zuber

FIGURE 3.11   The surface of a smooth block of diorite chipped into with a stone hammer-driven flint chisel (left of the tubular slot)

Source: Image by J. Stocks

FIGURE 3.12   Showing how the *nb* sign could be cut into rose granite with a flint chisel

Source: Image by J. Stocks

carved a 20 cm-high granite head in 36 hours with flint tools.[45] The experimental sign was completed with flint scrapers (Figure 3.13). These tools not only scrape the soft stones (Figure 3.14), but are also effective on the hard stones. This process inevitably takes longer and, upon granite, was accompanied by an acrid smell. Various sandstone rubbers of coarse and fine grades were employed to smooth the sign's surface (Figure 3.15).

FIGURE 3.13   Scraping the experimental *nb* sign with a flint tool

Source: Image by J. Stocks

FIGURE 3.14   Working soft limestone with a flint scraper

Source: Image by J. Stocks

In the tests carried out in 1999 at Aswan, Upper Egypt,[46] a rose granite block was prepared for the cutting of a second biliteral sign, *nb*, by pounding it with a dolerite hammer and grinding the surface smooth with sand and a flat quartzite rubber. This process, for an area of 400 cm², took a worker 4 hours to complete. After marking the sign to be 15 cm long and 3 cm at its widest point upon the flattened surface with chalk, stone hammer–driven flint chisels were used to cut

FIGURE 3.15   Smoothing the *nb* sign with a sandstone rubber

Source: Image by J. Stocks

into the feldspar crystals. This action again isolated the adjacent quartz and mica crystals, which were hacked away with further blows of the tools. Flint punches refined the surface left by the chisels. The chisels and the punches suffered considerable damage during their use, requiring frequent knapping to restore their edges and points. The sign was cut out to a depth of 4 mm, its volume of 12 cm^3 being removed in 2 hours, 30 minutes. The rate for cutting the sign was approximately 5 cm^3/hour, similar to the Manchester cutting experiments. The test chert chisels, punches, scrapers and gravers were made from nodules obtained from the Luxor region. However, these tools were unable to make any significant impression on the feldspar crystals: the hardness of chert critically falls below that of flint. The Manchester and Aswan experiments both confirmed the ability of the flint chisels and punches to work the rose granite, but that the chert tools' hardness fell just below this capability.

The experimental granite-working results indicate that ancient artisans could have chiselled and punched rose granite at the rate of approximately 15 cm^3/hour, or about three times the experimental rate. The explanation for this disparity is connected to the experimental conditions. First, the relatively small test pieces of granite rebounded when struck with the chisel, and this phenomenon counteracted some of the shock of a blow. As a result, a chisel's edge did not penetrate to its maximum possible amount. Conversely, large granite blocks, by virtue of their mass, assist the transmission of the blow into the stone. Second, the necessarily smaller flint tools, and consequentially lighter tool blows, employed on these relatively small pieces of granite. At the anticipated ancient stone removal rate of 15 cm^3/hour, a granite column *nb* hieroglyph could have been chipped out in 8 hours.

Anciently polished rose granite, because of the abundance of quartz crystals within its matrix, has a feel of glass. Therefore, the polishing of the specimen of

FIGURE 3.16   Polishing the granite with a leather lap and mud

Source: Image by J. Stocks

rose granite was attempted in the manner in which glass would be polished today, that is, by initially rounding the minute scratches and pits made by the grinding medium, in this case sandstone rubbers, and then polishing with a soft lap and paste. Leather was used as a hand-held lap for the experiments; it may have been used in ancient times. The Egyptians possessed a material which could have been in use for the initial polishing stages. This was a finely ground sand/stone/copper powder, a waste product from the tubular drilling and sawing of stone with sand abrasive. Chapter 4 will investigate this by-product more fully, and its possible uses to the craftworker.

Preliminary polishing of the rose granite involved mixing a quantity of the drilling powders, the by-product mentioned earlier, with liquid mud, and rubbing it onto the granite's surface with the leather lap. Lastly, to obtain a polish, mud only was utilized, again with the leather lap (Figure 3.16). Mud could have acted as a polishing medium in ancient times, as it is not unlike jeweller's rouge, which is used for polishing glass today. A fully polished surface would have cost ancient craftworkers much time and energy. The test polishing was not fully completed, and the total time for all the smoothing and the polishing operations was 80 minutes. It was noted that fine clay particles adequately fulfil the requirements of a polishing agent, giving a shallow, rounded shape to sharply defined pits and grooves, which display a frosted appearance on unpolished surfaces. With regard to the ancient *nb* sign, it is calculated that another 4 hours for polishing should be added to the 8 hours already stated, making a total of 12 hours in all (Figure 3.17).

The grooving in granite, previously mentioned, was imitated in the diorite and rose granite specimens with a flint tool possessing three faces and three edges. The experimental flint knapping created many such 'trifaces' of varying sizes.

FIGURE 3.17   The finished *nb* hieroglyph

Source: Image by J. Stocks

The point formed by the three edges may be driven with a mallet, and a groove is partly chipped and partly ground out of the hard stone's surface. Alternatively, the flint may be grasped with the hands and rubbed vigorously along the stone (Figure 3.18). The point can be sharpened by percussion-flaking two of the edges. While flint chisels and punches, followed by sandstone rubbers, effectively produced grooving in granite, this technology is included here for consideration; ancient craftworkers may have used it. The experimental groove in diorite measured 5 cm in length, 4 mm in width and 1 mm in depth. In rose granite, the groove length was 4 cm, the width 3 mm and the depth 1 mm. The time taken for each groove was approximately 2 minutes.

Another test for flint chisels, punches and scrapers was devised. A flat surface was prepared on a piece of hard, fine-grained sandstone. A test bronze chisel was used to produce the surface, but the chisel's edge became badly damaged. Flint produces a flat surface in such stone at a quicker rate. The Egyptian word for 'flint', the semi-ideogram *ds*, meaning 'sharp stone', consists of four signs; these are the consonants *d* (hand) and *s* (bolt), followed by the determinative signs for 'knife' (sharp) and 'stone'. The four symbols, each averaging 2 cm in length and 1 mm in depth, were cut into the sandstone with small flint chisels, punches and scrapers (Figures 3.19, 3.20) in 20 minutes. The floors of the signs had, at first, a pitted surface, which was caused by the pointed tools. Scraping with a flint microlith completely eradicated the pitting. A copper, or bronze, point small enough to have

FIGURE 3.18   An experimental groove in rose granite, cut with a pointed, 'trifacial' flint tool

Source: Image by J. Stocks

FIGURE 3.19   The hieroglyph for 'flint' (*ds*), incised into hard sandstone with flint chisels and punches

Source: Image by J. Stocks

FIGURE 3.20   Ancient hieroglyphs incised into hard sandstone

Source: Image by D. Stocks

cut this type of hieroglyph would not have stood up to the stresses imposed upon the metal.

Petrie was intrigued by the craftworker's ability to incise, or grave, hieroglyphs into fragments of a Fourth Dynasty diorite bowl he found at Giza. These incised lines were 1/150 inch (0.17 mm) wide.[47] Petrie was convinced that the lines were not scraped or ground out, but were ploughed through the diorite, leaving rough edges. Four materials were experimentally graved with a sharp-edged flint tool. These were granite, diorite, copper and bronze. The granite and the diorite could both be graved by forcefully drawing the tool across the materials' surfaces. The flint tool could be directed with a straight edge, or by the free use of the hand. Under magnification, the incisions closely matched the marks on the diorite fragments at Giza; the lines have rough edges. The copper and the bronze test samples were similarly scored by forceful strokes of the flint tool. Each incision in the copper sample became V-shaped in cross-section, with each edge raised above the surface. These experimental cuts closely resemble V-shaped incisions displayed on the surfaces of four copper razors in the British Museum (6079–82), inscribed with the name Idy.

Two model copper harpoon heads, from the Second Dynasty tomb of Khasekhemwy, were, according to Flinders Petrie, roughly cut out from sheet copper.[48] Forceful cutting with flints along a line, until the copper was completely severed, may well have been the technique employed by the ancient craftworker in making these models. H.H. Coghlan[49] tested flint tools upon a copper strip 3 mm thick and 13 mm wide, together with a small copper rod, 3 mm in diameter. He found that a flint chisel cut the copper strip in one minute, but the blade's edge became slightly notched. The rod was cut in three to four seconds with the same tool, without seriously damaging its edge. However, a serrated flint tool, used by

Coghlan as a saw on the same copper rod, was rendered useless in the five minutes needed to cut through the metal.[50] The present tests indicate that, although a mallet-driven flint chisel will cut into copper, and it is assumed that Coghlan drove his test chisel into the metal sample, continuous scoring of the metal by drawing a blade along the same line effectively cuts through copper without damaging the tool.[51]

The experimental use of the flint and chert knives, chisels and scrapers, for bark removal and handle carving, has already been mentioned. The intricate carving of any type of wooden object benefits from the employment of flint or chert tools, rather than with metal ones, and their sharp points and edges give extended service on all wood types, as with soft limestone.

Tools for keeping: tools for throwing away

The experiments with the flint tools suggest that this material was in extensive use for working all of the hard stones employed by the Ancient Egyptians. It is likely that flint knappers produced tools for working the hard stones which were separate from the production of durable flint tools for soft stoneworking and other purposes. This vital flint-knapping industry made flint tools that were deliberately designed for short lives. In other words, flint tools for working hard stones were dispensable tools. The modern term for such tools is 'throw-away'.

It has already been suggested that flint tools were used for working the limestone and granite at Giza in the Fourth Dynasty. With regard to the working of soft limestone into blocks, the employment of flint tools for the initial rough shaping makes sense. Why use expensively produced metal tools for this part of the operation when cheaply made, disposable stone tools are available? (It is *not* suggested that metal chisels were *not* in use for the final fitting work.) The experimental use of flint tools produced large numbers of microliths as they slowly disintegrated under each impact on the hard stone. Because of this, a search for undamaged ancient flint chisels and punches that were *definitely* used to shape hard-stone sculpture, vessels and building components is unlikely to be successful. By their very nature, the flint tools would eventually fragment into smaller and smaller pieces and be incorporated into the general debris at the work sites.

Although copper, bronze and iron were of great importance as tool-manufacturing materials to Ancient Egyptian craftworkers, the experimental working of the igneous stones suggests that flint and chert tools occupied a crucial place in the ancient workers' range of equipment. In addition to the cutting of hieroglyphs in hard stone, flint tools would have been invaluable for cutting small, incised hieroglyphs in softer stones, such as calcite, and this is supported by the archaeological evidence. For example, the experimental incising of lines into calcite closely match the hieroglyphs inscribed into the calcite statue of Menkaure in the Boston Museum of Fine Arts. Also, flint tools were probably in use for the carving of hard-stone columns and their complicated capitals, the chipping of hard-stone vessels to shape, and the carving of hard-stone sculptures.

It is likely that the craftworkers' use of flint and chert followed a distinctive pattern. There is tool manufacture itself – the creation of shapes and their cutting edges. But the worked materials themselves, which consisted of animal skins, flesh, plants, ivory, wood and, eventually, soft and hard stones, caused changes to tools' designs. For example, the carving of small wooden objects required tools of different designs than the flint adzes used so effectively for smoothing planks of wood and soft limestone surfaces. The developmental changes to flint tools were, therefore, the result of working different materials. Flint tools eventually assumed special shapes for specific purposes. For instance, the end-scraper probably developed into a chisel by driving it with a hammer or mallet, rather than just operating it with the hand. The technique of scraping stones with flint tools, a natural development from scraping skins and wood, was a vital one to ancient workers. (The use of sandstone rubbers on stone is analogous to the manner flint scrapers work on that material. Many sharp quartz crystals, exposed at the sandstone rubber's surface, effectively scrape minute particles from a stone's surface. At this level, though, these tiny quartz crystal scrapers are said to be grinding the surface of the stone.)

During the long occupation of various parts of Egypt, before the advent of a unified state, flint was in use for many purposes, some of which were referred to earlier in this chapter. It was the necessity to carve hard-stone vessels and statuary to shape (chisels and punches), and the hollowing of soft-stone vessels (crescentic borers), that forced new uses for flint upon the ancient worker. The large-scale employment of stone for building and for statuary, and as a material for the carving of reliefs and hieroglyphs, necessitated a huge increase in flint tool production. Many of flint's previous uses also remained in place. The test use of the flint tools demonstrated that this plentiful material possesses the characteristics of hardness, sharpness and toughness necessary successfully to work many different materials. For all these reasons, flint tools permeated the whole of Egyptian society at every level and throughout every period. Indeed, there had always been a flint for all seasons!

Notes

1 For example, a group of chert borers used to hollow Fourth Dynasty gypsum vessels at Umm-es-Sawan in the Fayum. A figure-of-eight-shaped borer and two crescent borers (now MM 8352–4) are called 'borers of chipped flint' on the information card. Caton-Thompson and Gardner also refer to the tools as 'flint' (G. Caton-Thompson and E.W. Gardner, *The Desert Fayum*, London: The Royal Anthropological Institute of Great Britain and Ireland, 1934, p. 105).

2 D.A. Stocks, 'Industrial technology at Kahun and Gurob: Experimental manufacture and test of replica and reconstructed tools with indicated uses and effects upon artefact production', unpublished thesis, University of Manchester, 1988, vol. II, pp. 246–73.

3 W.M.F. Petrie, *Kahun, Gurob and Hawara*, London: Kegan Paul, Trench, Trübner, and Co., 1890, p. 34.

4 For example, Twelfth Dynasty illustrations of handled flint knives (W.M.F. Petrie, *Tools and Weapons*, London: British School of Archaeology in Egypt, 1917, p. 23, pl. XXIV, K16–18). These knives are seen in a butchery scene in the Sixth Dynasty tomb of Mereruka at Saqqara (P. Duell (ed.) *The Mastaba of Mereruka*, Chicago, IL: The Oriental Institute, University of Chicago, 1938, vol. I, pl. 54, vol. II, pls 109A, 110).

5   Petrie, *Tools and Weapons*, p. 46, pl. LIII, S74 (from Meidum), S75–7 (from Giza), S82–5 (from Beni Hasan); W.M.F. Petrie, *Egyptian Architecture*, London: British School of Archaeology in Egypt, 1938, p. 30; W.C. Hayes, *The Scepter of Egypt*, New York: Metropolitan Museum of Art, 1953, vol. I, p. 290, Fig. 192.

6   H. Wild, *Le Tombeau de Ti*, Cairo: Government Press, vol. III, 1953, pls 120–4, 133; N. de G. Davies, *The Rock Tombs of Deir el Gebrâwi*, London: Egypt Exploration Fund, 1902, vol. II, pl. 16.

7   Petrie, *Tools and Weapons*, pl. LIII, S74, 75–7; MMA 15.3.832, from Lisht.

8   N. de G. Davies, *The Tomb of Rekh-mi-Rē' at Thebes*, New York: Metropolitan Museum of Art, 1943, vol. II, pl. LX.

9   Petrie, *Egyptian Architecture*, p. 30.

10 Ibid.

11 Ibid; C.C. Edgar, 'Sculptors' studies and unfinished works', *Catalogue Général des Antiquités Égyptiennes du Musée du Caire*, Cairo: Imprimerie de l'Institut Française d'Archéologie Orientale, 1906, p. v.

12 Petrie, *Egyptian Architecture*, p. 30.

13 The experimental knapping of flint produced many flakes with curved cutting edges.

14 J. Hill, *Theophrastus's 'History of Stones'*, London: J. Hill, 1774, books LXXII, LXXV.

15 Ibid., pp. 177, 181.

16 R. Engelbach, *The Problem with the Obelisks*, London: T. Fisher Unwin, 1923, p. 40.

17 R.F. Tylecote, *Metallurgy in Archaeology*, London: Edward Arnold, 1962, p. 244, table 80.

18 C.E. Pearson and J.A. Smythe, 'Examination of a Roman chisel from Chesterholm', *Proceedings of the University of Durham Philosophical Society* 9 (3), 1938, pp. 141–5.

19 Tylecote, *Metallurgy in Archaeology*, pp. 244–5, Fig. 63.

20 A. Bomann, 'Wadi Abu Had/Wadi Dib', in K.A. Bard (ed.) *Encyclopedia of the Archaeology of Ancient Egypt*, London and New York: Routledge, 1999, pp. 861, 863; D.A. Stocks, 'Roman stoneworking methods in the eastern desert of Egypt', in N.J. Higham (ed.) *Archaeology of the Roman Empire: A Tribute to the Life and Works of Professor Barri Jones*, Oxford: Archaeopress, 2001, pp. 283–6.

21 Bomann, 'Wadi Abu Had/Wadi Dib', p. 861.

22 A. Bomann and R. Young, 'Preliminary survey in the Wadi Abu Had, Eastern Desert, 1992', *JEA* 80, 1994, pp. 23–7, Fig. 2.

23 R. Engelbach, 'Evidence for the use of a mason's pick in Ancient Egypt', *ASAÉ* XXIX, 1929, pp. 19–24.

24 Stone chisel, pointed maul or 'pick' marks are to be seen in quarries dating to the Old and Middle Kingdoms, Early New Kingdom and Ramesside to the Thirtieth Dynasty. Similar tool marks are evident in the quartzite quarries of Gebel el-Ahmar (D. Arnold, *Building in Egypt: Pharaonic Stone Masonry*, New York: Oxford University Press, 1991, pp. 33, 40, Figs 2.7, 2.8, 2.9, 2.18, 2.19). For quarries, see J. Röder, 'Steinbruchgeschichte des Rosengranits von Assuan', *Archäologischer Anzeiger* 3, 1965, pp. 461–551; D. Klemm and R. Klemm, *Die Steine der Pharaonen*, Munich: Staatliche Sammlung Ägyptischer Kunst, 1981; J.A. Harrell and V.M. Brown, *Topographical and Petrological Survey of Ancient Egyptian Quarries*, Toledo, OH: University of Toledo, 1995.

25 Edgar, 'Sculptors' studies and unfinished works', pp. I–VIII; A. Lucas and J.R. Harris, *Ancient Egyptian Materials and Industries*, London: Edward Arnold, 1962, p. 68.

26 Stocks, 'Industrial technology', vol. I, pp. 87–8.

27 Davies, *Rekhmire*, vol. I, pp. 58–9, vol. II, pl. LX.

28 Ibid., vol. I, pp. 58–9, vol. II, pl. LX. Flint implements employed for quarrying and for cutting rock tombs are known (M.H.W. Seton Karr, 'How the tomb galleries at Thebes were cut and the limestone quarried', *ASAÉ* VI, 1905, pp. 176–84).

29 W.M.F. Petrie, *The Pyramids and Temples of Gizeh*, London: Field and Tuer, 1883, p. 213.

30 Arnold, *Building in Egypt*, p. 48.

31 For example, Petrie, *Tools and Weapons*, p. 43, pl. LXXVIII, showing part of a group of 23 iron tools dated to the seventh century BCE, including saws, bits for drilling wood, chisels, a punch, a rasp and a file, all from Thebes, Upper Egypt.

32 A. Zuber, 'Techniques du travail des pierres dures dans l'Ancienne Égypte', *Techniques et Civilisations* 30, 1956, pp. 195–215.

33 Engelbach, *The Problem*, p. 40.

34 D.A. Stocks, 'The working of wood and stone in Ancient Egypt: The experimental manufacture and use of copper, bronze and stone tools', unpublished dissertation, University of Manchester, 1982, pp. 164–97; Stocks, 'Industrial technology', vol. II, pp. 246–73.

35 D.A. Stocks, 'Testing Ancient Egyptian granite-working methods in Aswan, Upper Egypt', *Antiquity* 75, 2001, p. 93.

36 Old Kingdom gypsum (Mohs 2) vessels were bored with crescent-shaped chert, probably not flint, borers at Umm-es-Sawan in the Fayum (Caton-Thompson and Gardner, *The Desert Fayum*, p. 105). It is likely that flint or chert crescents were driven with the Twist/Reverse Twist Drill's inverted forked wooden shaft, which was lashed onto the main drill-shaft. See Chapter 5.

37 W. Shepherd, *Flint: Its Origin, Properties and Uses*, London: Faber, 1972.

38 Stocks, 'Testing Ancient Egyptian granite-working methods in Aswan, Upper Egypt', pp. 93–4.

39 R. Said, *The Geological Evolution of the River Nile*, New York: Springer-Verlag, 1981.

40 G.E. Carnarvon and H. Carter, *Five Years' Explorations at Thebes*, London: Egypt Exploration Society, 1912, p. 10.

41 N. Jenkins, *The Boat beneath the Pyramid*, London: Thames and Hudson, 1980, p. 81, pl. 55.

42 E. Naville, 'Excavations at Henassieh (Hanes)', *Egypt Exploration Fund Special Extra Report*, 1891, pp. 8, 9.

43 Stocks, 'Industrial technology', vol. II, pp. 246–73.

44 Compare CM JE33303 (larger marks), JE33301 (smaller marks) and JE33304 (smaller marks still) (Edgar, 'Sculptors' studies and unfinished works', pl. I).

45 Zuber, 'Techniques du travail des pierres dures dans l'Ancienne Égypte', p. 180, Figs 18–20.

46 Stocks, 'Testing Ancient Egyptian granite-working methods in Aswan, Upper Egypt', pp. 93–4.

47 Petrie, *Pyramids*, p. 173.

48 Petrie, *Tools and Weapons*, p. 37, pl. XLIV, V36, 37.

49 H.H. Coghlan, *Notes on the Prehistoric Metallurgy of Copper and Bronze in the Old World*, Oxford: Oxford University Press, 1951, pp. 81–2.

50 Ibid., p. 82.

51 Stocks, 'Industrial technology', vol. II, p. 269.

PART II

High priests of industry

The state's influence
on technology

4

THE ABRASIVE TECHNOLOGISTS

Flora and technology connections

The working of stone with copper chisels and adzes, with flint chisels, punches, scrapers and adzes, and with grinding stones and stone hammers only supplied part of the craftworker's capability to fashion all types of ancient stone artifacts. In order to enable Ancient Egyptian artisans to create the range of objects demanded of them during the Late Predynastic and Dynastic periods, other technology required development. Often, modern technology evolves from earlier techniques and materials, and it is likely that such fundamental developments also occurred in Ancient Egypt. Thus, two important tools for cutting the stones were added to the craftworker's tool kit, and these were the flat-ended copper tubular drill and the flat-edged copper saw, both used with a particulate abrasive. The tubular drill pre-dated the invention of the stonecutting saw, which probably owed its development to the introduction of hard stone for architecture in the Early Dynastic and Old Kingdom periods. The stonecutting saw is a direct development of the serrated woodcutting saw, itself a development from the serrated flint knife and sickle. No examples of copper stonecutting tubes and saws have survived to the present day, nor have any tomb representations of them been found.

In Ancient Egypt, people were influenced by the plants growing around them. The fact that certain plant shapes were copied in stone for architectural purposes has already been mentioned: Ancient Egyptian builders copied the flower of the lotus plant, in bud or fully open, and the leaves of palm trees as design ideas when creating stone column capitals. A particularly important native plant was the common reed. Another reed, *Arundo donax* (Spanish reed), also growing in Egypt, was not used to the same extent as the common reed. This reed grew along the river Nile in great abundance, and was in use for pens, arrows and small pieces of furniture. The leaves were used for making sleeping mats and the rhizomes for medicinal purposes.[1]

DOI: 10.4324/9781003269922-7

FIGURE 4.1   A large drill-hole in a rose granite block at Karnak, created by first drilling with a tube possessing a wall thickness of approximately 3 mm and then breaking out the core

Source: Image by D. Stocks

The common reed usually grows in marshy conditions, where it can attain 5 m in height;[2] it is much shorter in drier places. Large reeds have a diameter of several centimetres, and their stems are woody and strong. The slender, straight stem of the grass family of plants is hollow along its length, except at the leaf joints (nodes) which occur every few centimetres; these thin, internal leaf joint partitions completely block the tube's diameter. The partitions make the stem resistant to the wind. They can be removed, as previously described in Chapter 2, by breaking through them with a sharpened thinner reed, although this is not necessary for the manufacture of a tube in use as a drill. Provided the selected hollow section of the reed is left long enough to be engaged by a bow-string, or can be twisted clockwise and anticlockwise with the hand, it fulfils the requirements of a drill. The tubular drill produces a tubular-shaped slot, which surrounds a central core; this technology allows the removal of a small amount of the stone by drilling, but achieves the full-sized hole on removal of the core (Figure 4.1). It is likely that certain types of stone were first drilled with tubes made from reeds, which operated with a necessarily *dry* particulate abrasive at their cutting ends.

The introduction of long, hollow cylinders, or tubes, has greatly influenced human technical ability. By breaking through the leaf joint partitions in a reed stem, or indeed a bamboo cane or any other similar stem, thereby joining together the existing hollow sections to create a continuous tube, the ancient worker manufactured a radically new artifact. Today, tubes are made from a variety of materials, which include copper, brass, aluminium, mild and stainless steel and plastic. Tubes, or pipes, are in use for many purposes, such as conducting water, gas and oil to their destinations, as well as for scaffolding and hang gliders. The modified cane, wherever it first occurred, must be the progenitor of all long tubes.

The impetus for an important change in manufacturing technology originated with the production of hard- and soft-stone vessels. During the Badarian and Naqada I periods, hard-stone vessels, like the ones made of basalt, were laboriously hollowed by grinding with hand-held stone borers; sandstone borers, of varying coarseness, can be used without an abrasive substance, but other stone borers were probably utilized in conjunction with desert sand. Hand-held flint borers and scrapers were in use for the soft stones, such as soft limestone and gypsum, without the assistance of an abrasive material. It is likely that these tools, and the borers for hard stones, were continuously twisted and reverse twisted during their operation. The twist/reverse twist motion, a function of the lower arm and the wrist, is an important tool-driving ability. These techniques are fully explored in Chapter 5.

Sometime after the beginning of stone vessel manufacture, and before ca. 3600 BCE, when the casting of copper artifacts became established, workers probably employed the common reed as a tubular drill for initially hollowing the interiors of stone vessels manufactured from hard limestone and calcite: this technique considerably shortens the time needed to completely hollow out the interiors of stone vessels. It is likely that the common reed served as a pattern for Naqada II copper copies, which were able to drill into much harder stones than the reed tube. Tubular slots in various stone artifacts of Dynastic date, and which were made with copper tubular drills (the evidence for metal tubular drills will be examined shortly), together with the rapid increase in the manufacture of hard- and soft-stone vessels after ca. 3600 BCE, suggest that the idea for a tube made from copper could have arisen from a shape the craftworker had already seen and utilized – the tubular-shaped reed. The Egyptian coppersmith knew how to make tubes of copper during the Naqada II period, which is confirmed by a copper tubular bead (UC 5066), found in a grave at Naqada.

The reed was probably in use elsewhere for stone vessel manufacture. Indeed, it is likely that the common reed, found in abundance near to the Tigris and Euphrates rivers, was used as a drill for hollowing some of the early stone vessels in ancient Mesopotamia, before the introduction of copper tubes there. Peter Warren[3] suggests that reeds were employed for drilling stone vases in Minoan Crete, which utilized quartz sand as the abrasive material. Warren also mentions a blue/grey powder adhering to cores, which was analysed as emery. Warren did not favour metal drill-tubes for stoneworking in Minoan Crete, as they were absent, like the Egyptian ones, from the archaeological record. Joseph Shaw[4] also rejected Minoan metal drills and suggested that reed tubes were revolved upon sand or emery, which was lubricated with water or oil.

Abrasives and metals in use for the sawing and tubular drilling of stone

Before any experimental sawing and tubular drilling could commence, the most likely particulate abrasive material employed by ancient workers needed to be established. Emery and desert sand have been the subject of much discussion by

Egyptologists and others.[5] In this study, the archaeological and the environmental evidence, together with the results from these experiments,[6] and those of other experimenters,[7] were collectively assessed. The present experiments examined and evaluated the performance of the likely sawing and drilling abrasive under working conditions, and compared the results with the observed ancient sawing and drilling evidence.

The archaeological evidence for abrasives is inextricably linked to the evidence for copper stonecutting saws and tubular drills, and, therefore, both matters need investigating together. The ancient use of saws and tubular drills upon stone in Egypt was first recognized and recorded by W.M.F. Petrie. In the early 1880s, he examined saw marks on the basalt pavement on the eastern side of the Fourth Dynasty pyramid of Khufu at Giza,[8] and also investigated saw marks on the rose granite sarcophagi of Khufu and Khafre.[9] On Khufu's sarcophagus, Petrie noticed that straight, parallel striations ran horizontally along the sides. He stated that a saw about 9 feet[10] (2.7 m) in length was used to cut the granite to shape, allowing for the stroke of the tool. The normal stroke of a saw is approximately 30 cm, similar to the distance a bow-shaft travels when rotating a tubular drill: this is, of course, directly related to the reciprocating (to and fro) motion of the hand, a function of the arm's movement at its elbow and shoulder joints. Petrie located saw-slots in stone objects, and these showed that the saw thicknesses varied from 0.03 to 0.2 inch[11] (1–5 mm). Stonecutting saws were also in use on the Third Dynasty calcite sarcophagus of Sekhemkhet,[12] on the back of one of the triads of Menkaure,[13] and on stone blocks from the Fifth Dynasty pyramid complex of Nyuserre.[14] In order roughly to shape statuary, waste pieces were often sawn from the stone blocks.[15]

A particularly important example of sawing in rose granite is two striated, slanted saw-slots, forming a chevron, on the unfinished Fourth Dynasty sarcophagus of Hordjedef in the Cairo Museum (JE54938). The sawyers were trying to cut a section off the bottom of the sarcophagus for a lid: the already hollowed sarcophagus was never properly completed after the craftworkers unfortunately broke the lid after sawing halfway through the stone. The slots are 5 mm wide at the bottom of them, but taper outward to a width of 2 cm at their tops; the bottom of each slot is not flat, but laterally curved. (The later Aswan sawing experiments showed that these two phenomena are a consequence of the sawing action.) After earlier chevron cuts in this lid met at an apex on the centre-line, the saw was used to cut nearly down to the outer edges of the two original saw-slots. New striations, caused by the last sawing operation, are superimposed upon the striations made by the chevron-shaped cuts. Each of the three cuts was shorter than the full width of the block, requiring considerably less effort than sawing the full width in a single operation. Earlier workers used a similar method to saw Sekhemkhet's sarcophagus, which bears chevron-shaped marks on an exterior surface.[16]

On the back of the Fourth Dynasty basalt triad of Menkaure (CM JE46499), there are straight, horizontal, parallel striations, which look like saw marks. In this hard stone, these striations were caused by the side of a saw forcing a particulate abrasive substance against the walls of the slot as cutting progressed. Some of the striations are wider and deeper than others, and these can be explained by larger abrasive particles rubbing along particular striations. All of the saw marks seen on Egyptian stone artifacts display parallel striations that have an average depth and width of 0.25 mm. Although the saw is a reciprocating tool, the tubular drill can be thought of as part of a saw blade, but curved into a hollow cylinder.

W.M.F. Petrie[17] and G.A. Reisner[18] recorded that door pivot sockets in the Fourth Dynasty granite temples of Khafre and Menkaure had been created with tubular drills. Eye sockets and other parts of stone statuary were also drilled with tubes.[19] Stone cores, which always indicate the use of a tubular drill, have been located by various archaeologists, particularly Petrie.[20] Ancient holes in stone, and upon stone cores, have concentric striations around their circumferences, which are horizontal to the holes' and the cores' vertical axes (e.g. UC 18071, a calcite vase in the Petrie Collection), and these striations are, like the saw–slot striations, an average of 0.25 mm wide and deep. In particular, a tapered red granite core Petrie found at Giza (UC 16036) has a continuous striation which spirals for several rotations around its circumference. Petrie noticed that the striations cut through the softer feldspar and the harder quartz crystals in the granite without any variation in depth.[21] He rejected a loose cutting powder and thought this was good evidence to indicate the use of jewelled teeth, which were set into copper tubes as well as into copper saw blades.[22]

Tubular drills, driven by a bow, were employed for drilling out the interiors of calcite, granite and other hard-stone sarcophagi, but a detailed analysis of sarcophagus manufacture is reserved for Chapter 6. The bow-driven copper tubular drill was certainly used to drill the tapered holes in long tubular-shaped lug handles carved on the stone vessels of the Naqada II period: the experiments revealed that *only* bow–driven tubes produced tapered holes and cores. Good examples of these vessels with drilled lug handles are the Hathor Bowl in the Petrie Collection (UC 16245) and a syenite vase in The Manchester Museum (1776). Each of this vessel's two lug handles was drilled from each end, the tapering holes meeting in the middle: they have striations in them, also horizontal to their vertical axes. Similarly, four tapered holes, drilled into the lid of the rose granite sarcophagus of Prince Akhet-Hotep (Brooklyn Museum of Art 48.110) possess these striations. Each hole is 31 cm long and tapers from an average maximum diameter of 5 cm to an average minimum diameter of 4.5 cm (see Figure 6.2). They were probably used to lift the lid with thick ropes. There is strong evidence that tubes were used to drill single or multiple numbers of holes in stone vessels, and for making slots in stone artifacts. For example, eight tubular-shaped marks, left after the cores had been removed, are visible in an unfinished porphyry vase in the Cairo Museum (JE18758).

Petrie's measurements of the holes made by the tubular drills showed that tubular slot thicknesses ranged from 1/30 to 1/5 inch[23] (1–5 mm), similar to saw thicknesses. Petrie also stated that tubular drills varied from 1/4 inch to nearly 5 inches in diameter[24] (approximately 6 mm to 12 cm); it is likely that 6 mm-diameter drill-tubes possessed 1 mm-thick walls, and that wall thicknesses increased slightly with larger diameter tubes. A small drill-tube, about 8 mm in diameter, with a

1 mm-thick wall, was used to drill an uncatalogued Old Kingdom calcite vase in the Petrie Collection. The unbroken parallel-sided core is about 6 mm in diameter and 5 cm long, and it remains in a parallel-sided hole approximately 8 mm in diameter and 7.5 cm deep. A bow, therefore, was not used for driving the drill-tube. Much larger drill-tubes were possible, exemplified by a number of 45 cm-diameter slots, used in dressing down a limestone platform situated in front of some Twelfth Dynasty tombs at Deir el-Bersheh.[25] Woodcutting saws and wood drills were made from copper, but what evidence is there to indicate that this material was in use for stonecutting saws and tubular drills?

At Giza, Petrie[26] noticed green staining on the sides of some Fourth Dynasty saw-cuts in stone, which he ascribed to bronze, but was more likely to have been copper in the Fourth Dynasty. Grains of sand, also stained green, were found in a saw-cut at Giza by Petrie.[27] In a piece of basalt, from the pavement on the eastern side of the Great Pyramid, Petrie noticed a saw-cut with the sawing dust and sand still left in it.[28] Tubular drill marks exist on a block of stone from the Fifth Dynasty complex of Nyuserre, which bears traces of verdigris left from the use of a copper drill-tube.[29]

Alfred Lucas examined a hole made by a tubular drill in a fragment of alabaster (CM JE65402), of Third Dynasty date, from the Step Pyramid at Saqqara. In the hole, there was a compact mass of what was almost certainly the abrasive powder of a light green colour. The powder consisted of naturally rounded, very fine grains of quartz sand, and the colour was due to a copper compound, evidently from the drill used.[30]

Also at Saqqara, Lucas examined a large drill core about 8 cm in diameter, of coarse-grained red granite with green patches on the outside from the copper of the drill.[31] G.A. Reisner[32] found fine gritty powder, tinged green, in holes made by a tubular drill in two unfinished Fourth Dynasty stone artifacts. In a hole drilled by a tube into a granite doorpost of Ramesses II (MMA 13.183.2) are minute bronze particles. The hole is 7.5 cm in diameter and 10.3 cm deep. The stump of a core left in the hole shows that a tube was used to drill it, and the particles indicate that it was made from bronze; it is likely that bronze tubes eventually superseded copper ones. As a matter of interest, tubular drills made from hardened steel, with serrations at their cutting ends, are still in use today for making large holes in wood and sheet plastic.

The finding of fine sand particles, tinged green, is good evidence to indicate that the saw-cuts and the tubular holes in hard- and softer-stone artifacts were made with copper or bronze saws and tubular drills utilizing desert sand abrasive at their cutting edges. (Note: when exposed to the air, new copper's salmon pink colour turns a deeper red, then reddish brown, followed by a thin coat of oxide which gradually becomes green, due to the formation of a carbonate of copper.) Lucas thought that the abrasive should have been a local product, and was generally finely ground quartz sand, used wet, and that vast quantities of the abrasive must have been consumed. Cyril Aldred[33] and J.H. Breasted[34] also supported the use of sand abrasive for cutting hard stone. Lucas rejected the use of emery, an impure variety of corundum, as there is no evidence of its occurrence in Egypt. He also rejected Petrie's theory that for the drilling and sawing of the hard stones, jewelled points were set into copper tubes and saws. Petrie was unwilling to accept that sand could cut granite, stating that for cutting the soft alabaster, plain sand was amply hard, and that where alabaster vases had been cut, of the early dynasties at Hierakonpolis, and of Greek times at Memphis, large quantities of sand and alabaster dust had been found.[35] J.E. Quibell and F.W. Green[36] found sand that had been used as an abrasive material in a vase grinder's workshop at Hierakonpolis; they dated this workshop to the Old Kingdom period.

Pliny, the Roman historian, stated:

> The cutting of marble is effected apparently by iron, but actually by sand, for the saw merely presses the sand upon a very thinly traced line, and then the passage of the instrument, owing to the rapid movement to and fro, is in itself enough to cut the stone.[37]

The experimental use of copper and bronze flat-edged saws indicates that Pliny could have witnessed the process, but whether he was writing about Egyptian stone-sawing practices is not known. However, it seems likely that flat-edged iron saws eventually replaced the earlier Egyptian copper and bronze tools as this material came into fuller use after the Twenty-sixth Dynasty. Some tests were made with a mild steel (similar to wrought iron's characteristics) flat-edged saw to establish its cutting capabilities. Although marble's hardness is Mohs 4–5, and not as hard as granite, the tests show that Ancient Egyptian craftworkers *necessarily* sawed stones above the hardness of Mohs 3 with a flat-edged copper saw using sand as the abrasive.[38]

The sand environment in Egypt: effects on human activity

At first glance, quartz sand (Figure 4.2) is a nuisance to any form of civilized life. In Ancient Egypt, as now, there were vast quantities of dry sand moving in response to the pressure of the wind. The Ancient Egyptians suffered from several sand-induced ailments, including severe wear to their teeth, caused by sand-contaminated bread, and eye and lung diseases attributable to the fine dust raised from wind-blown sand. The Ancient Egyptians would have noticed that windblown sand erodes stone, and although the Egyptians suffered from the effects of sand upon their physical well-being, the craftworker was able to utilize quartz sand for several purposes.

What are the properties of desert sand noticed by ancient workers? Desert sand is almost always completely dry. To an Ancient Egyptian, the largest area of the environment was dry, inhospitable sand, and an ancient craftworker's perception of this desert environment, and its suggested uses for technology, must profoundly have been affected by its characteristics when in a fully dry condition.

Dry sand flows under the effects of pressure and gravity until equilibrium is reached. In fact, it acts much like a fluid. (Very wet sand will flow, but the experiments firmly dismiss wet, *coarse* sand as an abrasive for the saws and the drill-tubes.)

FIGURE 4.2   Crystals of quartz in sand

Source: Image by J. Stocks

A simple example combining these two phenomena is the manner a human foot, with a fairly high load upon a relatively small area, first causes the sand to flow outward, but after the weight has been removed it flows back into the depression left by the foot; the shape of the foot is not delineated, but an elongated hollow is formed. This flowing property of dry sand is of considerable significance to the sawing and the tubular drilling of stone.

A graphic example of how dry sand flows under pressure was demonstrated by Rick Brown and NOVA/WGBH Boston[39] at a granite quarry situated some 25 miles north-west of Boston, Massachusetts. Brown constructed a very large box made from concrete blocks, and completely filled it with dry sand. A 25-tonne granite obelisk, placed horizontally upon the sand, but partly upon an adjacent ramp, slowly forced the sand to flow out of two apertures cut into the base of the box, causing the obelisk to rotate and gently to descend onto a pedestal. Braking ropes prevented an uncontrolled descent of the obelisk.

Quartz crystals in sand caused serious damage to the teeth of the Ancient Egyptians. Frank Leek examined Ancient Egyptian teeth. He found that teeth were badly worn and flattened, largely due to eating bread heavily contaminated with quartz fragments from wind-blown sand.[40]

It is reasonable to assume that wind-blown sand crystals were present in Egyptian bread before the introduction of tubular drilling technology. Early Egyptian craftworkers may have recognized that the erosion of their hard teeth was caused by grinding them together on sand fragments, and this could have been a factor that influenced the introduction of sand as an abrasive for grinding stone with tools.

The lack of emery in Egypt, the existence of desert sand in vast quantities, the impracticability of mounting jewelled points into copper saws and drill-tubes, the finding of sand powders mixed with copper compounds associ-ated with sawing and tubular drilling activities in both soft and hard stones, and the present experimental evidence, which shows that sand will grind very hard stones, including igneous varieties, all clearly point to sand being the primary source of the abrasive in use with copper saws and tubular drills. Craftwork-ers were able to supply tubes and saws with cutting teeth by the million, and the cost to the state was just the chore of collecting it. The actual use of the sand for grinding did, however, cause considerable damage to the health of craftworkers.

Drilling stones with reed tubes

Experimental tests[41] were made upon the following stones: soft and hard limestone, calcite, hard sandstone (coarse-grained), hard sandstone (fine-grained) and blue gran-ite (close-grained). All of the tests were carried out in Manchester, except for the test upon the fine-grained sandstone, which took place in Aswan, Upper Egypt.

Each test utilized a 1 cm-diameter reed tube, which possessed 2 mm-thick walls. The tube was rounded at the top, for the capstone, and driven with a bow (Figure 4.3); a load of approximately 1 kg/cm^2 was applied upon the tube. The drill-tubes were tested with dry and wet sand abrasive. Overcutting of the holes, due to the lateral motion imposed by the bow, was allowed for when calculating the cutting rates for each drill-tube. Therefore, the *volumes* of the reed stem worn off a tube, and the stone drilled out, were used to obtain a ratio between the two materials, rather than measuring a tube's lost length and a hole's increased depth.

FIGURE 4.3   Test drilling soft limestone, with a bow-driven reed tube and dry sand abrasive

Source: Image by J. Stocks

TABLE 4.1 Reed tube cutting ratios and rates

A. With dry sand abrasive			B. With wet sand abrasive	
Stone type	Ratios of wear rates reed: stone		Cutting rates (cm³/hour)	
	dry	wet	dry	wet
soft limestone	1: 3	1: 1.5	12	12
gypsum	1: 3	1: 1.5	12	12
steatite	1: 3	1: 1.5	12	12
hard limestone	1: 2	2: 1	8	4
calcite	1: 2	2: 1	8	4
slate	1: 2	2: 1	8	4
hard sandstone:				
coarse-grained	–	–	–	–
fine-grained	1: 2	–	8	–
granite	–	–	–	–

The results are shown in Table 4.1. Dry sand abrasive caused some splintering to the tube, and the stem spread slightly outward. However, the drill retained its tubular shape and effectively drilled the soft and hard limestone and the calcite samples.

The reed drill-tube used with wet sand abrasive soon softened and spread outward and inward, thus completely filling the originally hollow interior with softened stem material. Despite this alteration to the tube's configuration, it performed useful work upon the soft limestone, but performed poorly upon the hard limestone and the calcite. However, because the drill had assumed the shape of a solid stalk, instead of a tube, penetration into the soft limestone was reduced, even though the volumetric rate of drilling remained similar to that of the tube in use with dry sand. The use of the reed tubes upon the coarse-grained hard sandstone and granite, utilizing wet or dry sand abrasive, so badly damaged them that no useful cutting could be achieved.

Copper: a new material for an old purpose

After the introduction of truly smelted and cast copper after ca. 3600 BCE, the stone vessel worker was able to imitate the hollow reed by beating thick sheets of cast copper into thinner sheets and rolling them into tubes around wooden, cylindrical formers made from tree branches; larger diameter tubes may have been cast to shape. Possibly, these tubes were cast by creating vertical, open, tubular-shaped moulds in damp sand, initially made by a reed tube acting as a pattern. Later, the wooden pattern/core method of manufacturing cast tubes could have been introduced, whereby a solid cylinder of wood, the pattern, is pushed vertically into the dampened sand, and then withdrawn. A slightly smaller, cylindrical, dried mud core is then centrally positioned into the hole left by the pattern and pushed into the mould's sand bottom (Figure 4.4). The tubular mould can now be filled with molten copper and the core

FIGURE 4.4   A tubular-shaped mould in sand, ready for filling with molten copper

Source: Image by J. Stocks

knocked out after cooling has taken place. This method[42] showed that the *minimum* tube wall thickness that could be cast was 4 mm (Figure 4.5).

In Chapter 2, the casting of copper into open, horizontal moulds in sand was mentioned (see Figure 2.15). In an experiment,[43] the minimum thickness of copper just covering the bottom of a mould was 5 mm, a similar dimension that Petrie ascribed to the maximum width of saw slots in stone objects, and for the maximum thickness of drill-tube walls. This thickness ensured the rigidity of long saws. However, thinner, as thin as 1 mm, shorter saw blades, both serrated and flat-edged, must have been made from copper plates that had been beaten down from an original minimum cast thickness of approximately 5 mm.

Examples of copper beaten into tubes and other artifacts have been found. Alfred Lucas[44] cleaned the cylindrical copper sockets in which the upright poles of the canopy of Queen Hetepheres, the mother of Khufu, rested. A socket was made by forming sheet copper into a cylinder, and hard soldering the overlapping joint with a silver-based solder. A piece of copper water pipe, 102 cm in length, 4.7 cm in diameter and with a wall thickness of 1.4 mm, was found at the Fifth Dynasty pyramid complex of Sahure.[45] Two Sixth Dynasty statues of Pepi I and his son were constructed from copper beaten around a wooden core.[46] Most parts were made from beating the copper to a thickness of 1–2 mm, although other parts were

FIGURE 4.5 Two failed copper tubular castings

Source: Image by J. Stocks

as thick as 4–5 mm, and these may first have been cast to shape. Although small-diameter copper tubular drills were fabricated from beaten cast sheets, 5 mm-thick copper sheet is extremely difficult to form into tubes. Consequently, it is more likely that furnace workers directly cast larger drill-tubes.

Copies of the reed tube shape made from sheet or cast copper gave four immediate advantages. First, tubes can be manufactured to reasonably accurate diameters and lengths and uniform wall thicknesses. Second, copper tubes made from beaten copper sheet have thinner walls (as thin as 1 mm), and this means that less stone needs to be removed from a hole. Third, tests showed that copper tubes can drill granite, diorite and porphyry, in addition to the softer stones; and, fourth, copper drills wear out much more slowly than reed drills (compare Table 4.1 with Tables 4.2 and 4.3).

The reed as a blowpipe, and the copy of the reed tube in copper, fundamentally changed the direction of Ancient Egyptian technology, and the development of Egyptian civilization. Without the blowpipe in the Predynastic period, it is unlikely that the furnaces could have been made hot enough for the length of time required to melt useful amounts of copper for casting: a primitive furnace, solely dependent upon the wind for its air, is unlikely to have matched the melting capability of furnaces fed with air through several blowpipes. Without the ability to cast copper sheets large enough to work into tubes, or directly to cast them, the craftworker could not have expanded stone vessel production in hard stone during the Naqada II period. The rapid expansion of hard-stone vessels during this period indicates the replacement of the reed tube with a copper copy.

TABLE 4.2 Manchester copper and bronze saw and bow-driven tube cutting ratios and rates – average of all experiments

Stone type	Ratios of metal: stone wear rates			Cutting rates (cm³/hour)			
	by volume		by weight	copper		bronze	
	copper tools	bronze tools	copper and bronze tools	tube	saw	tube	saw
rose granite	1: 3	1: 3	1: 0.9	1.5	4	1.3	3
diorite	1: 3	1: 3	1: 0.9	2	5	1.8	4.5
hard sandstone	1: 20	1: 23	1: 7	9	22	10	25
hard limestone	1: >100	1: >100	1: 8	15	37	14.5	36
calcite	1: >100	1: >100	1: 12	30	75	30	75

Note: the specific gravity of copper = 8.94 g/cm³, approximately 3.3 times the stones' specific gravities. See Table 4.4 for the specific gravities of the stones.

TABLE 4.3 Aswan copper saw and tube cutting data in rose granite

A. Saw

	slot depth	slot length	time taken	saw depth lost	volume of copper lost	weight of copper lost	volume of stone sawn	weight of stone sawn
wet sand	8 cm	75 cm	30 hours	32 mm	170 cm³	1520 g	360 cm³	972 g
dry sand	3 cm	95 cm	14 hours	7.5 mm	52 cm³	463 g	170 cm³	459 g

	cutting rate	saw stroke length	ratio 1	ratio 2	ratio 3
wet sand	12 cm³/hour	90 cm	1: 2	1: 0.6	1: 2.5
dry sand	12 cm³/hour	115 cm	1: 3.3	1: 1	1: 4

Note: The three ratios expressing the volumes, weights and depths of the copper worn off the saw (separately with the wet and dry sand abrasive) to the volumes, weights and depths of the sawn granite are recorded as 1, 2 and 3 respectively.

B. Tube

	hole depth	time taken	tube length lost	volume of copper lost	weight of copper lost	volume of drilled stone	weight of drilled stone
dry sand	6 cm	20 hours	9 cm	22.4 cm³	200 g	104 cm³	280 g

	cutting rate	revs/min.	ratio 1	ratio 2	ratio 3
dry sand	5.2 cm³/hour	120	1: 4.6	1: 1.4	1: 0.66

Note: The three ratios expressing the volume, weight and length of the copper abraded off the drill-tube to the volume, weight and depth of the drilled granite are recorded as 1, 2 and 3 respectively.

A copper tube would have been relatively short due to manufacturing constraints, but, by forcibly driving a long wooden shaft part-way into a tube, a bow's string or rope could be engaged to turn the drill, the upper part of the shaft revolving in a hand-held capstone. Large-diameter shafts may have been waisted, allowing a bow-rope, continually stretched by use, to be engaged upon a larger circumference of the waisted section, thus improving the bow-rope's grip without the nuisance of stopping work and shortening the rope. Also, a copper tube's outside diameter is necessarily larger than its wooden shaft's diameter, letting a tube penetrate to the bottom of sarcophagi and tall stone vessels. As the tube penetrates ever deeper, successive stone cores can be broken off, allowing the tube further to drill into the artifact. When a drill-tube wears down to a length no longer viable for effective drilling, it is a simple matter to fit a new tube to the original shaft. A worn-down drill-tube, and also a worn stonecutting saw blade, must have been returned to the foundry and melted down with additional copper for making new tubes and saws. Metals, such as copper and bronze, were precious commodities to the Ancient Egyptians because of the difficulties of mining the ores, smelting them and transporting the ingots to other places of work. This is indicated by the strict checks kept on the weight of state-owned bronze tools issued to the workers of Deir el-Medina, who cut the royal tombs in the Valley of the Kings, thereby discouraging and reducing the theft of the metal.[47]

The construction and use of the experimental Manchester saws and tubular drills

Eight copper tubes, one bronze tube, a copper saw and a bronze saw were tested upon the soft and hard limestones, calcite, hard sandstone (coarse-grained), blue granite (close-grained), rose granite (coarse-grained) and diorite.[48] The specific gravities of the stones are contained in Table 4.4. A mild steel saw was used to test cut the granite and the hard limestone.[49]

TABLE 4.4 Specific gravities of some Egyptian stones

Stone type	Mohs hardness	Specific gravity (g/cm³)
basalt	7	2.9
calcite	3–4	2.7
diorite	7	2.7
dolerite	7	2.9
flint	7	3
hard limestone	5	2.6
hard sandstone	5	2.6
porphyry	7	2.7
quartzite	6–7	2.7
rose granite	7	2.7
slate	4–5	2.6
soft limestone	2.5	2.4
syenite	7	2.7

TABLE 4.5 Experimental mild steel (wrought iron) saw cutting ratios and rates

Stone	Ratio of steel: stone wear rate (by weight)	Cutting rate (cm³/hour)
granite	1: 2	3
hard limestone	1: >100	30

TABLE 4.6 Average quantities of sand consumed by the experimental copper saws and drill-tubes

Stone type	Mohs hardness	Specific gravity (g/cm³)	Quantity of sand (g) consumed per cm³ of sawn and drilled stone
calcite	3–4	2.7	45
diorite	7	2.7	200–250
hard sandstone	5	2.6	60
hard limestone	5	2.6	50
rose granite	7	2.7	200–250

The experimental sawing of the granite with the low carbon content (less than 0.3 per cent carbon) annealed mild steel saw (VPN 131), similar to annealed wrought iron's characteristics, indicated that iron saws effectively could have cut through this stone. The steel saw's rate of cutting was lower than the copper and bronze (annealed hardnesses of VPN 42 and 75 respectively) saws' cutting rates. The tests suggested that an iron saw needed to be as soft as possible, allowing the angular quartz crystals to embed themselves more easily into the metal, thus increasing its efficiency as a cutting tool. However, the saw required a pressure of 3 kg/cm² in order to obtain an optimum sawing rate.

Based upon the experimental steel saw cutting rate of 3 cm³/hour for granite, and the experience gained from the large-scale sawing tests in Hamada Rashwan's granite quarry during March 1999[50] (see below), the estimated ancient rate for sawing the granite with a long, weighted, wrought iron saw operated by two workers is approximately 18 cm³/hour. The ratio of the weight of the metal worn off the experimental saw to the weight of the sawn granite was 1:2. The steel sawing results for the granite and the hard limestone are contained in Table 4.5.

The test copper and bronze tube diameters ranged from 1–8 cm, with wall thicknesses of 0.6–5 mm; they were employed to establish the drilling techniques, the cutting rates and the ratios of the copper and bronze worn off the tools to the volumes of stone drilled out. The amounts of sand consumed in sawing and drilling each stone type were also recorded in Table 4.6. All of the drill-tube experiments, except for the 8 cm-diameter copper tube, were performed in Manchester between 1981–1982; the 8 cm-diameter copper tube was tested in a rose granite quarry in Aswan, Upper Egypt, during March 1999.[51] A copper saw and a bronze saw, which both possessed 5 mm-thick edges, were each tested in Manchester to establish the sawing techniques, and for comparison with the drilling results. The leaded bronze tube, and the saw of this metal, were also tested, and the results achieved were similar to those obtained with the copper and bronze tubes. Also in Aswan, the tests included sawing a long slot into a granite block with a stone-weighted, flat-edged copper saw. The Manchester sawing and drilling results are recorded in Table 4.2 and the Aswan sawing and drilling results in Table 4.3.

The copper and bronze saw cutting results closely matched the tubular drilling results for these two metals. It will be noticed, in comparing the results in Table 4.5 with the results contained in Tables 4.2 and 4.3 that the harder steel cuts less efficiently than the softer copper and bronze tools: for the purposes of testing, cast copper and bronze tubes and saws were left to cool slowly, which fully annealed them. The beaten copper sheets were annealed before bending them into tubes.

All of the tubular drills were fitted with round wooden shafts. Each shaft was manufactured from prepared and seasoned tree branches, the bark of which had been removed by flint scrapers. The experiments proved that the drill-shafts remained firmly fixed in their respective tubes, no matter what diameter they measured; the friction between the shaft and the tube was quite sufficient to hold them together during use. Some tubes were fitted with straight-sided shafts, but others were fitted with waisted shafts, which permitted the stretched bow-strings or ropes to remain tightly wrapped around them. The experiments indicate that ancient craftworkers probably adopted this tube/shaft configuration, similar to the waisted drill-stock's design. Each drill-shaft was rounded at the top end to allow free rotation in one of three capstones, which acted as a bearing. The small Manchester saws were fitted with wooden handles, but the Aswan saw's stone weights, fastened by ropes to each end, also served as handles for the sawyers.

Two tools were needed to drive the drill-tubes; these were the bow and the capstone (Figure 4.6). Four bows were constructed from seasoned tree branches. The two main test bows were shaped like the ancient woodworker's bow, partly bent or curved at one end of the shaft, and having lengths of 39 cm (Figure 4.7) and 73 cm respectively. Each bow-string measured 2 mm in thickness. The other two bows were arc-shaped, one being 1.26 m in length, with a rope thickness of 6 mm, the other being 1.63 m in length, with a rope thickness of 1.3 cm. Hemispherical holes were carved into the three capstones with flint chisels, punches and scrapers. The holes were smoothed with sandstone rubbers. The three capstones weighed 510, 700 and 1,225 g respectively. A load of 1 kg/cm^2, placed upon the drills' end-faces and the saws' edges, was found to obtain the best cutting results. This pressure, mainly applied by the arm, also took account of personal fatigue. The total load, therefore, changed to suit different drill-tube diameters, or saw lengths.

The bow-strings and the bow-ropes were each tied into slots, cut for the purpose in each end of each bow. It is not possible to determine which materials were used to make ancient bow-strings and bow-ropes for driving drill-tubes. Possibly, halfa grass, papyrus, flax fibre or palm fibre were all in use. Sufficient slack was left in a bow-string so that, when the bow-shaft was bent a little, the bow-string made one complete turn around the drill-shaft, thus keeping the bow-shaft and the bow-string under tension. The bow-string's grip on the drill-shaft adequately resisted

FIGURE 4.6 One of the reconstructed capstones

Source: Image by J. Stocks

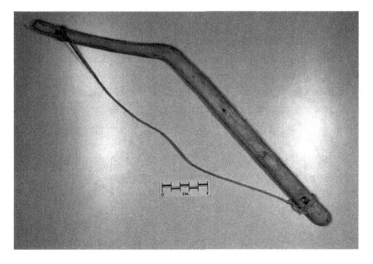

FIGURE 4.7 A 39 cm-long bow for driving small reconstructed tubular drills

Source: Image by J. Stocks

FIGURE 4.8   Drilling diorite with a bow-driven bronze tube and sand abrasive

Source: Image by J. Stocks

the friction generated at the drill's end-face; no slipping of a bow-string took place with the smaller diameter drill-tubes. However, this problem did arise with the 8 cm-diameter drill-tube.

The two test arc-shaped bows are dissimilar in shape to the angled, or curved, woodworkers' bow-shafts displayed in some tomb representations.[52] Larger bows, which were needed for driving the large diameter tubular drills, have been lost to us like the drill-tubes they drove. These ancient bows may have been shaped like the woodworker's bow, or arc-shaped, a design seen in certain Eighteenth Dynasty Theban tombs.[53]

Two types of sand were obtained for the experiments. Measurements of 150 quartz crystals, from the first sand type, showed that their lengths fell between 0.69 and 0.16 mm. The second sand type contained larger crystals, and measurements of 100 of them revealed that their lengths mainly fell between 1.27 and 0.13 mm, except for a few crystals, whose lengths were slightly longer than 1.27 mm. The coarser sand was employed upon the granite and the diorite, the finer sand upon the hard sandstone, hard and soft limestone and calcite. (The results for soft limestone are included for comparison with the reed tube's ability to cut this stone.) A large proportion of quartz crystals in sand are angular in shape, but an even greater proportion are roughly spherical. The angularity of quartz crystals proved to be an important factor in drilling and sawing the stones.

The sand abrasive in use for the Manchester sawing and drilling experiments was mainly utilized in the dry condition (Figure 4.8), but some tests were carried out with wet sand. In Aswan, one edge of the saw used wet sand to cut a slot in the rose granite, while the opposite edge of the saw used dry sand to cut a second slot. The large Aswan drill-tube used dry sand, but a short test with the sand wet revealed that this

FIGURE 4.9   Close-up of a copper tubular drill, engaged in the drill-hole. Notice that the hole is slightly overcut due to the lateral forces imposed during the drilling action

Source: Image by J. Stocks

test, and the others, established that it is counter-productive to the type of sawing, drilling and boring undertaken by the Ancient Egyptians. To our Twenty-first-century way of thinking, metal drills should be cooled by a mixture of water and soluble oil. The experiments have demonstrated that problems caused by heat generated by friction do not arise, and quartz sand's rate of cutting, particularly when used with metal tubes, is slightly better with the sand dry, rather than with it wet. Measurements of the temperature of the test drill-tubes, under load for several minutes, showed a constant drill temperature of approximately 80–100°C. Copper is a good conductor of heat, and this ability to conduct heat upward from the drilling area helps to keep a drill's temperature low. The experiments with the flat-edged copper saws, in use with sand abrasive, indicate that annealed copper cuts more effectively than hammered copper. (Copper and bronze drill-tubes need to remain fully annealed, whereas a modern, high-speed steel twist drill needs cooling to keep its hardness intact.)

The key factor enabling copper drill-tubes to operate is that individual quartz crystals embed themselves into the softer copper for a fraction of a second, and are swept around, or along in the case of a saw blade, the stone's surface. The crystals striate the stone. These actions take place many times a second, causing a tubular-shaped hole (Figures 4.9, 4.10, 4.11), or a slot, gradually to be cut out of the stone.

FIGURE 4.10 A tubular hole in diorite

Source: Image by J. Stocks

FIGURE 4.11 A tubular hole in rose granite

Source: Image by J. Stocks

Work experience demonstrates that spherical sand crystals roll around and act as a form of bearing – similar to tiny ball bearings. These actions help the operators to turn a drill or to push a saw. However, at any one moment, larger, angular crystals are retained in the softer copper and are forced to striate the stone.

A rotating copper drill-tube may be thought of as a kind of gyratory crusher or a grinding mill. However, while a normal mill is designed to grind large particles down with a minimum of wear to the harder grinding surfaces, the aims of the tubular drilling of stone are to maximize the wear to the lower grinding surface (the stone) and to minimize the wear to the upper grinding surface (the copper tube). The sand crystals, the particles of stone and the copper particles from the tube are ground down by the milling action into smaller and smaller sizes. Although the crystals pit and abrade a copper tube's end-face (Figure 4.12), and a copper saw's flat edge (Figure 4.13), they abrade many stone types at a faster rate,

FIGURE 4.12   The striated and pitted cutting surface of a copper tubular drill

Source: Image by J. Stocks

FIGURE 4.13   The striated flat edge of a stonecutting saw blade

Source: Image by J. Stocks

except for the igneous stones, where the ratio, by weight, of the copper worn off the saws and tubes to the sawn or drilled stone is 1:0.9. (The ratio by volume is about 1:3, where the specific gravities of copper and stone are 8.94 g/cm³ and 2.7 g/cm³ respectively.) The ratios obtained from the softer, non-igneous stones are more advantageous (see Table 4.2).

Wet sand is troublesome to work with inasmuch as that, when it is used up, that is, reduced to fine proportions, it is difficult to remove from a stone vessel. Used,

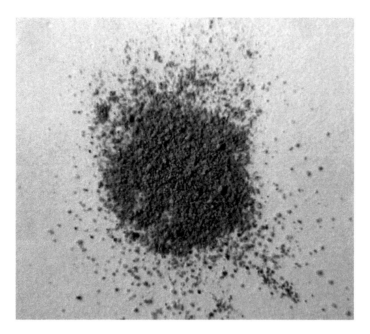

FIGURE 4.14 The waste product, sand/copper/stone powder, obtained from drilling granite with a copper tube and sand

Source: Image by J. Stocks

dry sand may easily be poured out and fresh supplies immediately admitted. The essence of drilling with the sand abrasive is the continually smooth replacement of the worn crystals with new ones at the cutting face, and wet or drying-out sand prevents this. Very wet, or fluid, sand will interchange, but when considering deep holes in heavy sarcophagi, a new factor comes into play concerning the removal of the used sand from the hole. The tests showed that the sand, after being ground by the drilling action for some time, turns into a very fine powder. It has the texture of finely milled flour. Experiments have shown that if the quantity of sand in operation is ground until all the sand is turned into a finely ground homogeneous powder (Figures 4.14, 4.15), then a significant number of the particles are within the size range of 50–150 microns, with the odd particle measuring about 200 microns. Most of the particles are less than 50 microns in size. However, a further short period of grinding reduces the bigger particles to sizes lying between 50 and 80 microns (Figure 4.16). Some drilling of the stone still proceeds, even with this exceedingly fine powder. However, the powder, now exhausted as an effective abrasive for tubular drilling, can be used for polishing stone, for drilling stone beads and for making blue faience, frits and pigment.[54]

After scoring the stone, worn and shattered particles cross under a drill-tube's end-face and pack into the space between the top of the core and the bottom of the wooden drill-shaft, although some of the powder is trapped between the tube and the hole wall. A few large quartz crystals sometimes pass under the drill-tube's

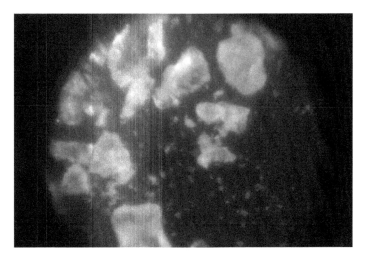

FIGURE 4.15 The finely ground powder, looking through a light microscope. The field of view is 1 mm across

Source: Image by J. Stocks

FIGURE 4.16 Scanning electron micrograph of finely ground granite derived powder. Many of the quartz and stone fragments are between 50 and 80 microns in size

Source: Image by B. Oswald

FIGURE 4.17 Striations cut into a stone core

Source: Image by J. Stocks

end-face and are carried up into the tube with the fine powder. Likewise, large crystals are trapped on the outside of the tube, where the coarse sand is initially introduced. The gyratory actions of the bow-driven drill-tube force these crystals to cut striations into the core (Figure 4.17) and into the wall of the hole. Because the drill is spinning two or three revolutions clockwise, and then anticlockwise, these heavier crystals are swirled around in the powder. Naturally, they too, in their turn, are ground down to a powder. The reciprocating motion of a saw also forces larger particles suspended in the fine powder to score the side walls of the slot. The experimentally produced striations were similar to those seen in ancient stone artifacts.

The powder, because of its fineness, is cohesive and sticks together in one mass, even though completely dry, remaining in position inside the drill-tube as it is withdrawn from the hole. The powder can, therefore, be withdrawn from deep holes in sarcophagi. Wet sand powder, owing to its weight and fluidity, cannot be withdrawn; it sinks to the bottom. Naturally, the tubular hole eventually becomes filled with used powder, and further drilling operations are considerably frustrated.

It must have been a matter of judgement and practice as to when an ancient driller withdrew a tube loaded with the used powder and discarded it, before recharging the hole with fresh sand. Table 4.7 gives percentage contents of sand, stone and copper in average samples of powder obtained from the sawing and drilling of the granite, hard limestone and calcite. These stones have been deliberately

TABLE 4.7 Indicated average percentages (by weight) of the sand, stone and copper in the waste powders

Stone type	Sand	Stone	Copper
calcite	94.1	5.43	0.46
granite	97.7	1.1	1.2
hard limestone	94.46	4.93	0.61

singled out for analysis, because the subsequent faience experiments indicate that the powders obtained from the igneous stones, like granite, porphyry, basalt and diorite, could be the basis for ancient glazes, and that the powders obtained from the hard limestone and the calcite might be the basis for ancient faience cores.

In 1983, Leonard Gorelick and John Gwinnett[55] found that they could reproduce regular, concentric lines, or striations, on granite cores *only* when a copper tube was used with emery (hardness Mohs 9) in a water slurry or in olive oil. The concentric striations were also visible using corundum and diamond. Gorelick and Gwinnett also reported that wet or dry sand or crushed quartz (Mohs 7), used in conjunction with a copper tube, did not produce concentric striations around granite cores. However, in 1992, they modified this view by reporting that crushed quartz usually produced fewer lines, which were roughly cut out. In effect, the harder, sharper emery was able to cut more deeply into the side wall and therefore to drill more rapidly than quartz abrasive.[56] This is to be expected, since emery is much harder than quartz. However, the striations produced by the emery particles appeared to be radically different from the striations cut into the drill-holes in the lid of Prince Akhet-Hotep's Fourth Dynasty granite sarcophagus, which Gorelick and Gwinnett were trying to replicate in their 1983 experiments.

Note: the percentage content of each component material changes slightly in any drilling or sawing powder from a particular stone. The main reason is the variability of the type and the amount of sand used as the abrasive. This affects the quantity of copper worn from a drill-tube or a saw and the amount of the stone drilled or sawn by the tools.

They stated that their drill-tube rotated at a constant 1,000 revolutions/ minute. This must be assumed to be in one direction. The approximately 4.5 cm-diameter tube used for the tapering holes in Prince Akhet-Hotep's sarcophagus lid was driven with a bow. This size of drill-tube could only have been driven at the approximate rate of 200 revolutions/minute, two to three clockwise revolutions, followed by two to three anticlockwise revolutions. A constant rate of 1,000 revolutions/ minute in one direction cannot be compared to the much lower rate of 200 revolutions/ minute, where the drill's rotation reversed each stroke of the bow. The whole nature of the drilling action is different. Although Gorelick and Gwinnett mention the use of a bow-drill, they do not indicate if any of their drill-holes were made with a bow-driven tube. Therefore, all the holes produced in Gorelick and Gwinnett's experiments were parallel, not tapered.

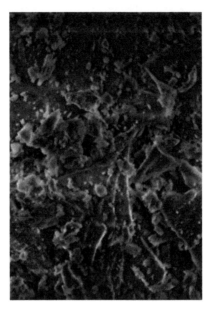

FIGURE 4.18 Scanning electron micrograph of minute angular particles in the granite-derived powder. Most of the quartz and stone fragments are between 0.5 and 5 microns in length

Source: Image by B. Oswald

It is clear from the drilling experiments that the random movement of the large sand crystals contained within the finely powdered sand, particularly in deep holes, *gradually* scrape striations into the stone. Striations seen in ancient artifacts were not immediately scraped to their full depths and widths by a single crystal. Striations are caused by many crystals over a period of time: in particular, striations in rose granite cross, without check, the interface between adjacent feldspar and quartz crystals in this stone. As a core and a hole wall are worn away by the gyration of the drill-tube, some existing striations are abraded away, but these are deepened again by new sand crystals. These striations generally run horizontally around a core and the hole's wall, but some striations cross existing ones at various angles. The spiral striation, seen by Petrie on the granite core from Giza (see note 21), can be explained in this way. Gorelick and Gwinnett's scanning electron micrographs (SEM)[57] of the epoxy model made from a silicone impression of the bottom of one of the drill-holes in Prince Akhet-Hotep's sarcophagus lid show that the concentric striations were not always regular and parallel. Some fade into adjacent lines, while others converge and diverge: they are rough in appearance. The present experiments demonstrate that the crystals in the dry sand do indeed produce concentric striations in granite cores, and in the holes' walls, that are similar to the depths and the widths of ancient striations.

The scanning electron microscope revealed that much of the powder consists of extremely fine particles. Many of these particles lie within the size range of 0.5–5 microns, particularly in the hard-stone powders (Figure 4.18). Breathing fine particles of stone and quartz of this size range causes lung damage to craftworkers.[58] The particles, which are mainly inert quartz, embed into the lung tissue, which can only isolate them by surrounding each one with scar tissue. This tissue does not permit carbon dioxide and oxygen to pass through the lung's walls. After prolonged exposure, lung efficiency is progressively diminished, causing severe incapacitation and, subsequently, death. It is likely that Ancient Egyptian workers suffered severe silicosis as a result of their work with the sand, and that their life expectancy was somewhere around 30 years. This estimate is supported by extant tomb representations. Nearly all the depicted stone vessel drillers are young. Today, industrial grinding still causes injury and death to workers.

The experimental drilling of the rose granite and the diorite produced light grey–coloured powders. Black granite and basalt would produce darker grey powders; they may look and feel like powdered emery. Possibly, these darker grey quartz-based powders have mistakenly been identified as powdered emery. Powders from the drilling and the sawing of limestone and calcite are nearly white in colour, dependent upon the original colour of the sand abrasive. Anciently produced sand/stone/copper powders, a waste product, may well have been collected for use in other manufacturing operations: for the polishing of stone artifacts, for the drilling of the stone beads, and as a basic material for the manufacture of some faience cores, of blue and green faience glazes, and of blue frits and pigment. These matters will be investigated in Chapters 6, 8 and 9.

The Aswan sawing and drilling experiments

While the small-scale Manchester tests established the initial sawing and drilling data, it is now instructive to see how the large-scale tests proceeded in Aswan. In March 1999, an opportunity arose to saw and drill the rose granite in a quarry located on the edge of the southern Egyptian town of Aswan. Several Egyptian quarry workers operated a 1.8 m-long copper saw and an 8 cm–diameter copper drill-tube, which was taken to Egypt with its driving bow. These sawing and drilling experiments were undertaken to test two theoretical propositions:[59] that two- and three-worker teams were required to drive large ancient saws (Figure 4.19) and tubular drills (Figure 4.20) respectively. The saw and the drill-tube were tested upon the rose granite under realistic ancient conditions, and the results compared with those obtained from the previous experiments conducted with the much smaller reconstructed copper saws and drills in Manchester.[60] Each Aswan tool used locally obtained sand as the cutting abrasive.

The unused 1.8 m-long copper saw blade, stood on its edge, measured 15 cm in depth and 6 mm in thickness and weighed 14.5 kg. The quarry workers had previously, and unnecessarily, fitted a heavy wooden frame to this saw blade, as well as notching it numerous times along the cutting edge with an electric abrasive wheel; no doubt, they understandably were influenced by modern working practices. Nevertheless, for comparison with a completely flat edge acting on dry sand abrasive, it was decided to test the notched edge with very wet, fluid sand along a

FIGURE 4.19 A painting illustrating how ancient workers could have sawn granite and other hard stones

Source: Image by J. Stocks

FIGURE 4.20 A painting showing how ancient workers could have drilled granite and other hard stones with large-diameter drill-tubes

Source: Image by J. Stocks

granite block's width of 75 cm, its surface initially pounded flat along the line of sawing.

Two workers pushed and pulled the saw from opposite sides of the block. The blade rocked from side to side during each forward and backward movement, creating a V-shaped slot.[61] At a depth of 8 cm, the V's cross-sectional shape measured 2.5 cm at the top and 6 mm at the bottom, each side angled at 7° to the vertical.

This V-shaped slot is similar to the two partially sawn slots seen in Hordjedef's rose granite sarcophagus in the Cairo Museum, and saw-slots cut into a basalt pavement block near Khufu's pyramid at Giza.[62] The laterally curved bottoms of these slots are a further consequence of the rocking action of the ancient saw blade, which itself would have assumed a laterally curved shape along its cutting edge. These phenomena occurred in the wet and the dry sand sawing experiments.

Long parallel striations of varying depths and widths, similar to those seen in ancient stone objects, were visible on the sides and the bottom of the slot, and upon the saw's individual flat edges between the notches. There was extensive pitting to the sides of the saw, also seen in the subsequent dry sawing test. In both the wet and the dry tests, the extra granite abraded to form the V-shape has been disregarded when calculating the cutting rate. It was noticeable that the sand *had* to be kept fluid; drying-out sand rapidly increased an already significant effort to move the saw. The used sand powder slurry poured over each end of the slot, its copper content largely washed away into the ground below.

For the tests with the dry sand abrasive, the wooden frame was removed and the blade reversed to allow its completely flat top edge to operate on the stone; the granite block's width at the point of sawing was 95 cm. The blade was now weighted with four stones (see Figure 6.3), two tied on to each end of the blade (first suggested in 1986);[63] these four stones, weighing 32 kg, also acted as handles for the sawyers. The saw's total weight of 45 kg placed a load of nearly 1 kg/cm^2 upon the blade's edge in contact with the granite.

Similar parallel striations to ancient ones, and to those obtained in the Manchester sawing tests, were visible on the sides and the bottom of the slot, and upon the saw's continuous flat edge. The angular crystals embedded into the edge and striated the stone under the blade and along the saw-slot's walls, sometimes causing new striations, at other times reinstating old ones, as the blade moved backwards and forwards along the stone. The rate of dry cutting was just over 12 cm^3/hour, similar to the wet abrasive result. It was noticeable that the effort to reciprocate the saw using the dry sand was easier than for the wet sand abrasive. The used dry sand powder, grey in colour, poured over each end of the slot, its copper content intact.

In Table 4.3, the three ratios expressing the volumes, weights and depths of the copper worn off the saw (separately with the wet and dry sand abrasive) to the volumes, weights and depths of the sawn granite are recorded as 1, 2 and 3 respectively. The ratios obtained from sawing with the flat-edged blade and dry sand show an improvement to the ratios achieved with the notched saw and wet sand.

The tubular drilling of a rose granite block required the assembly of the four component parts of the drilling equipment: the 8 cm-diameter copper tube, the round wooden drill-shaft partly force-fitted into it, the driving bow and rope, and a capstone bearing in which to rotate the upper end of the drill-shaft (see Figure 6.6). The capstone took one hour to shape and hollow, using flint chisels and punches, from locally obtained hard sandstone. The top of the shaft was carved into a cone, with a rounded top; drilling experience demonstrated reduced friction if the top of the cone rotated in the apex of the bearing. This was lubricated

FIGURE 4.21   In the foreground, the team of three workers is drilling a block of rose granite with an 8 cm-diameter copper tube. In the background, two sawyers operate the flat-edged copper saw

Source: Image by D. Stocks

with grease, in place of the likely ancient tallow. Preliminary tests in Manchester indicated that a very stiff bow-shaft was needed to place sufficient tension on the 1.3 cm-thick bow-rope, necessary to prevent slippage on the wooden drill-shaft.

A small area of the rose granite's surface was prepared by pounding it with a dolerite hammer until it became flat and smooth. The end of the tube, smeared with red water-based paint (probably red ochre in ancient times), made a circular mark by pressing it on the stone's surface. The dolerite hammer drove a flint chisel along the circular line to make a groove. (There is evidence in the Petrie Collection of such a circular groove in an unfinished, unprovenanced and uncatalogued alabaster vessel.) This groove allowed the tube to be located for the initial grinding operation, achieved by fastening two temporary stone weights to the top of the drill-shaft, which was continuously twisted, by hand, clockwise and anticlockwise on dry sand abrasive. Hand grinding continued until the groove attained a depth of 5 mm, a measurement at which the bow could spin the located tube without it jumping out.

A team of three workers operated the drill (Figure 4.21), one worker at each end of the bow to drive it, the third worker holding the capstone (first suggested in 1986).[64] The bow-rope was sufficiently loosened to enable two complete turns to be made around the drill-shaft (Figure 4.22), which placed a bending stress upon the bow-shaft. This gave 50 cm of tight contact between the rope and the drill-shaft's circumference. The 8 cm-diameter tube, with 1 mm thick walls, optimally required a total load of 2.5 kg acting upon its end-face. A greater load than this caused the drillers unnecessary work, and even bent the rigid bow-shaft, slackening the tension in the rope.

FIGURE 4.22   The bow-rope double turned around the drill-shaft

Source: Image by D. Stocks

The workers' normal reciprocating strokes, each approximately 50 cm in length, turned the drill-shaft at a rate of 120 revolutions/minute. The driller pushing the bow simultaneously assisted the other driller pulling it; these actions automatically reversed at the end of each stroke. Resisting the reciprocating strokes was not too difficult for the worker holding the capstone, although keeping it completely still was impossible. A small amount of dry sand, trickling around the tube as drilling progressed, found its way down to the cutting face. Later measurements showed that about 250 g were used by the saw, and the drill-tube, to remove 1 cm^3 of the granite, similar to the Manchester results. Water in the sand abrasive made the drill-tube more difficult to turn and washed away the copper particles. Further, used wet sand powder, probably containing lime, is troublesome to remove from a tubular hole, rapidly setting as a rudimentary mortar if drilling is suspended for a short time. Dry sand powder was easy to remove; it stuck together inside the drill-tube and periodically could be withdrawn from the hole.[65]

The gyratory actions of the drill-tube's exterior wall wore the hole into a taper which sloped inward to its bottom, and the tube's interior wall wore the core into a reversed taper, i.e. narrower at the top and wider at the bottom (Figure 4.23). The tubular slot, importantly, also became tapered. Additionally, the drill-tube's lateral movements across the slot, caused by the bow's reciprocating action, overcut it; this

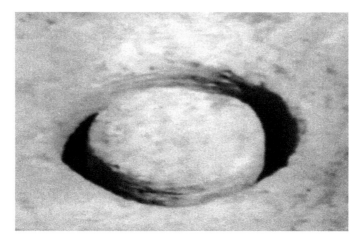

FIGURE 4.23 The core within the tubular-shaped hole

Source: Image by Terry Dowker

FIGURE 4.24 Flat-tapered chisels being used to remove the core from the tubular hole

Source: Image by Terry Dowker

phenomenon reduced as the hole deepened. The drilling results are summarized in Table 4.3. The three ratios expressing the volume, weight and length of the copper abraded off the drill-tube to the volume, weight and depth of the drilled granite are recorded as 1, 2 and 3 respectively.

The core was removed from the drilled granite by soundly hammering two adjacently placed flat tapered chisels vertically into the tapered slot: the slot and the chisels' tapers fitted almost perfectly (Figure 4.24). The chisels acted on a short arc of the top of the core's circumference, using its length as a lever. This forced the core over, causing the brittle granite at the bottom of the core, and directly

FIGURE 4.25   The striated granite core

Source: Image by Terry Dowker

FIGURE 4.26   Striations in the hole wall

Source: Image by Terry Dowker

below the chisels, to be placed under such tension that it parted completely, allowing the core to be extracted in a single piece (Figure 4.25). Horizontal striations similar to the ancient ones on rose granite were visible both in the wall of the hole (Figure 4.26), and upon the core.

Discussion

The experimental sawing of the rose granite with the wet and dry sand abrasive indicate that the stone was cut at roughly equal rates. However, there is no requirement for a stonecutting saw to be notched, or serrated like a wood saw. In fact, notches[66] and serrations are counter-productive to sawing with a loose abrasive, wet or dry. Any copper removed to notch the saw is wasted, reducing the area of the cutting edge. The wooden frame is unnecessary to place tension on such a rigid blade, and in a tall block of stone the frame eventually limits the depth to which the saw can cut. However, stone weights at either end allow a saw to cut through the stone without restriction.

The drawbacks with wet sand are an increase in the effort to move the saw, the provision of the water and the consequential loss of the copper particles from the waste powders. On the other hand, dry sand can be used in locations far from water, an important consideration in Egypt. For dry sand, the ratios of the average weights of the copper worn from the Aswan tools to the average weights of the sawn and the drilled granite are similar to the results obtained from the Manchester sawing and drilling experiments. The Aswan sawing and drilling rates were respectively six and three times faster than the Manchester rates.

Observations, and experience in Aswan using the tubular drill, suggest that an expert three-worker team could drill tubular holes up to 12 cm in diameter. The Aswan drill-tube and the wooden shaft, bow-shaft and capstone needed no adjustment or repair during the drilling period. Only the bow-rope needed occasional tightening; the rope lasted 18 drilling hours before becoming badly frayed, when it was replaced.

The abundance of quartz sand, and the regular supply of copper for making saws and tubes, allowed Ancient Egyptian craftworkers to achieve two of the most formidable stoneworking operations: namely, the sawing and the drilling of the rose granite. All tools were important to Ancient Egyptian craftworkers, but it is fair to say that the flat-edged copper saw and the flat-ended copper tube were crucial to the successful manufacture of stone vessels, sarcophagi, statuary and architectural blocks, particularly those made from the hardest stones.

Notes

1 V. Täckholm and G. Täckholm, *Flora of Egypt*, Königstein: Otto Koeltz Antiquariat, vol. I, 1973, pp. 204–7, 213–16.
2 Ibid., p. 210.
3 P.M. Warren, *Minoan Stone Vases*, Cambridge: Cambridge University Press, 1969, pp. 158–61; P.M. Warren, 'The unfinished red marble jar at Akroteri, Thera', *Thera and the Aegean World* I, 1978, p. 564.
4 J.W. Shaw, 'Minoan architecture: Materials and techniques', *Annuario della Scuola Archeologica di Atene* 49, 1971, pp. 69–70, Figs 61–3.
5 For example, W.M.F. Petrie, *The Pyramids and Temples of Gizeh*, London: Field and Tuer, 1883, pp. 173–4; W.M.F. Petrie, *The Arts and Crafts of Ancient Egypt*, Edinburgh and London: T.N. Foulis, 1909, p. 73; W.M.F. Petrie, *Tools and Weapons*, London: British School of Archaeology in Egypt, 1917, pp. 44–5; J.H. Breasted, *A History of Egypt*,

New York: Smith, Elder and Co., 1906, p. 93; H.H. Coghlan, *Notes on the Prehistoric Metallurgy of Copper and Bronze in the Old World*, Oxford: Oxford University Press, 1951, p. 85; A. Lucas and J.R. Harris, *Ancient Egyptian Materials and Industries*, London: Edward Arnold, 1962, pp. 43, 71–4; G.A. Reisner, *Mycerinus, the Temples of the Third Pyramid at Giza*, Cambridge, MA: Harvard University Press, 1931, p. 180; C. Aldred, *Egypt to the End of the Old Kingdom*, London: Thames and Hudson, 1965, p. 59; L. Gorelick and A.J. Gwinnett, 'Ancient Egyptian stone drilling: An experimental perspective on a scholarly disagreement', *Expedition* 25, 3, 1983, pp. 40–7.

6 D.A. Stocks, 'Industrial technology at Kahun and Gurob: Experimental manufacture and test of replica and reconstructed tools with indicated uses and effects upon artefact production', unpublished thesis, University of Manchester, vols I, II, 1988.

7 For example, L. Gorelick and A.J. Gwinnett, 'Ancient Egyptian stone drilling'.

8 Petrie, *Pyramids*, pp. 174–5, pl. XIV, 3, 4.

9 Ibid., pp. 46, 84, 106, 174–5, pl. XIV, 1.

10 Ibid., p. 84.

11 Ibid., pp. 174–5.

12 M.Z. Goneim, *The Buried Pyramid*, London: Longmans, Green and Co., 1956, p. 108.

13 CM JE46499.

14 L. Borchardt, *Das Grabdenkmal des Königs Ne-User-Re*, Leipzig: Hinrichs, 1907, p. 142.

15 For example, two calcite statues of Menkaure (Reisner, *Mycerinus*, pp. 111, 116) and a quartz crystal statuette in the Petrie Collection, University College London (Petrie, *Arts and Crafts*, Fig. 89).

16 Goneim, *The Buried Pyramid*, p. 108.

17 Petrie, *Tools and Weapons*, p. 44; Petrie, *Pyramids*, pl. XIV, p. 8.

18 Reisner, *Mycerinus*, p. 86.

19 Ibid., pp. 117, 118.

20 Examples are a granite core from Giza (Petrie, *Pyramids*, pl. XVI, 7), a 3.2 cm-diameter diorite core from Saqqara (Lucas and Harris, *AEMI*, p. 69) and a 9 cm-diameter granite core from Giza, with a saw-cut on its top surface (Boston Museum of Fine Arts 13.5078).

21 Petrie, *Pyramids*, p. 174, pl. XVI, 7; Petrie, *Tools and Weapons*, pp. 44–5, pl. LII, 59.

22 Petrie, *Pyramids*, p. 174, pl. XVI, 4, 12.

23 Ibid., p. 175.

24 Ibid.

25 Ibid., p. 176.

26 Ibid., p. 174.

27 Ibid.

28 Ibid., pp. 174–5, pl. XIV, 3.

29 Borchardt, *Ne-User-Re*, p. 142.

30 Lucas and Harris, *AEMI*, p. 74.

31 Ibid., p. 69.

32 Reisner, *Mycerinus*, p. 180.

33 Aldred, *Egypt to the End*, p. 59.

34 Breasted, *A History*, p. 93.

35 Petrie, *Tools and Weapons*, pp. 45–6.

36 J.E. Quibell and F.W. Green, *Hierakonpolis II*, London: British School of Archaeology in Egypt, 1902, p. 17.

37 D.E. Eichholz, *Pliny Natural History*, London and Cambridge, MA: Harvard University Press, 1962, p. 41.

38 Stocks, 'Industrial technology', vol. I, p. 136.

39 M.J. Fisher and D.E. Fisher, *Mysteries of Lost Empires*, London: Channel 4 Books, 2000, pp. 93–7.

40 F.F. Leek, 'The dental history of the Manchester mummies', in A.R. David (ed.) *Manchester Museum Mummy Project. Multi-disciplinary Research on Ancient Egyptian Mummified Remains*, Manchester: Manchester University Press, 1979, p. 75.

41 Stocks, 'Industrial technology', vol. I, pp. 137–40, vol. II, p. 344; D.A. Stocks, 'Technology and the reed', *The Manchester Archaeological Bulletin* 8, 1993, pp. 58–68.

42 Stocks, 'Industrial technology', vol. I, pp. 58–60.

43 Ibid., vol. I, p. 57.

44 Lucas and Harris, *AEMI*, pp. 215–16.

45 L. Borchardt, *Das Grabdenkmal des Königs Śa͗ḥu-re*, Leipzig: Hinrichs, vol. I, 1910, p. 78.

46 Quibell and Green, *Hierakonpolis II*, pp. 46–7, pls L–LVI.

47 J. Černý, 'Egypt from the death of Ramesses III to the end of the Twenty-first Dynasty', in I.E.S. Edwards (ed.) *The Cambridge Ancient History*, Cambridge: Cambridge University Press, 1975, vol. II, no. 2, p. 621.

48 Stocks, 'Industrial technology', vol. I, pp. 133–6.

49 Ibid., vol. II, p. 343.

50 D.A. Stocks, 'Testing Ancient Egyptian granite-working methods in Aswan, Upper Egypt', *Antiquity* 75, 2001, pp. 89–91, Fig. 1.

51 Fisher and Fisher, *Mysteries of Lost Empires*, pp. 64–5. Stocks, 'Testing Ancient Egyptian granite-working methods in Aswan', pp. 91–3, Figs 2, 3.

52 For example, N. de G. Davies, *The Tomb of Rekh-mi-Rī'at Thebes*, New York: Metropolitan Museum of Art, 1943, vol. II, pls LII, LIII.

53 Ibid., vol. II, pl. LIV.

54 D.A. Stocks, 'Stone vessel manufacture', *Popular Archaeology* 7 (4), 1986, p. 17; D.A. Stocks, 'Ancient factory mass-production techniques: Indications of large-scale stone bead manufacture during the Egyptian New Kingdom Period', *Antiquity* 63, 1989, pp. 528, 530; D.A. Stocks, 'Indications of Ancient Egyptian industrial interdependence: A preliminary statement', *The Manchester Archaeological Bulletin* 4, 1989, pp. 21–6; D.A. Stocks, 'Derivation of Ancient Egyptian faience core and glaze materials', Antiquity 71, 1997, pp. 179–82.

55 L. Gorelick and A.J. Gwinnett, 'Ancient Egyptian stone-drilling: An experimental perspective on a scholarly disagreement', *Expedition* 25 (3), 1983, pp. 40–7.

56 L. Gorelick and A.J. Gwinnett, 'Minoan versus Mesopotamian seals: Comparative methods of manufacture', *Iraq* LIV, 1992, p. 62.

57 Gorelick and Gwinnett, 'Ancient Egyptian stone-drilling: An experimental perspective on a scholarly disagreement', Figs 5, 6.

58 A. Curry, C. Anfield and E. Tapp, 'The use of the electron microscope in the study of palaeopathology', in A.R. David (ed.) *Science in Egyptology*, Manchester: Manchester University Press, 1986, pp. 58–9, Fig. 2.

59 D.A. Stocks, 'Sticks and stones of Egyptian technology', *Popular Archaeology* 7 (3), 1986, p. 28, top and bottom illustrations.

60 Ibid., pp. 24–9; Stocks, 'Industrial technology', vol. I, pp. 100–43.

61 Suggested by R.G. Moores (R.G. Moores, 'Evidence for use of a stone-cutting drag saw by the Fourth Dynasty Egyptians', *JARCE* 28, 1991, p. 143).

62 CM JE54938; Moores, 'Evidence for use of a stone-cutting drag saw by the Fourth Dynasty Egyptians', p. 143, Figs 6, 7. In his Fig. 6, Moores measured the angle of the slot's side walls to the vertical to be about 8°.

63 Stocks, 'Sticks and stones of Egyptian technology', p. 28, top illustration; Stocks, 'Testing Ancient Egyptian granite-working methods in Aswan, Upper Egypt', p. 90, Fig. 1.

64 Stocks, 'Sticks and stones of Egyptian technology', p. 28, bottom illustration.

65 Ibid., p. 27.

66 Hypothetically suggested by R.G. Moores (Moores, 'Evidence for use of a stone-cutting drag saw by the Fourth Dynasty Egyptians', p. 147).

5
MAKING STONE VESSELS

Stone vessels by the thousand

The technology for hollowing stone vessels was fully established in the Predynastic period. During the Badarian and Naqada I periods, hard-stone vessels were necessarily, and laboriously, hollowed with hand-held stone borers, used in conjunction with desert sand abrasive; in these periods, hand-held flint borers were probably in use for very soft stone (e.g. gypsum), without sand abrasive. G. Caton-Thompson and E.W. Gardner[1] found crescent-shaped chert tools (1/4 to 3/4 crescents) that were used to bore out the interiors of the gypsum vessels at an Old Kingdom workshop at Umm-es-Sawan in the Fayum (Figure 5.1); the crescents were frequently found caked in gypsum.

Some holes in soft limestone (e.g. MMA 14.7.146, from the mastaba of Perneb), probably bored with crescent-shaped flints, were discovered at Saqqara by C.M. Firth, J.E. Quibell and J.-P. Lauer.[2] Flint and chert crescents caused the striations in very soft stone to vary considerably in depth, width and direction, and a broken gypsum vessel in the Robert H. Lowie Museum, Berkeley, California (6–10016), illustrates these features. However, the tests on calcite showed that it is too hard effectively to be bored with flint or chert crescents (Figure 5.2),[3] and the additional experiments with the reed tubular drills suggest that these tools could have been in ancient use for drilling the stone vessels made from calcite, in addition to the hard limestone vessels, before the introduction of copper tubes in the Naqada II period. When flint and chert crescents are forced against hard-stone vessel walls, the scraping action breaks their edges.[4]

Badarian cemeteries have yielded few stone vases, but from Naqada I they become more common, and were manufactured in a variety of shapes and stones. Basalt jars with flat bases, some with perforated lugs under the rim for suspension, and which may be copies of Badarian ivory vases, were made in this period.[5]

DOI: 10.4324/9781003269922-8

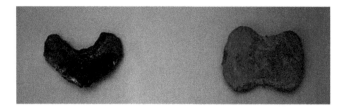

FIGURE 5.1   An Old Kingdom crescent-shaped flint borer, BM 59998 (left), probably used for hollowing gypsum vessels, and a striated figure-of-eight-shaped quartzite borer from Abydos, BM 37278 (right), dated to the First Dynasty

Source: Image by J. Stocks. © Copyright the British Museum

FIGURE 5.2   A replica crescent-shaped chert borer

Source: Image by J. Stocks

Similar shapes have been found at Merimde, Lower Egypt. In the Naqada II period, a popular stone vase shape was the oblate spheroidal (a flattened sphere) type, which was made with a rim and two perforated tubular-shaped lugs. Good examples of this shape (Figure 5.3) can be seen at The Manchester Museum (1776, made of syenite – a type of diorite from Aswan), and at the Petrie Museum, University College London (UC 15587, made of breccia). Taller, bulbous lugged jars from the Predynastic period were made of porphyry, diorite, breccia, serpentine, calcite and limestone. An excellent example is a limestone/breccia double-handled jar from the Naqada II period (MMA 12.183.2). Striations are in evidence inside the vessel's mouth.

Stone-vessel manufacture declined somewhat near to the end of the Naqada II period, although contemporary, good-quality vessels made of granite, diorite, basalt, gneiss, limestone and calcite were found at Ma'adi,[6] and some of these were

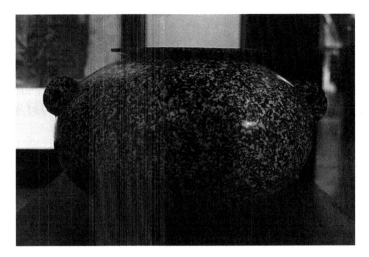

FIGURE 5.3   A Naqada II oblate spheroidal-shaped syenite vessel from Hierakonpolis (MM 1776), with drilled lugs. The vessel's internal diameter, height and wall thickness are 50 cm, 34 cm and 3 cm respectively

Source: Image by J. Stocks from the Manchester Museum, The University of Manchester

used for trade. The industry continued to flourish in Early Dynastic times. A fine example of this period is a squat jar (MMA 24.7.5), made of diorite. However, by the end of the Old Kingdom not only did the number of stone vessels decrease, but also the percentage of the vessels made from the hardest stones.[7] The numbers of the softer-stone vessels, in particular those made of calcite, increased dramatically. For example, stored in various chambers beneath Zoser's Step Pyramid at Saqqara were tens of thousands of stone vessels, many of them made of calcite, but other vessels of schist, porphyry, breccia, quartz crystal and serpentine were in evidence.[8]

The experimental working of the hard stones indicated that the exterior shaping of all hard-stone vessels, including those manufactured of basalt, diorite, porphyry, breccia, granite, and even the softer calcite, in every period, must have been completed with flint chisels, punches and scrapers. The incisions and the other marks obtained with the experimental flint chisels, punches and scrapers on the calcite and the igneous stones matched the marks on a variety of ancient stone artifacts manufactured from similar stones. Even soft limestone and gypsum vessels, which could have been shaped with copper tools, probably needed awkward places shaping with flint scrapers; necks, rims and the undercutting of vessels' shoulders all required skilled carving techniques using exceptionally sharp tools.

Although some stone vessels were cylindrically shaped, and only required a tubular drill for hollowing, many vessels were bulbous. Some excellent examples of bulbous vessels were recovered by G. Brunton and W.M.F. Petrie[9] from Tomb 8, which lies to the south of Senusret II's pyramid at Lahun. These vessels, now in The Metropolitan Museum of Art, New York, consist of four calcite canopic jars (16.1.45–48) and a calcite magic water jar (21.2.62); they all belonged to Princess

Sit-Hathor-Yunut, a daughter of Senusret II. Each canopic jar is 25.7 cm tall, 14 cm in diameter at its base, with a shoulder diameter of 21.7 cm. The magic water jar is 42 cm tall, 10 cm in diameter at its base, and 28 cm in diameter at its shoulders and possesses walls which are 1.2 cm thick. Each jar required widening below the shoulder using boring processes that were separate from the drilling of the interior with tubes. All of the jars represent stone vessel manufacturing at its best, and are likely to have been created in the nearby workers' town of Kahun.

What were the key factors enabling such ancient work to be accomplished? What were the common elements joining the production of brittle calcite vessels with the hollowing of the harder stone vessels, and which were of many shapes and sizes? What tool was common to all these endeavours?

The tomb evidence for stone vessel making

Similarities between the Uruk and the Jemdet Nasr periods of Mesopotamia (ca. 3600–2900 BCE) and the Naqada II and Early Dynastic periods of Egypt (ca. 3600–2890 BCE) include cylinder seals, the recessed panelled façade design in architecture, the use of pictographs and decorative art, and the shapes of stone vessels. And craftworkers from Mesopotamia and Egypt necessarily developed similar tools and techniques for manufacturing stone vessels. In order to explore these similarities, the use of a reconstructed Ancient Egyptian tool in making a limestone vase was investigated.

It is generally thought that the cold beating, or forging, of truly smelted and cast copper into tools and other artifacts first occurred in Egypt ca. 3600 BCE,[10] castings being made in rudimentary open moulds at this period.[11] Cold-forged, cast copper tools were also manufactured in Mesopotamia.[12] The technique of beating copper into sheets must have existed in both Egypt and Mesopotamia, where vessels of this metal were found at Ur by Leonard Woolley.[13] Sheet copper was essential for the making of copper tubes, indispensable tools for drilling out hard-stone vessels.

Certainly in Egypt, and probably also in Mesopotamia, copper tubular drills were used for the initial hollowing of the interiors of the vases and jars made from hard stones,[14] although, as in Egypt, the stonecutting copper tubular drill has never been located in Mesopotamia. Striations are clearly visible on the inside *vertical* walls (made with tubular drills, not stone borers) of vessels from Mesopotamia and Egypt, caused by the sand abrasive employed with the drills. Subsequently, Mesopotamian and Egyptian bulbous vessels – those considerably wider internally than at the mouth – were further hollowed by grinding with another tool, a stone borer of elongated form (Figure 5.4). The mid-point of its long axis was made to narrow equally from both sides. Seen from above, the borer assumes the shape of a figure-of-eight, enabling a forked shaft to engage with the waist (Figure 5.5). The top is normally flat, the bottom curved. In Egypt, this particular borer has been discovered at Hierakonpolis, a site associated with Late Predynastic and Early Dynastic stone vessel production;[15] Mesopotamian figure-of-eight-shaped stone borers were discovered by Woolley at Ur.[16] A previously made tubular hole, after

FIGURE 5.4   A reconstructed elongated figure-of-eight shaped stone borer

Source: Image by J. Stocks

FIGURE 5.5   The reconstructed elongated stone borer engaged with a forked shaft

Source: Image by J. Stocks

core extraction, could be enlarged with successively longer figure-of-eight borers until the correct internal form was achieved.

Circular borers were used to grind Mesopotamian stone bowls, and a Meso-potamian stone borer for this purpose, from Ur (BM 124498),[17] has striations on its curved underside surface and a piece cut out from each side of its upper, flat surface, also for retaining a forked shaft. At Ur, figure-of-eight-shaped stone borers were common in the Uruk and Jemdet Nasr periods, and Woolley thought that the constricted part of this stone borer was engaged by a forked wooden shaft *driven with a bow*.[18] Borers made of diorite are common in Mesopotamia and Egypt; other stones utilized in Egypt included chert, sandstone and crystalline limestone.

Striations on Mesopotamian vessels, and on the bottom surfaces of stone borers, are similar to the striations seen on their Egyptian counterparts – generally 0.25 mm wide and deep caused, as discussed in Chapter 4, by quartz sand abrasive. This material has been connected to Egyptian stone borers by N. de G. Davies, J.E. Quibell and F.W. Green. Davies pointed out that the cutting edge was horizontal and the surface near it was scored by parallel grooves, suggesting that sand was the real excavating medium.[19] The undersides of figure-of-eight-shaped borers found by Quibell and Green[20] at Hierakonpolis have been scored at both ends by parallel striations. These striations describe an arc, centred upon each borer's vertical turning axis (see Figure 5.1, right).

Neither the forked wooden shafts, nor the tools that drove them, have been discovered in Mesopotamia or Egypt. However, the tool is depicted as a hieroglyph, the first known one occurring in the Third Dynasty at Saqqara.[21] During the Old Kingdom, the ideogram used in words for 'craft, 'art', and other related words, represent this hieroglyph as a *forked central shaft* with two stone weights, or bags of sand, fastened underneath an inclined, curved, tapering handle.[22] This fork engaged with a stone borer, depicted in side elevation, so concealing its figure-of-eight, or circular, shape. The forked shaft ideogram, therefore, shows only the visually interesting and informative view of the fork and borer, rather than the ambiguous view of a tube, which would appear to be part of the shaft; this follows Ancient Egyptian artistic protocol. The weights placed a load upon a tool's cutting surface. There are no known representations from Mesopotamia.

Different forms of the tool are illustrated in a number of Egyptian tombs constructed between the Fifth and the Twenty-sixth Dynasty. In these illustrations, the vessel obscures the lower, working end of the tool's shaft, but sometimes a second shaft is shown lashed to the central shaft. By the Middle Kingdom, the double-stone method of weighting the tool is shown alongside a single, perforated, hemispherical stone weight, in which the central shaft is located.[23] In New Kingdom times, the ideogram representing the tool had changed to a forked shaft lashed to a central shaft, with one hemispherical stone weight.[24] In a Twenty-sixth Dynasty tomb representation,[25] two weights are again in evidence, and this reflects the Twenty-sixth Dynasty's interest in the Old Kingdom period. Also, separate hanging weights are much easier to make and fit than a centrally drilled hemispherical weight. From the Fifth Dynasty, a forked shaft was secured by a thin rope to the central shaft of a tool (Figure 5.6), as seen in a painted Twelfth Dynasty tomb representation (Fitzwilliam Museum, Cambridge E55.1914, a limestone fragment from Lahun).

Another type of Egyptian stone borer – an inverted truncated cone with two slots cut opposite each other in the upper, horizontal surface – was employed to shape a vessel's mouth; there is an uncatalogued cone borer with similar cutouts in the Petrie Collection. As previously mentioned, crescent-shaped flint and chert tools, also engaged by forked shafts, were used exclusively for cutting soft stones, such as gypsum, without sand abrasive. In extended use, the forks of the

FIGURE 5.6   A Twelfth Dynasty representation depicting a forked shaft fastened to a
            central shaft

Source: Drawing by D. Stocks from Fitzwilliam Museum E55.1914. Courtesy of the Fitzwilliam
Museum

FIGURE 5.7   A proposed drilling version of the tool for making stone vessels, which has
            a copper tube force-fitted to its central shaft

Source: Image by D. Stocks

reconstructed tools showed wear.[26] A worn forked shaft could be replaced simply
by lashing a new one to the central shaft, much as a drill-bit is changed in a modern
electric drill. As the destruction of a *forked central* shaft would have rendered the
whole tool useless, it may have evolved from this original configuration. A central
shaft fitted with a tube and weights probably lasted for many years.

The tool for the preliminary drilling operations would have had a copper tube
force-fitted to its central shaft (Figure 5.7). Some tomb illustrations may display a

central shaft fitted with a tube, which is being used to drill adjacent holes in wide-mouthed vessels to remove the central mass.[27] It is likely that the drilling tool did not change in form, except for the manner in which it was weighted; a tubular drill would not have damaged its wooden shaft during use, and a succession of new tubes could be fitted to the same shaft time and time again.

Several archaeologists have expressed opinions about the use of a tubular drill for drilling stone vessels. W.M.F. Petrie stated that the interior of a stone vase was cleared by a tube-drill of the size of the mouth.[28] J.E. Quibell observed that cylindrical drills were used in vase-making, and that cores of diorite and granite have been found, together with the ends of drill holes in alabaster.[29] G.A. Reisner proposed a connection between a tubular drill of copper and the tool that drove it. He says, when writing about copper tubes, that the tube may have been weighted with stones and worked by a crank handle.[30] Alfred Lucas also concurred with the suggested fitting of a tube to a tool dedicated to vase manufacture.[31]

Ten tomb representations of the drilling/boring tool have been identified. Depicted upon a Fifth Dynasty limestone relief from a tomb at Saqqara[32] is a single standing worker operating the tool. It has two large weights, fastened by a rope to the shaft. The lower shaft entering the vessel appears to be joined to the central shaft by an obliquely placed stick, which passes through a collar. In the Fifth Dynasty tomb of Ti at Saqqara[33] are two artisans, who are hollowing vessels of quite different shapes. Each vessel requires internal widening at some point. The weights are indistinct. Incorporated into the scene are two representations of a single, forked shaft engaged with a figure-of-eight-shaped borer, depicted in side elevation. The stone weights are contained in nets, probably made from string.

In the Sixth Dynasty tomb of Mereruka at Saqqara,[34] two squatting workers are depicted hollowing differently shaped vessels. Each drilling tool has two weights. The left-hand worker grips the central shaft above and below the weights, possibly drilling a series of holes into the vessel to weaken its central mass. The right-hand driller grips the handle with the left hand. The whole of this tool, below the weights, is in the stone vessel. A representation in the Sixth Dynasty tomb of Aba at Deir el Gebrâwi[35] shows a standing artisan gripping a tool with both hands, above and below the two weights.

In the Twelfth Dynasty tomb-chapel of Ukh-hotp's son Senbi at Meir[36] is an illustration of two squatting workers hollowing stone vessels (Figure 5.8). The

FIGURE 5.8   An illustration of the drilling tool in the Twelfth Dynasty tomb-chapel of Ukh-hotp's son Senbi at Meir

Source: Drawing by D. Stocks after A.M. Blackman, *The Rock Tombs of Meir*, London: Egypt Exploration Society, 1914, pl. V

FIGURE 5.9 A representation of the drilling tool in the Twelfth Dynasty tomb of Pepionkh at Meir

Source: Drawing by D. Stocks after A.M. Blackman and M.R. Apted, *The Rock Tombs of Meir*, London: Egypt Exploration Society, 1953, part V, pl. XVII

FIGURE 5.10 An Eighteenth Dynasty representation of a seated driller hollowing a calcite vessel. From the tomb of Rekhmire at Thebes

Source: Drawing by D. Stocks after N. de G. Davies, *The Tomb of Rekh-mi-Rē' at Thebes*, New York, 1943, vol. II, pl. LIV. Courtesy of the Metropolitan Museum of Art

left-hand tool appears to possess a centrally placed weight, but in the tomb of Pepionkh at Meir,[37] also from the Twelfth Dynasty, two craftworkers are utilizing tools fitted with two stone weights. However, two other workers are illustrated in the same scene each using a tool fitted with a single, hemispherical stone weight (Figure 5.9). This scene indicates an important change to the tool's design.

The Eighteenth Dynasty tomb of Rekhmire at Thebes[38] depicts a seated driller hollowing a calcite vessel (Figure 5.10). The tool is gripped below the single, hemispherical stone weight with the right hand, while the other hand steadies the vessel. Although the tomb artist has made a mistake in drawing the craftworker's right hand, it is intended to show that the worker's hand grips the longer shaft, which is lashed to a shorter shaft upon which the weight is fixed. The Eighteenth Dynasty tomb of Two Sculptors at Thebes[39] depicts a seated driller also hollowing a calcite vessel (Figure 5.11); the artisan is obliged to grip the handle with both hands because the hemispherical stone weight is close to the vessel's top surface. In the Eighteenth Dynasty tomb of Puyemre at Thebes,[40] two operators twist tools, both of which possess a single, central weight (Figure 5.12).

FIGURE 5.11   A representation of a seated driller in the Eighteenth Dynasty tomb of Nebamun and Ipuky at Thebes

Source: Drawing by D. Stocks after N. de G. Davies, *The Tomb of Two Sculptors at Thebes*, New York, 1925, pl. XI. Courtesy of the Metropolitan Museum of Art

FIGURE 5.12   An illustration of two workers in the Eighteenth Dynasty tomb of Puyemre at Thebes

Source: Drawing by D. Stocks after N. de G. Davies, *The Tomb of Puyemrê at Thebes*, New York, 1922, vol. I, pl. XXIII. Courtesy of the Metropolitan Museum of Art

Lastly, in the Twenty-sixth Dynasty tomb of Aba at Thebes,[41] a standing artisan drills a vessel (Figure 5.13). The tool now possesses two weights again, and the worker grips the long shaft under the weights with both hands.

Analysis of the pictorial evidence

The evidence of the hieroglyphs and the tomb representations clearly show that the drilling tool was in use at least from the Third to the Twenty-sixth Dynasty. The central drill-shaft was round, having been manufactured from a suitable tree branch. The tapered and angled top part, or handle, of the central shaft seems to correspond

FIGURE 5.13   A standing worker depicted in the Twenty-sixth Dynasty tomb of Aba
at Thebes

Source: Drawing by D. Stocks after N. de G. Davies, *The Rock Tombs of Deir el Gebrâwi*, London: Egypt
Exploration Fund, 1902, vol. I, pl. XXIV

to the angle and shape of a branch which grows from a larger stem, this stem acting
as the central shaft. The main stem was cut away just above the branching stem and
smoothed. The forked shaft, made from a branch by equally shortening the two stems
forming the fork, was inverted before lashing it to the tool's central shaft.

The tomb evidence shows a clear progression from the Old Kingdom drill,
weighted with two stones or sandbags, to the Middle Kingdom period, where drills
with two weights are used alongside drills with a single, hemispherical stone. The
single weight may have been exclusively in use during the New Kingdom Period,
but in the Twenty-sixth Dynasty, which saw a revival of the Old Kingdom culture,
two weights were adopted once more. It is obvious that the drill needed to be
weighted and balanced, but it is also clear that the weights were situated near to the
top of the tool to allow it to penetrate deeply into a vessel.

The drilling tool was investigated by R.S. Hartenberg and J. Schmidt, Jr. in
1969.[42] They concluded that the tool rotated in one direction, and that the handle was used as some form of crank. Their tests were carried out on a bent tube
weighted with two house bricks. However, the present tests, on tools reconstructed
from materials in use by ancient craftworkers, demonstrate that not only does a
continuous rotary action cause the drill to wobble alarmingly, but is difficult for
a human to perform and, indeed, to control. The stone weights fly outwards and
increase the wobbling action. Such use of the tool must cause serious damage to
any vessel, not to mention the extreme tapering of the cores and the hole when
in use with a tubular drill. This is at variance with the archaeological evidence for
parallel-sided cores and holes in ancient vessels. This proposed use of the tool must
firmly be rejected.

The experiments clearly demonstrated that the tool's weights were for placing
a load on the tubular drills, stone borers or crescentic flint/chert borers, and that
the tool was first twisted clockwise, and then anticlockwise to its starting position.
No other action produces parallel-sided cores with tubular drills. The tombs of

Mereruka and Aba (Sixth Dynasty) both depict a worker holding the handle above and below the weights. This grip is the most comfortable manner of twisting and reverse twisting the tool, but the experiments show that all the other depicted methods of using the tool are effective for operating it.

The pictorial, archaeological and experimental evidence, therefore, confirm that this ancient implement was in use as a *combined* drilling and boring tool. The tests indicate that the tool was first used upon a stone vessel with a central shaft fitted with a copper tube and, later in Dynastic times, a bronze tube, which was twisted clockwise, and then anticlockwise to its starting position. In view of its actual operating procedure, the tool has been named the Twist/Reverse Twist Drill (TRTD), calling it a 'drill', even though its other function was for boring.

The rate at which each twist and reverse twist of the shaft takes place is enhanced by the drill possessing a centrally located single weight, rather than with two tied weights on each side of the shaft. It should be noted here that the name of the Twist/Reverse Twist Drill refers only to the central drill-shaft, the lashed-on forked shaft and the stone weight(s). Tubular drills, stone borers of differing shapes and flint crescents are attachments to this tool. All of the tomb representations show that stone vessels were always carved to shape *before* the drilling and boring commenced, and this procedure was followed in making the experimental barrel-shaped vase.

A twist/reverse twist drill attachment tool

The figure-of-eight-shaped stone borer was a key attachment to the TRTD. A clear example of this type of boring may be seen in a vertically sawn translucent Twelfth Dynasty calcite Duck Jar (MM 5341), found by E. Mackay in the Southern Pyramid, Mazghuneh (Figures 5.14, 5.15). The unsmoothed boring marks in one half of the jar are effectively illuminated by the display case lighting shining softly through the stone. The complete vessel was 46 cm high, 24 cm in diameter at its widest point and 11.5 cm in diameter at its mouth. The craftworker was unable, because of the vessel's internal depth and narrow neck diameter, to smooth away the ridges between the boring grooves left by the employment of successively longer, and shorter, figure-of-eight-shaped borers.

An unfinished, unprovenanced, Predynastic granite vessel in the Liverpool Museum, UK, further demonstrates this technique. This oblate spheroidal vase (Liverpool Museum 1973.1.199) appears to have been tubular drilled part-way down and the hole subsequently enlarged with hand-held borers, these used in conjunction with sand abrasive. This enlargement, directly under the shoulders, was probably prepared for the admission of the first figure-of-eight-shaped borer. The problem of undercutting a cylindrical hole in a narrow-necked vase has been mentioned by Petrie. He identified two sandstone borers, used along with sand, for boring out the interior of vases. The hour-glass form of one of them enabled it to be slipped vertically through a neck, and then turned flat to drill a wider hole. It was rotated by a forked stick holding the contracted part.[43] Also, there must have been a series of such grinders of increasing lengths.[44]

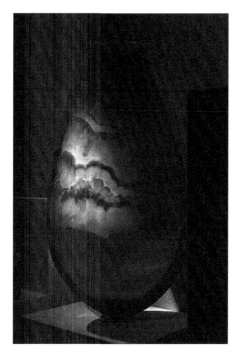

FIGURE 5.14   A translucent Twelfth Dynasty calcite Duck Jar (MM 5341), found in the Southern Pyramid, Mazghuneh

Source: Image by J. Stocks from the Manchester Museum, The University of Manchester

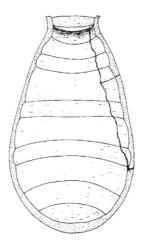

FIGURE 5.15   A drawing of the Duck Jar, showing the large grooves made by figure-of-eight-shaped stone borers (from MM 5341)

Source: Drawing by D. Stocks after the Manchester Museum, The University of Manchester

Not all workers were prepared to acquiesce to the difficulties of widening a stone vessel below the neck. An evasion of the difficulty began in the First Dynasty by making a vase in two halves.[45] The bottom half was drilled and finished upright, whereas the top half was first drilled upright but subsequently made wider in an upside-down position. The halves were then glued together. This technique was also adopted in the Twelfth Dynasty.

Reconstructed twist/reverse twist drills

Reconstructed TRTDs were manufactured from suitable tree branches, which had been allowed to season. The bark was first removed with a flint scraper. Each branch was adapted by cutting away the central stem above the place where it forked; the remaining part was sawn to length and carved into a taper. The following TRTDs and the accompanying attachments were manufactured for experimental use.

In all, ten TRTDs were fitted with tubular drills. All of these tools were weighted with two stones (Figure 5.16), except for a 3 cm–diameter TRTD shaft (Figure 5.17), which was fitted with a single stone weight (after the Eighteenth Dynasty tomb representations). The weight was drilled through its vertical axis

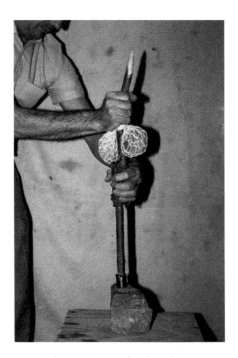

FIGURE 5.16 A reconstructed TRTD, weighted with two stones, driving a copper tubular drill

Source: Image by J. Stocks

FIGURE 5.17   A reconstructed TRTD, fitted with a single stone weight

Source: Image by J. Stocks

with a tube fitted to another TRTD, the finished weight being adjusted to be a force-fit on the drill-shaft, just under the inclined handle. Two test TRTDs established the working procedures, the cutting rates and the ratio of the metal worn from a drill-tube to the amount of stone it drilled. One of these was fitted with a copper tube, the other with a bronze tube (90 per cent copper, 10 per cent tin). Each drill-tube's external diameter measured 2.8 cm, and each shaft was weighted with two stones. The smallest diameter drill-tube made in the whole series was 2.2 cm, the largest one being cast to a diameter of 7 cm (Figure 5.18).

Three TRTDs were fitted with lashed-on forked shafts (Figures 5.19, 5.20); they drove a flint crescent and two figure-of-eight-shaped stone borers. The smaller stone weights, for the smaller TRTDs, were hung in coarse nets knitted from string. The largest TRTD's stone weights, each weighing 3 kg, were secured with ropes positioned into grooves ground into the stones (see Figure 5.21).

FIGURE 5.18 A 7 cm-diameter cast copper drill-tube, fitted to the lower end of a TRTD central shaft

Source: Image by J. Stocks

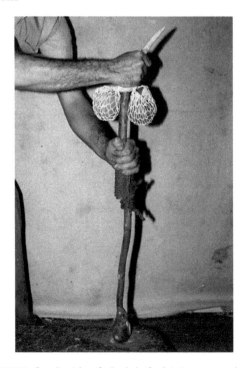

FIGURE 5.19 A TRTD, fitted with a forked shaft, driving a stone borer

Source: Image by J. Stocks

FIGURE 5.20   Close-up of a forked shaft lashed tightly to a central shaft

Source: Image by J. Stocks

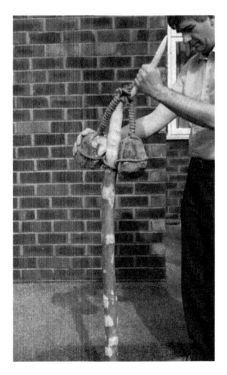

FIGURE 5.21   A clockwise twist of a large drill-shaft

Source: Image by J. Stocks

The twist/reverse twist drill tests[46]

Tubular holes produced by bow-driven tubes in large, hard-stone artifacts are nearly circular in shape, but the difficulties of making stone vessels with thin walls excluded this technique. It was found that the mechanical stresses imposed upon the thin stone walls by gyratory forces in bow-drilling breaks the vessel. Also, the to-and-fro movement of a bow caused sand trapped outside the tube to enlarge the hole out toward the external wall of the vessel, particularly in softer stones; ancient vessels were always shaped in advance of the drilling and boring operations, and, clearly, hole elongation would have meant the failure of each vessel.

In the tests, it was best to twist the tool first clockwise, by approximately 90°, and then anticlockwise to its starting position (Figures 5.21, 5.22). One hand grips the inclined and tapered handle; the other hand grips the central shaft, just below the weights. The curved handle fits the semi-clenched hand perfectly, and must have been chosen and carved for this purpose. Once the hands are comfortably gripping the handle and the shaft, they are not moved from that position, except for rest or to renew the sand abrasive. This comment applies only to the tubular

FIGURE 5.22 An anticlockwise twist of a large drill-shaft

Source: Image by J. Stocks

drills and the circular stone borers which, even when partially rotated, cut out the stone around the whole of their circumferences. The twist/reverse twist motion produced cores with parallel sides. In using a figure-of-eight stone borer, and a crescentic borer, the craftworker must periodically change the position of the hands on the tool *after* a full clockwise or anticlockwise twist, in order to grind out the stone evenly around the whole circumference of a vessel.

The twist/reverse twist action is comfortable and, once the arm and hand muscles are adapted to this type of work, not tiring for the operator; continuous test drilling was carried on for several hours without any ill effects. The physiological aspects of protracted lengths of time spent twisting the TRTD demonstrated a considerable use of the forearm musculature. The upper arm and the shoulder muscles also become strengthened. In particular, each hand and wrist receives a punishing regime which serves to increase the normal gripping action of the hand. However, years of this work probably caused some form of repetitive strain injury to stone vessel workers. Tomb scenes show most workers seated close to the point of drilling. They must constantly have inhaled considerable quantities of fine dust into their lungs. Ancient stone vessel drillers, continually employed upon this work, are not likely to have enjoyed good health, and probably suffered an early death.

The volume of soft limestone removed from the barrel-shaped vase by the 4 cm- and the 2.2 cm-diameter drill-tubes was approximately 6 cm^3/hour each. The volumetric rate of stone removal remains roughly constant for any diameter drill-tube. Larger diameter tubes, possessing a greater area of contact with the stone at their end-faces, cannot be twisted at a similar rate to the smaller diameter tubes. The reason for this is a necessary increase of weight upon the larger diameter tubes, which in turn causes a consequential rise of inertia, together with a commensurate increase of friction between the copper tube and the sand abrasive. This leads to increased operator fatigue and, although theoretically more stone should be drilled from the hole by a drill-tube end-face possessing a greater area of contact, a natural slowing down of the twist/reverse twist actions takes place, and this keeps the volume of stone removed similar for every diameter drill-tube.

The TRTD cutting rate for both granite and diorite was 0.4 cm^3/hour, whereas the bow-driven tube rate equalled 2 cm^3/hour. The TRTD cutting rate for calcite was 6 cm^3/hour, the bow-driven tube rate being 30 cm^3/hour. Therefore, the TRTD tests demonstrated that this type of drilling is five times slower than for bow-driven tubular drilling in all of the stones tested.

Making stone vessels in ancient Mesopotamia

The experiments with the *bow-driven* copper tubes indicated that using a bow to drive a figure-of-eight-shaped stone borer was probably extremely difficult. In order to investigate this possibility, a figure-of-eight borer and a circular borer were tested by this method. Each test borer was admitted into a previously prepared hole, which imitated the interior of a partly bored stone vessel.[47] A forked shaft engaged each borer in turn. The figure-of-eight borer immediately jammed in the hole, mainly caused by a massive amount of friction between the borer and the sand abrasive. However, it is suspected that this was exacerbated by an out-of-balance centrifugal force acting upon one end of the borer as the bow-rope began to twist it, forcing the tool into the wall of the hole. Turning problems occurred with the circular borer; in this case, the even higher sand-induced friction caused the bow-rope to slip upon the forked shaft. The experiments do not support the driving of Mesopotamian stone borers with a bow-driven forked shaft.

Egyptian representations of the stone vessel drilling and boring tool show its extreme simplicity of form; nowhere in Egyptian representations of stone vessel production does the ancient artist ever display a stone borer being driven with a bow. In fact, tomb artists never showed a tubular drill being driven with a bow, although the use of bow-driven tubes must have been well known. The experiments demonstrated that the twist/reverse twist technique provided the only satisfactory method that *any* ancient stone vessel artisan could have employed for driving the tubular drills and stone borers. In particular, the figure-of-eight stone borer can only be driven with the leverage and control of the Twist/Reverse Twist Drill, and the finding of such borers in Mesopotamia indicates the use of some form of this tool.

Manufacturing a limestone barrel-shaped vase[48]

The experimental vase was carved to shape from a rough block of soft limestone with large and small copper adzes, flat and crosscut copper chisels, a mallet, flint chisels, punches and scrapers and sandstone rubbers. No set measurements were adhered to, the shape of the vase being achieved by acting upon intuitive judgements. The shoulders of a barrel-shaped vase are wider than its flat bottom; it made sense to align the narrower base surface directly under the centre of the projected top surface, and ensure parallelism between them. The top and the bottom surfaces were finished before any further shaping took place.

The initial shaping of the curved sides now commenced (Figure 5.23). Copper adzes were utilized to pare away the limestone from the top to the bottom. However, a hand-held, adze-shaped flint blade could also have been employed for this operation: if this vessel had been manufactured from granite or porphyry, flint chisels and punches would have been used to chip away the stone. During this shaping, constant checking of the relationship between the top and the bottom surfaces to the curved sides became necessary. The second phase of the barrel form could now begin. Using small copper chisels, a mallet, and flint scrapers of different shapes and sizes allowed the shoulders and neck gradually to be carved into shape (Figure 5.24). After checking the final form of the vase, sandstone rubbers of graded textures were used to smooth the whole of its surface. The final smoothing, however, was deferred until the completion of the hollowing. The vase measured 10 cm in diameter and 10.7 cm in height, with a neck diameter and height of 7.5 cm and 1 cm respectively (Figures 5.25, 5.26).

FIGURE 5.23   Shaping the exterior of the test stone vase

Source: Image by J. Stocks

FIGURE 5.24   Carving the vase's neck to shape with a flint scraper

Source: Image by J. Stocks

The first stage of hollowing commenced with a tubular drill, initially part-way into the vase. It was decided to tubular drill it, even though soft limestone was probably hollowed with crescent borers in ancient times. This method appeared to be the safest way for a beginner to practise the hollowing tasks. In Chapter 4, an unprovenanced and uncatalogued calcite vessel in the Petrie Collection was

FIGURE 5.25 The finished exterior of the vase

Source: Image by J. Stocks

FIGURE 5.26 The tools used to shape the vase

Source: Image by J. Stocks

mentioned; this vessel has a circular groove upon its top surface. The groove is likely to have been made in order to locate a tubular drill, which prevented the tube from 'wandering' around the surface. The experimental vase was similarly prepared (Figure 5.27). First, the drill–tube was correctly positioned, so that a mark

FIGURE 5.27   The chiselled and scraped groove in the vase's top surface, for locating a copper tube in readiness for drilling

Source: Image by J. Stocks

could be made around its circumference, which allowed a groove to be chipped out with a flint chisel and mallet, just inside the circular mark. In fact, two grooves were so prepared, one within the other, in order that two different diameter tubes could be used for the drilling.

There is evidence that different-diameter tubular drills, rotated upon the same axis, were utilized on stone in ancient times. In the Petrie Collection is a tubular-shaped basalt core; horizontal striations are in evidence on its internal and external surfaces. The core's date and provenance are unknown. The core does not taper at all; its internal and external sides are perfectly parallel. Petrie ventured an opinion that the core came from an enlarged hole in basalt; a lesser hole had been cut and found too small, and then a larger hole was made, detaching a tube of basalt.[49] A different interpretation may be presented to explain its shape. Possibly, the lesser hole, after the removal of the solid core left by the smaller tubular drill, was deliberately enlarged, reducing the risk of breaking a vessel by trying to remove a larger, solid core (Figure 5.28). The use of this technology in the experimental vase showed that the tubular-shaped core breaks upon removal; soft stone is liable to fracture easily. But hard stone, such as basalt, may occasionally have survived removal intact. Both ends of the Petrie Collection basalt tube are flat. One might have expected the tube to possess a jagged end, where it was broken out from the hole. Nevertheless, there are solid cores in the Petrie Collection which have flattened and polished ends,[50] although the purpose for this is unclear. However, the tubular core could have been drilled through the top part of a vase being manufactured in two pieces; this would account for each end being flat.

There is other evidence for the use of different diameter tubular drills upon the same axis. Petrie mentions a marble eye for inlaying, made with two tube

FIGURE 5.28 Two tubular holes drilled on the same axis in limestone, demonstrating the tubular core so formed

Source: Image by J. Stocks

drill-holes, one within the other, showing the thickness of the small drills.[51] This technique was probably used regularly by Egyptian workers for stone vessel production. The careful removal of each successive core enhances the successful completion of a vessel in brittle calcite, not to mention the harder stones in use by Egyptian artisans.

The experimental vase was now drilled to a depth of 3.5 cm with the 4 cm and the 2.2 cm-diameter tubular drills (Figures 5.29, 5.30). The cores were carefully removed with a mallet and a copper chisel. Pieces of the solid core were removed first, followed by the tubular core (Figures 5.31, 5.32). The soft mallet blows were directed toward the centre of the vase. Other experimental work with the smaller tubular drills upon some sandstone and limestone specimens showed that the twist/reverse twist forces, exerted upon a slim stone core by the finely ground sand powder trapped between the core and the drill's interior wall, caused it to fracture at its base. Care was taken to eliminate any lateral forces acting upon the core during these tests. The twist/reverse twist driven tube can also, very carefully, be forced to one side to snap off a slim core. The only other alternative is with a wedge. However, although this technique was employed for the drilling of sarcophagi (see Chapters 4 and 6), a wedge utilized to snap off a core in a vessel could break it. A broken calcite mortar (UC 16038) possibly suffered such a fate, although this mortar could have been drilled with a bow-driven tube; the core is tapered.[52]

The vase now required undercutting at the shoulders, and then hollowing to follow its external shape. There are several ways that this could have been achieved in ancient times. First, tubular drill the vase completely to the bottom, and then bore out the remainder of the stone with figure-of-eight-shaped stone borers. Second, tubular drill the vase to a point just below the shoulder, and introduce a

FIGURE 5.29   Drilling the vase with a 4 cm-diameter copper tube

Source: Image by J. Stocks

FIGURE 5.30   Weakening the core with a smaller-diameter tubular drill

Source: Image by J. Stocks

FIGURE 5.31 The removal of the small solid core preceded the breaking of the tubular
stone core

Source: Image by J. Stocks

FIGURE 5.32 The tubular core is now removed

Source: Image by J. Stocks

FIGURE 5.33 Scraping a groove under the vase's shoulder with a hook-shaped flint tool

Source: Image by J. Stocks

first figure-of-eight-shaped borer to force a sideways cut. This first borer would be slightly longer than the diameter of the tubular drill; the use of flint scrapers to scrape a slight groove in the wall of the hole would help in the introduction of this first figure-of-eight borer. Each successively longer figure-of-eight borer would further increase the undercutting to a point where downwards penetration became necessary. The tubular drilling and the core removal would recommence until the final depth was reached. However, flint scrapers and hand-held borers may have been used exclusively to undercut the shoulders before the first figure-of-eight borer was admitted. As the first short figure-of-eight borers deepened this initial undercut, successively longer and longer borers could be accommodated. This proposed technology follows the apparent initial techniques employed in the unfinished Liverpool Museum vase.

Third, tubular drill the vase to a point just below the shoulders, then use only successively larger figure-of-eight borers until the bottom is reached. This method is not supported by the striations seen on extant figure-of-eight borers, which are under the borers' extremities, not under their central parts. This indicates that such borers were always used to widen an existing hole. The second alternative was chosen for this particular vase, although methods need to be reviewed when taking into account other vessels' shapes and stones.

A groove was now scraped with a hand-held, hook-shaped flint scraper around the vase's internal circumference at a depth of 2 cm (Figures 5.33, 5.34). A first figure-of-eight borer, slightly longer than the hole diameter of 4 cm, was slipped lengthways, that is, with its long axis vertical, into the hole, and brought to a nearly horizontal position (Figures 5.35, 5.36). One end of the borer was located in the scraped groove. There is a difference with oblate, spheroidal-shaped vessels, where

FIGURE 5.34 The groove ready for admitting a borer

Source: Image by J. Stocks

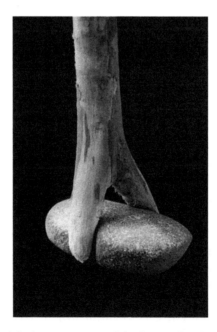

FIGURE 5.35 A forked shaft engaging one of the figure-of-eight borers used for enlarging the vase's bulbous shape

Source: Image by J. Stocks

a vase's internal diameter is considerably larger than its height. A long figure-of-eight borer could not have been admitted vertically and turned to a horizontal position. However, the unusually large mouth size meant that a worker could admit

FIGURE 5.36   The figure-of-eight borer engaged into the groove

Source: Image by J. Stocks

a big hand-held borer, and this may have been the manner in which this type of vase was internally ground to shape.

The limestone vase was now filled with dry sand abrasive up to the level of the borer, and a forked shaft engaged with it. Gradual twist and reverse twist actions, together with a new grip every few twists, allowed the borer to settle into a fully horizontal position (Figure 5.37). The scraped groove was further cut sideways and downwards by these actions. The dry sand abrasive slowly eroded the vase interior, and also the borer. Occasionally, the sand powder was poured out of the vase, and fresh supplies admitted.

Ancient vases were probably held by friction in a socket hollowed into an earthen bench, or in the ground. Some earthen bench sockets have been found in an ancient vase grinder's workshop at Hierakonpolis by Quibell and Green,[53] although their illustration shows a vase grinder in an earthen socket. All of the tomb representations depict stone vessels standing without support; conventions in tomb drawing may have ignored the true method of fastening vessels down for drilling and boring them.

Sometimes, craftworkers are shown steadying the vase with one hand. In the Twelfth Dynasty Tomb-Chapel of Ukh-hotp's son Senbi at Meir, one driller is saying to another worker: do you observe that this *mnhw* does not keep steady without its gum?[54] The driller making the statement is holding a TRTD handle in the right hand, and the vase with the left hand. The worker is possibly suggesting that the stone vessel should be stuck down during the drilling work.

FIGURE 5.37 Hollowing out the vase, with the stone borer in a horizontal position

Source: Image by J. Stocks

Tubular drilling continued to the bottom of the test vase, whereupon the cores were removed. Figure-of-eight borers finished the hollowing of the vase. A series of raised ridges, or cusps, were created as each successive borer ground away a groove into the vase's wall. These were smoothed away by long, hand-held sandstone rubbers, the bottom being smoothed with a rounded stone borer, in use with sand abrasive. It is likely that an ancient stone vessel worker gathered many stone borers of different shapes and sizes over a lifetime's work. Just as a modern blacksmith keeps any special tool for possible future use, many borers in ancient tool collections would have been kept for such a purpose. The maximum internal diameter of the vase measured 8 cm, its minimum diameter being 5.5 cm, with a mouth diameter of 4.5 cm and a depth of 10 cm (Figures 5.38, 5.39). The total time for manufacture was 22.5 hours.

Discussion

The earliest historical evidence for the TRTD comes from the Third Dynasty. The latest dated scene showing the tool is from the Twenty-sixth Dynasty, the tomb of Aba at Thebes, but it is reasonable to assume that the TRTD was in use to the end of Dynastic history. The rapid increase of stone vessel production in the Naqada II period, and the evidence of the craftworkers' ability to make tubes of copper, are good grounds to suggest that this increase in stone vessel production was a direct result of joining the copper tube to the TRTD. It is likely, therefore, that the TRTD, with its twin rôles of tubular drilling and stone boring, commenced use in the Naqada II period.

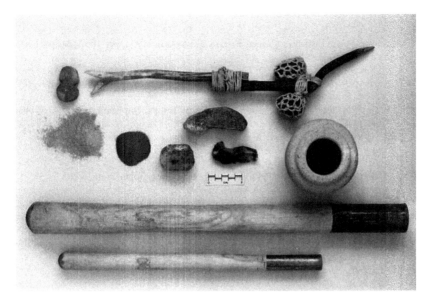

FIGURE 5.38   The tools used to drill and bore the vase

Source: Image by J. Stocks

FIGURE 5.39   The finished vase's interior

Source: Image by J. Stocks

Notes

1 G. Caton-Thompson and E.W. Gardner, *The Desert Fayum*, London: The Royal Anthropological Institute of Great Britain and Ireland, 1934, pp. 105, 131, pls LXVIII, 1–25, LXIX, 1–12.

2 C.M. Firth, J.E. Quibell and J.-P. Lauer, *The Step Pyramid*, Cairo: Imprimerie de l'Institut Française d'Archéologie Orientale, 1935–1936, vol. I, pp. 124, 126, vol. II, pls 86 (6), 93 (1–2).

3 D.A. Stocks, 'Technical and material interrelationships: Implications for social change in Ancient Egypt', in W. Wendrich and G. van der Kooij (eds) *Moving Matters: Ethnoarchaeology in the Near East. Proceedings of the International Seminar held at Cairo, 7–10 December 1998*, Leiden: Leiden University, 2002, p. 111.

4 Ibid.

5 B. Adams, *Predynastic Egypt*, Princes Risborough: Shire Publications, 1988, p. 33.

6 M. Amer, 'Annual report of the Maadi excavations, 1930–32', *Bulletin of the Faculty of Arts* I, 1933, pp. 322–4; M. Amer, 'Annual report of the Maadi excavations, 1935', *CdÉ* XI, 1936, pp. 176–8; M.A. Hoffman, *Egypt before the Pharaohs: The Prehistoric Foundations of Egyptian Civilization,* London and Henley: Routledge and Kegan Paul, 1980, p. 203.

7 A. Lucas and J.R. Harris, *Ancient Egyptian Materials and Industries*, London: Edward Arnold, 1962, p. 422.

8 J.E. Quibell, 'Stone vessels from the Step Pyramid', *ASAÉ* 35, 1935.

9 G. Brunton, *Lahun I, The Treasure*, London: British School of Archaeology in Egypt, 1920, pl. XIV; W.M.F. Petrie, G. Brunton and M.A. Murray, *Lahun II, The Pyramid*, London: British School of Archaeology in Egypt, 1923, pl. XXIV. For the forms of stone vessels, see B.G. Aston, *Ancient Egyptian Stone Vessels*, Heidelberg: Heidelberger Orientverlag, 1994.

10 Hoffman, *Egypt before the Pharaohs*, p. 207.

11 W.M.F. Petrie, *Tools and Weapons*, London: British School of Archaeology in Egypt, 1917, p. 6.

12 P.R.S. Moorey, *Materials and Manufacture in Ancient Mesopotamia: The Evidence of Archaeology and Art, Metals and Metalwork, Glazed Materials and Glass*, Oxford: British Archaeological Reports, International Series S237, 1985, pp. 40–6.

13 C.L. Woolley, *Ur Excavations*, Oxford: The Trustees of the British Museum and the Museum of the University of Pennsylvania, Philadelphia, PA, vol. IV, 1955, pp. 30–1.

14 C.L. Woolley, *Ur Excavations*, Oxford: The Trustees of the British Museum and the Museum of the University of Pennsylvania, Philadelphia, PA, vol. II, 1934, p. 380; G.A. Reisner, *Mycerinus, the Temples of the Third Pyramid at Giza*, Cambridge, MA: Harvard University Press, 1931, p. 180; Lucas and Harris, *AEMI*, p. 74.

15 J.E. Quibell and F.W. Green, *Hierakonpolis II*, London: British School of Archaeology in Egypt, 1902, p. 6, pl. LXII.

16 Woolley, *Ur Excavations*, vol. IV, p. 75, Fig. 15b.

17 Ibid., p. 185, pl. 13.

18 Ibid., p. 14, Fig. 5.

19 N. de G. Davies, *The Tomb of Rekh-mi-Rē' at Thebes*, New York: Metropolitan Museum of Art, 1943, vol. I, p. 49, note 22.

20 Quibell and Green, *Hierakonpolis II*, pls XXXII, LXII.

21 Firth, Quibell and Lauer, *The Step Pyramid*, vol. I, pl. 93.

22 A. Gardiner, *Egyptian Grammar*, Oxford: Griffith Institute, Ashmolean Museum, 1976, p. 519, sign U25; M.A. Murray, *Saqqara Mastabas*, London: British School of Archaeology in Egypt, vol. I, 1905, p. 65, pl. XXXIX; L. Borchardt, 'Beiträge zu 'GRIFFITH' Benihasan III', *ZÄS* XXXV, 1897, p. 107.

23 A.M. Blackman and M.R. Apted, *The Rock Tombs of Meir*, London: Egypt Exploration Society, part V, 1953, pl. XVII.

24 Gardiner, *Egyptian Grammar*, p. 518, sign U24; Davies, *Rekhmire*, vol. II, pl. LIV.

25 N. de G. Davies, *The Rock Tombs of Deir el Gebrâwi*, London: Egypt Exploration Fund, 1902, vol. I, pl. XXIV.
26 D.A. Stocks, 'Industrial technology at Kahun and Gurob: Experimental manufacture and test of replica and reconstructed tools with indicated uses and effects upon artefact production', unpublished thesis, University of Manchester, 1988, vol. I, pp. 168–213.
27 P. Duell (ed.) *The Mastaba of Mereruka*, Chicago, IL: The Oriental Institute, University of Chicago, 1938, vol. I, pl. 30.
28 W.M.F. Petrie, *Social Life in Ancient Egypt*, London: British School of Archaeology in Egypt, 1923, pp. 153–4.
29 Quibell, 'Stone vessels from the Step Pyramid', pp. 77–8.
30 Reisner, *Mycerinus*, p. 180.
31 Lucas and Harris, *AEMI*, p. 67, note 1.
32 CM JE39866.
33 G. Steindorff, *Das Grab des Ti*, Leipzig: Hinrichs, 1913, pl. 134.
34 Duell, *Mereruka*, vol. I, pl. 30.
35 Davies, *Gebrâwi*, vol. I, pl. XIII.
36 A.M. Blackman, *The Rock Tombs of Meir*, London: Egypt Exploration Society, 1914, pl. V.
37 Blackman and Apted, *The Rock Tombs of Meir*, pl. XVII.
38 Davies, *Rekhmire*, vol. II, pl. LIV.
39 N. de G. Davies, *The Tomb of Two Sculptors at Thebes*, New York: Metropolitan Museum of Art, 1925, pl. XI.
40 N. de G. Davies, *The Tomb of Puyemrê at Thebes*, New York: Metropolitan Museum of Art, 1922, vol. I, pl. XXIII.
41 Davies, *Gebrâwi*, vol. I, pl. XXIV.
42 R.S. Hartenberg and J. Schmidt, Jr., 'The Egyptian drill and the origin of the crank', *Technology and Culture* 10, 1969, pp. 155–65.
43 Petrie, *Tools and Weapons*, p. 45, pl. LII, 72, 73.
44 W.M.F. Petrie, *The Funeral Furniture of Egypt [and] Stone and Metal Vases*, London: British School of Archaeology in Egypt, 1937, p. 3.
45 Ibid., p. 3, pl. XXIX, examples 627, 629, 632.
46 Stocks, 'Industrial technology', vol. I, pp. 188–92.
47 Ibid., vol. I, p. 189; D.A. Stocks, 'Making stone vessels in ancient Mesopotamia and Egypt', *Antiquity* 67, 1993, pp. 600–1.
48 Stocks, 'Industrial technology', vol. I, pp. 192–212.
49 Petrie, *Tools and Weapons*, p. 45, pl. LII, 61.
50 Provenance and date unknown.
51 W.M.F. Petrie, *The Pyramids and Temples of Gizeh*, London: Field and Tuer, 1883, p. 176, pl. XIV, 11. Tubular drills were used in a similar fashion for creating eyes in statuary (R. Engelbach, 'Evidence for the use of a mason's pick in Ancient Egypt', *ASAÉ* 29, 1929, p. 21).
52 Petrie, *Pyramids*, pl. XIV, 9. Found at Kom Ahmar by Professor Sayce, a colleague of Petrie.
53 Quibell and Green, *Hierakonpolis* II, pl. LXVIII.
54 Blackman, *The Rock Tombs of Meir*, p. 30, pl. V.

6

THE DEVELOPMENT OF STONE SARCOPHAGUS MANUFACTURE

Shaping stone sarcophagi: surface decoration tools and techniques

The creation of sarcophagi from single blocks of stone evolved from Early Dynastic wooden coffins, these being made of planks of wood held together with dowels.[1] The coffins were often decorated with a symbolic recessed 'palace-façade' design, in reality a house façade derived from earlier reed buildings (Figure 6.1). This recessed design appears on wooden coffins and stone sarcophagi of all periods,[2] which were often carved with hieroglyphs and reliefs, both internally and externally.[3]

Monolithic sarcophagi were first introduced in the Third Dynasty, being constructed of soft white limestone.[4] Later in this dynasty, sarcophagi made of calcite were manufactured for Zoser and Sekhemkhet. In the Fourth Dynasty, Khufu's craftworkers manufactured the first sarcophagus of granite. Subsequent sarcophagi were made of these three stones, along with basalt, quartzite and greywacke.[5] Soft limestone, calcite and granite represent ascending degrees of difficulty in making sarcophagi. The Manchester and Aswan test cutting, sawing and drilling results, analysed in Chapters 2, 3 and 4, allow new light to be shed upon the difficulties that ancient craftworkers encountered during the manufacture of stone sarcophagi.

The results of the experiments with the replica copper chisels and adzes support the shaping and hollowing of soft limestone sarcophagi with these tools, but it is possible that they were also worked with flint chisels, adzes and scrapers;[6] the 15 cm-long flint chisel found in Khufu's boat pit at Giza would have been ideal for this work. Flint chisels, punches and scrapers were vital for carving the hieroglyphs and reliefs on the internal and external surfaces of hard-stone sarcophagi and their lids (e.g. the bas-relief of a panther skin on the lid of the Fourth Dynasty rose granite sarcophagus of Uriren, CM JE48078; the incised hieroglyphs inside greywacke and granite sarcophagi, Musée du Louvre N345 D9, N346 D10 respectively), and

DOI: 10.4324/9781003269922-9

FIGURE 6.1 Palace-façade design on the rose granite sarcophagus of Akhet-Hotep, excavated by the Harvard University-Museum of Fine Arts, Boston, Expedition to Giza (Mastaba G7650, pit C)

Source: Brooklyn Museum of Art 48.110 Charles Edwin Wilbour Fund. Courtesy of the Brooklyn Museum of Art

also to shape hard-stone anthropoid (mummiform) sarcophagi from the Middle Kingdom onward.[7]

Some lids were sawn from the bottoms of previously shaped stone sarcophagi (e.g. Hordjedef's Fourth Dynasty rose granite sarcophagus, CM JE54938): such a detached lid automatically fits its sarcophagus. Lifting holes were sometimes drilled in a lid's raised end sections (Figure 6.2) with a bow-driven tube (e.g. a Third Dynasty calcite sarcophagus, CM JE28102). Other lids generally were left with their lifting bosses still attached (e.g. an Old Kingdom rose granite sarcophagus, CM JE6156; a Fifth Dynasty limestone sarcophagus of Ra-ur, CM JE51950). Two wedge-shaped saw-slots are visible in Hordjedef's granite sarcophagus, which still has at least half of its broken lid attached; these slots are set at an angle of approximately 45° to each side of the sarcophagus, forming the shape of a chevron. As previously explained in Chapter 4, these wedge-shaped slots were caused by a long, heavy, flat-edged copper saw blade rocking from side to side during its reciprocating movements, progressively creating wear to the slot's sides.

In order for the slanted slots to be cut, Hordjedef's sarcophagus was first stood upon its end, and then tilted over to an angle of about 45°, probably on deep sand, which would have rendered the operation as safe as possible. After the first cut reached the centre-line of the lid, the sarcophagus had to be tilted over through 90° to accomplish the other slanted cut. Following this cut, which created the chevron, the sarcophagus was stood fully upright and the saw used to cut down nearly to the outer edges of the two original saw-slots, starting at the chevron's apex (Figure 6.3). Each of the three cuts was significantly shorter than the full width of the block, requiring considerably less effort than sawing the full horizontal

FIGURE 6.2   Lifting holes drilled into the lid of Akhet-Hotep's rose granite sarcophagus, excavated by the Harvard University-Museum of Fine Arts, Boston,
Expedition to Giza (Mastaba G7650, pit C)

Source: Brooklyn Museum of Art 48.110 Charles Edwin Wilbour Fund. Courtesy of the Brooklyn
Museum of Art

FIGURE 6.3   A stonecutting saw needed to be slightly longer than the width of a block
of stone, to allow for its reciprocating movement

Source: Image by D. Stocks

width. These procedures could be repeated until the lid became detached. In this case, however, a disaster befell the workers. They must have allowed the sawn, and therefore detached, half of the lid to strike a solid object, or to be placed under considerable pressure, which immediately broke it off at the point of sawing. One can imagine the panic following this occurrence!

The striations from the very last horizontal saw-cut, made with the sarcophagus standing on one end, are still clearly visible where the lid has broken away. These striations on Hordjedef's sarcophagus, and other evidence for copper saws in use with sand abrasive,[8] indicate that a flat-edged copper saw cut Hordjedef's and Sekhemkhet's sarcophagi to shape, the saw being slightly longer than the depth of the sides and the width of the top and the bottom surfaces. However, the horizontal striations running lengthwise along both sides of Khufu's sarcophagus indicate that they were sawn with the sarcophagus standing on its bottom. In Chapter 4, mention was made of W.M.F. Petrie's suggestion that the saw in use for Khufu's sarcophagus, used horizontally along its full exterior length of 2.276 m, must have been about 9 feet long (2.7 m),[9] allowing for it to be moved to and fro: this assumes that the two ends had already been sawn off the block of granite. The employment of a long blade for Khufu's sarcophagus reduced the amount of work needed to level the surfaces, whereas the use of a shorter saw to cut Hordjedef's Fourth Dynasty granite sarcophagus left very uneven surfaces, creating an abrupt change in level at the point where a subsequent saw-cut interfaced with a previous cut.

Hollowing hard-stone sarcophagi interiors

The use of stone mauls for pounding calcite, granite, basalt, quartzite or greywacke from the interiors of sarcophagi is impracticable: the force of the blows would soon have cracked the already-shaped stone blocks. The use of flint chisels and punches would have taken far too long to remove such a large mass of stone. Therefore, Egyptian craftworkers employed the copper tubular drill for hollowing Sekhemkhet's calcite sarcophagus, a tool that had served them well since Naqada II times for hollowing the hard-stone vessels, and drilling the holes in their lug handles. M.Z. Goneim,[10] the excavator of Sekhemkhet's pyramid, discovered that his calcite sarcophagus had been tubular drilled from one end, rather than from its long, top surface, as in Khufu's sarcophagus. Later in Dynastic history, huge hardstone sarcophagi were manufactured for the burial of the Apis bulls. At Saqqara, in the early 1850s, Auguste Mariette found 28 granite and diorite bull sarcophagi in the Serapeum; they each weigh over 80 tonnes. The burials date from the Nineteenth Dynasty. It is likely that each sarcophagus was sawn to shape and hollowed with bronze tubular drills,[11] similar to royal sarcophagi.

Petrie[12] recorded the internal and external measurements of Khufu's sarcophagus. The metric equivalents of the internal length, width and depth were 198.3 cm, 68.1 cm and 87.4 cm respectively, and the external length, width and height were 227.6 cm, 97.8 cm and 105 cm respectively. The weight of the shaped block,

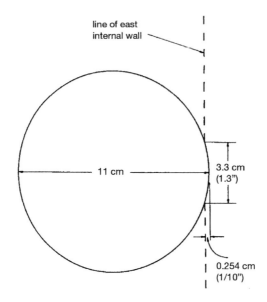

FIGURE 6.4 The calculated external diameter of the copper tube in use for drilling Khufu's sarcophagus, with W.M.F. Petrie's measurements of the curved mark in the internal wall

Source: Image by D. Stocks

before hollowing, was 6,310 kg, where granite's specific gravity is 2.7 g/cm³. The removed stone weighed 3,186 kg, leaving a finished weight of 3,124 kg.

A curved mark visible in the inside of the eastern wall of Khufu's sarcophagus was measured by Petrie[13] to be 1/10 inch (2.54 mm) deep, 3 inches (7.6 cm) long, and 1.3 inches (3.3 cm) wide, the bottom of the mark being at a depth of 8.4 inches (21.3 cm) below the top of the stone block.[14] Trigonometrical calculations, using Petrie's measurements (Figure 6.4), indicate that a tubular drill measuring 11 cm, very close to a measurement of six royal fingers, or one and a half royal palms, in diameter was employed for drilling the granite.[15] The metric measurement of a royal finger's width is 1.87 cm, calculated by dividing the number of fingers, 28 in a royal cubit, into a metric length of 52.31 cm,[16] although Dieter Arnold has calculated the royal cubit to be 52.5 cm by measuring existing buildings.[17] Cubit rods measuring 52.5 cm are known, but they date to the New Kingdom.[18]

An 11 cm-diameter copper tube fits almost exactly 18 and six times into the internal length of 198.3 cm (26.5 royal palms) and the internal width of 68.1 cm (nine royal palms) respectively of Khufu's Fourth Dynasty rose granite sarcophagus (Figure 6.5). In Hordjedef's Fourth Dynasty rose granite sarcophagus an 11 cm-diameter tube fits almost exactly 19 and eight times into the internal length of 208 cm (28 royal palms) and the internal width of 88.5 cm (12 royal palms)[19] respectively. In another rose granite sarcophagus, probably from the Fourth Dynasty (number 42 in the Egyptian Museum, Cairo, when measured by the author), an

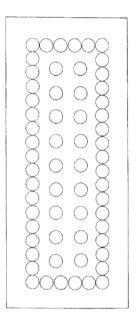

FIGURE 6.5   The proposed method of drilling Khufu's sarcophagus with 62 holes, 44 for the perimeter, 18 to weaken the central mass

Source: Image by D. Stocks

11 cm–diameter tube fits almost exactly 16 and six times into the internal length and width of 176 cm (23 royal palms) and 68 cm (nine royal palms)[20] respectively. These findings are also supported by dividing an 11 cm–diameter tube into the internal length and width of the Twelfth Dynasty rose granite sarcophagus of Senusret II at Lahun, which fits precisely 19 and six times into the internal length of 209.5 cm (28 royal palms) and the internal width of 67.4 cm (nine royal palms) respectively, and measured by Flinders Petrie.[21] The manufactured internal dimensions of these four granite sarcophagi indicate that a six royal finger–diameter drill-tube became a standard size for drilling igneous stone sarcophagi, and that the internal length and width of a sarcophagus was obtained by centralizing the required nearest whole number of drill-tube diameters, when just touching each other,[22] leaving an adequate amount of stone after drilling around the perimeter to form the side and end walls. The length and width of a mummified pharaoh's outermost coffin determined the required number of 11 cm-diameter holes.

The Aswan tubular drilling experiments indicated that the ancient use of an 11 cm-diameter copper tube was close to the largest tube that could be revolved by a team of three drillers: the two bowyers carrying out the drilling frequently interchanged with the centre drill-shaft steadier, each of the three operators able to continue more effectively, and continuously, with this strenuous procedure. Second, and discussed later in this chapter, an 11 cm-diameter drill-tube's ratio of stone drilled out as powdered sand/granite/copper particles to the hole's volume after core removal is a highly favourable ratio, which required a relatively small amount of granite to be drilled out of the interior of a granite sarcophagus.

In February 2005, with the permission of the Supreme Council of Antiquities, Cairo, a measurement of the distance from the vertical centre-line of the curved mark seen on the inside of the eastern wall of Khufu's sarcophagus, as it now rests in the Great Pyramid (the right-hand side of Figure 6.5), to the inside of the northern wall (the top of Figure 6.5) found it to be 37.5 cm.[23] In the indicated line of 18 touching holes drilled along the eastern wall of the sarcophagus, the calculated position for the centre-line of the fourth hole from the inside of the northern wall is 38.5 cm (the centre-lines of the third and fifth holes would be 27.5 cm and 49.5 cm respectively). Allowing for a discrepancy, such as not drilling the hole vertically *along* the wall, just as the curved mark demonstrates that the tubular drill was not truly vertical *across* the wall during the drilling operation, the measured distance of 37.5 cm is close to the calculated fourth hole position in a chain of 18 holes drilled along the inside of the eastern wall, corroborating the use of an 11 cm-diameter drill for hollowing out Khufu's granite sarcophagus. The chain-of-touching-holes perimeter drilling method is still used today to make large, often irregular-shaped, holes in resistant materials.

There is evidence that tubular drills were used to chain-drill multiple numbers of holes in stone vessels: for example, eight touching tubular-shaped marks, seven around the circumference, with one in the centre, left after the cores had been removed, are visible in an unfinished porphyry vessel CM JE18758 (see Chapter 4).

The bottom of the curved mark probably represents a maximum initial penetration of the tubular drill, owing to adverse frictional forces, when the core must have been broken off, allowing the drill-tube further to penetrate into the stone. The experimental use of an 8 cm-diameter drill-tube in Aswan showed that frictional forces generated at the flat-ended cutting face by the rotation of the tube, and by used sand powder clogging the spaces between the core and the hole wall, increased the force required to turn the tube. However, this compressing of the product of the tubular drilling of stone inside the drill-tube, a dry, finely ground cohesive powder,[24] allows it periodically, and vitally for the introduction of fresh sand, to be withdrawn from deep holes.

The experiments indicated that a three-worker team was required to drive an 11 cm-diameter tube. The Aswan drilling tests confirmed that two drillers needed to push and pull a large bow, with the third member steadying a hemispherical capstone placing pressure on the drill's cutting face (Figure 6.6). As previously mentioned, the drilling and sawing experiments suggest that a pressure of 1 kg/cm² upon a saw's and a tubular drill's cutting edges is necessary. Consequently, long stonecutting saws were probably weighted with stones at each end of the blade. The Aswan sawing experiments confirmed that inertia, exacerbated by the friction generated in a long, deep slot, would have required two ancient workers to overcome it, one at each end of the saw.

FIGURE 6.6   The copper tube used to drill out Khufu's granite sarcophagus was a little larger in diameter than this reconstructed tubular drill. The lubricated capstone is on the left

Source: Image by D. Stocks

In Khufu's sarcophagus, all 44 perimeter holes were probably drilled first, followed by the removal of their cores by hammering a tapered metal chisel vertically into the side of the tubular slot nearest the now isolated central mass; this strategy would have protected the walls from damage. The central mass could now be weakened by a further 18 holes (see Figure 6.5), instead of a possible maximum 64 central holes (108 altogether) all touching each other. The true number of holes in the central mass can never be known, but craftworkers always try to minimize unnecessary work. In the 18-hole proposition, their cores and interconnecting columns of stone are sufficiently isolated to allow them to be broken away with stone mauls, without damaging vibration being transmitted to the sarcophagus walls. The removal of a first level of stone, down to about 21 cm, lets a drill-tube penetrate further, beginning, as before, with the perimeter holes. Between four and six levels would be required to reach the bottom, dependent upon the lengths of the drill-tubes. The cusps left in the walls after drilling, and the broken-off cores and the columns on the bottom, were probably removed by dressing with flint chisels and punches. Smoothing was possibly accomplished with coarse sandstone rubbers, followed by the application of the finely ground sand/stone/copper waste powders from the sawing and tubular drilling processes. Polishing could have been achieved with leather laps and mud.

Discussion

The data in the preceding section can now be used in conjunction with the indicated ancient sawing and drilling rates to determine the approximate expenditure of copper, sand and time for the manufacture of Khufu's sarcophagus. On the basis of the Manchester and Aswan experimental drilling and sawing results, it is estimated that the ancient sawing and drilling rates for granite sarcophagi were approximately 30 and 12 cm³/hour respectively, and for calcite sarcophagi were 450 and 180 cm³/hour respectively.[25] Even though the area of contact with the stone is much greater for a saw than for a drill-tube, the reciprocating action for sawing is less tiring than converting the same action into a rotary motion. Possibly, to save time, two two-worker teams sawed the opposite sides, the ends, and the top and the bottom at the same time. Similarly, three three-worker teams had sufficient space simultaneously to drill the sarcophagus – a team at each end and one in the middle.

Using the 62-hole proposition for Khufu's sarcophagus, the intimated employment of two sawing and three drilling teams, the likely 5 mm saw and tube wall thicknesses and the calculations based upon the indicated ancient cutting rates suggest the times for consecutively sawing and drilling to be four and ten months respectively, with a further few months for dressing and polishing the sarcophagus and making its lid, a total of approximately 28,000 worker-hours. (Naturally, the drilling times, and the consumed copper and sand, would proportionally be greater for 108 holes; the use of *single* two-worker and three-worker sawing and drilling teams would also increase the total manufacturing time.) The calculated weight of the copper lost from the saws (168 kg) and the tubes (266 kg) amounts to 434 kg, *an average* daily rate of copper loss from the saws and drills of approximately 1 kg.

The weights of the sand used for the sawing and the drilling is estimated to be about 14.5 and 22.5 tonnes respectively, a total of 37 tonnes. The huge amounts of the waste powders obtained from making a sarcophagus from igneous stone, containing many copper particles, may have been stored for later use as an abrasive for stone polishing, stone bead drilling and for making some blue and green faience glazes, frits and pigment.[26] Each granite, or diorite, Apis bull sarcophagus must have consumed significantly greater quantities of copper, or bronze, sand and time in manufacturing it than the amounts expended on Khufu's granite sarcophagus, an indication of the importance attached to the burial of the Apis bull at the Serapeum.

The total weight of the removed stone was 3,186 kg, but the weight of the drilled stone, if using the proposed 62 holes, would be 242 kg. The ratio of the weight of the drilled granite to the total weight of the removed granite is 242:3186 or 1:13, and the ratio for the weight of the copper lost from the drill-tubes to the total weight of the removed granite is 266:3186 or 1:12. Expressed as the volume of the copper lost to the volume of the removed stone, the ratio is 1:40 (where copper's specific gravity is 8.94 g/cm^3, 3.3 times the specific gravity of granite). The efficiency of this method of safely hollowing stone sarcophagi is indicated by these favourable ratios.

The chiselling, adzing, scraping, sawing and drilling tests on soft limestone, calcite and granite reveal a significant difference between the tool materials, employed techniques and the consumption of copper, sand and time for manufacturing sarcophagi made from these three types of stone. In particular, there was a steep rise in the use of copper, sand and time for the making of igneous stone sarcophagi, commencing in the Fourth Dynasty. It is also clear, from the Manchester and Aswan sawing and drilling experiments, that the quantities of the copper ground off the ancient stonecutting saws and the drill-tubes used for sarcophagi manufacture, particularly those made of the igneous stones, accounted for a substantial proportion of the copper production in Ancient Egypt.

Notes

1 W.B. Emery, *Archaic Egypt*, Harmondsworth: Penguin Books, 1984, pls 24, a, b, 25, b.
2 A.J. Spencer, *Death in Ancient Egypt*, Harmondsworth: Penguin Books, 1982, p. 166.
3 For example, the Twenty-sixth Dynasty sarcophagus of the Adoratrice of Amun at Thebes, Ankhnesneferibre (BM 32). The lid is inscribed with hieroglyphs and a figure of Ankhnesneferibre in relief, while the underside of the lid is inscribed with hieroglyphs and a figure of the goddess Nut (T.G.H. James, *An Introduction to Ancient Egypt*, London: Book Club Associates, 1979, pp. 76, 166, Figs 25, 59).
4 W.M.F. Petrie, *Royal Tombs of the Earliest Dynasties*, London: Egypt Exploration Fund, vols I, II, 1900–1901; G.A. Reisner, *Early Dynastic Cemeteries of Naga ed-Dêr*, Los Angeles, CA: University of California Publications, 1908, vol. I; A.C. Mace, *Early Dynastic Cemeteries of Naga ed-Dêr*, Los Angeles, CA: University of California Publications, vol. II, 1909; E. Naville, *Cemeteries of Abydos*, London: Egypt Exploration Society, vol. I, 1914; T.E. Peet, *Cemeteries of Abydos, Part II, 1911–1912*, London: Egypt Exploration Society, 1914; Spencer, *Death*, p. 167.
5 For example, the sarcophagus of Menkaure (basalt); the sarcophagi of Senusret I, Amenemhat III and Tutankhamen (all of quartzite); the sarcophagus of Ankhnesneferibre (greywacke).
6 W.M.F. Petrie, *Egyptian Architecture*, London: British School of Archaeology in Egypt, 1938, p. 30; D.A. Stocks, 'Industrial technology at Kahun and Gurob: Experimental manufacture and test of replica and reconstructed tools with indicated uses and effects upon artefact production', unpublished thesis, University of Manchester, 1988, vol. II, pp. 246–73.
7 For example, the black granite mummiform sarcophagus of Merymose, Viceroy of Kush under Amenhotep III (BM 1001).
8 W.M.F. Petrie, *The Temples and Pyramids of Gizeh*, London: Field and Tuer, 1883, pp. 174–5; G.A. Reisner, *Mycerinus, the Temples of the Third Pyramid at Giza*, Cambridge, MA: Harvard University Press, 1931, p. 180; A. Lucas and J.R. Harris, *Ancient Egyptian Materials and Industries*, London: Edward Arnold, 1962, p. 74; D.A. Stocks, 'Sticks and stones of Egyptian technology', *Popular Archaeology* 7 (3), 1986, pp. 24–9; Stocks, 'Industrial technology', vol. I, pp. 100–43; D.A. Stocks, 'Testing Ancient Egyptian granite-working methods in Aswan, Upper Egypt', *Antiquity* 75, 2001, pp. 90–1, Fig. 1.
9 Petrie, *Pyramids*, p. 84.
10 M.Z. Goneim, *The Buried Pyramid*, London: Longmans, Green and Co., 1956, p. 124.
11 Tubular drills were made of bronze in the Nineteenth Dynasty. A tubular hole in a Ramesside granite door jamb contained particles of bronze (MMA 13.183.2). See D.

Arnold, *Building in Egypt: Pharaonic Stone Masonry*, New York: Oxford University Press, 1991, p. 286, Fig. 6.20, note 65 in Chapter 6.

12 Petrie, *Pyramids*, p. 86.
13 Ibid., p. 84.
14 W.M.F. Petrie, 'On the mechanical methods of the Ancient Egyptians', *JRAI* 13, 1884, p. 93.
15 Stocks, 'Industrial technology', vol. I, pp. 148–50, Figs 23, 24.
16 Howard Carter's measurement of the cubit was 52.31 cm (H. Carter, 'Report on the tomb of Zeser-Ka-Ra Amenhetep I, discovered by the Earl of Carnarvon in 1914', *JEA* 3, 1916, p. 150); Petrie's measurement of the cubit was 52.37 cm (Petrie, *Pyramids*, p. 181). For the purpose of calculating the width of a royal finger for this study, Carter's measurement has been used.
17 D. Arnold, *The Temple of Mentuhotep at Deir el-Bahari: From the Notes of Herbert Winlock*, New York: Metropolitan Museum of Art, 1979, p. 30.
18 R. Lepsius, *Die alt-aegyptische Elle*, Berlin: Buchdruckerei der Königl. Akademie der Wissenschaften, 1865, pp. 13–17.
19 Measured by the author.
20 Measured by the author.
21 W.M.F. Petrie, *Illahun, Kahun and Gurob*, London: David Nutt, 1891, pp. 3–4.
22 Petrie, *Pyramids*, p. 176, pl. XIV, 13; Petrie, 'On the mechanical methods of the Ancient Egyptians', p. 93.
23 D.A. Stocks, 'Auf den Spuren von Cheops' Handwerkern', *Sokar* 10 (1), 2005, pp. 4–9.
24 Stocks, 'Sticks and stones of Egyptian technology', p. 27.
25 D.A. Stocks, 'Stone sarcophagus manufacture in Ancient Egypt', *Antiquity* 73, 1999, p. 921, table 1.
26 D.A. Stocks, 'Stone vessel manufacture', *Popular Archaeology* 7 (4), 1986, p. 17; D.A. Stocks, 'Ancient factory mass-production techniques: Indications of large-scale stone bead manufacture in the New Kingdom Period', *Antiquity* 63, 1989, p. 528; D.A. Stocks, 'Derivation of Ancient Egyptian faience core and glaze materials', *Antiquity* 71, 1997, pp. 180–1.

7

MASTER MASONRY FITTERS

Masonry fitters' tools

The fitting of large numbers of stone blocks together, which commenced with Zoser's pyramid and other parts of his funerary complex at Saqqara in the Third Dynasty, reached a zenith in the Fourth Dynasty at Giza, where Khufu's masons closely fitted the large core- and casing-blocks into the Great Pyramid (Figure 7.1). The system used by ancient masons to make truly flat surfaces on stone blocks, sarcophagi and obelisks has never fully been understood. Some tools and tomb

FIGURE 7.1   Large limestone casing-blocks at the foot of the northern side of the Great Pyramid

Source: Image by D. Stocks

DOI: 10.4324/9781003269922-10

FIGURE 7.2 A replica wooden frame for testing horizontal level, shaped like the upper-case letter 'A'

Source: Image by J. Stocks

illustrations of the techniques have survived, and the later described experiments with replica ancient tools, and their assessment, were helpful in interpreting the available archaeological evidence.

Craftworkers used lengths of string soaked in red ochre for the marking of levelling-lines on stone masonry,[1] and string was also needed for plumb lines, which were in use with some important tools. At first, plumb bobs were grooved to retain the string,[2] but from the Fourth Dynasty a hole was drilled for this purpose.[3] The holes appear to be made for 2 mm-diameter string. W.M.F. Petrie found a number of plumb bobs, the earliest coming from the Third Dynasty site of Meidum.[4]

Three ancient tools were dependent upon the plumb line, and these were the wooden frame for testing horizontal level, shaped like the upper case letter 'A' (Figure 7.2), the vertical testing frame (Figure 7.3), also made of wood, and a surveying instrument carved from bone called the *merkhet*. Texts inscribed on the walls of the Graeco-Roman temples of Dendera and Edfu indicate that the *merkhet*, a horizontal bar having a plumb line hanging from a transverse hole drilled into a raised part at one end, was used in conjunction with a sighting instrument, the *bay*, for determining true north; the *bay* was made from a straight palm-rib, a V-shaped slot being cut into the wider end. I.E.S. Edwards,[5] referring to the accuracy of the alignment of the two main pyramids at Giza, suggested that the *bay* was stood upright at the centre of an accurately levelled circular wall built on a projected pyramid's horizontal rock bed. A particular star, sighted through the V-shaped slot, would have its rising position marked on the wall directly in line between the observer and the star. A few hours later, the same star's setting position would be marked on the wall. Resting a *merkhet* on the top of the wall allowed the plumb line perpendicularly to transfer

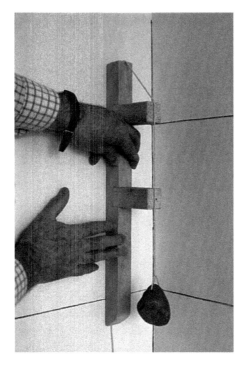

FIGURE 7.3 A replica wooden vertical testing frame

Source: Image by J. Stocks

the marks to the ground: a line bisecting the angle formed between them pointed to true north. Models of the horizontal and vertical testing tools were found in the Nineteenth Dynasty tomb of the architect Senedjem at Deir el-Medina.[6]

The 'A' frame was made from three pieces of wood. Two were joined at the apex to form an angle of 90°, both free ends being cut at an angle of 45°. The third piece was fastened on horizontally, so as to complete the 'A' shape. A hole drilled at the apex, for threading the plumb line, was knotted at the back to secure it. In calibrating a replica tool,[7] the two free ends of the frame needed to touch the surface of still water. A vertical mark was made on the horizontal bar, exactly behind the hanging plumb line. After calibration, the replica tool tested a horizontal surface, already confirmed to be truly level with a modern spirit level. The replica 'A' frame proved to be just as reliable as the modern instrument, and there is good reason to suppose that ancient frames were so calibrated and accurate.

A replica vertical testing device was also constructed.[8] Here, it was important to make the two horizontal pieces exactly the same length before fastening them to the vertical length of wood. (A simple outside calliper was probably in use – see the later section concerning the Kahun set of rods and string for a detailed explanation of this technique.) A hole was made in the top of the vertical piece, and another hole drilled at an angle of 45° through the end of the upper horizontal piece, the

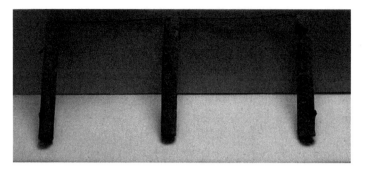

FIGURE 7.4   Three wooden rods (MM 28) found at Kahun by W.M.F. Petrie

Source: Image by J. Stocks from the Manchester Museum, The University of Manchester

plumb line being threaded through the two holes, with the bob hanging freely. In a test upon a modern wall, the string just touched the bottom horizontal piece, indicating that the wall was truly vertical. Provided each piece of timber was accurately made and fitted together, an ancient instrument automatically became calibrated at the end of the construction process. The replica tool's precision is comparable to a modern spirit level.

Although there is no direct evidence to prove that these two frames were in use at the Great Pyramid, the evidence for plumb lines predating the Fourth Dynasty, and the ability of the masons to create truly horizontal and vertical surfaces at Giza, support this proposition.

The stonemason used a set square to help test the accuracy of the inside or outside of a corner forming an angle of 90°; the same set square can do both jobs. A model set square was located with the two previously described tools from the tomb of Senedjem (CM JE27259). This set square consists of two straight pieces of wood, one with an extra piece acting as a foot, fixed to form a right angle. A wooden straight edge was possibly in use for stoneworking. However, in the tomb of Rekhmire,[9] this tool is being used for woodworking, not for stoneworking.

A crucial tool for testing surface flatness of stone blocks, consisting of three short wooden rods of equal length, two of them originally connected at the top with a piece of thin string, was found by Petrie at Twelfth Dynasty Kahun (Figure 7.4);[10] this set of rods is the earliest known example of this tool. The two joined rods, when placed vertically upon a stone's surface, were pulled apart to make the string taut. The third rod was held against the string to test for surface flatness under it.

For moving and fitting stone blocks together, the Egyptian mason used a sloppy gypsum mortar for three essential purposes. First, mortar was used as a lubricant for sliding the large casing-blocks together in the Great Pyramid; core-blocks were similarly moved by this method.[11] Second, Somers Clarke and Reginald Engelbach noticed that the spaces between badly fitting core-blocks in Khufu's pyramid were filled with small pieces of stone, which were buried in a matrix of gypsum mortar.[12]

Third, Clarke and Engelbach also drew attention to the difficulty of ensuring that blocks on a lower course evenly supported the blocks above them.[13] Egyptian masons, skilled though they were, could not precisely fit the top surface of a lower block to the bottom surface of a block resting upon it. The mortar used for sliding the two blocks together automatically filled slight hollows in the blocks' surfaces, which later set hard, evenly transmitting the weight of the top block upon the supporting block's surface. This phenomenon prevented the blocks from cracking.

Some problems confronting the mason

In the early stages of stoneworking development, Egyptian masons were handling stone blocks of manageable size and weight. The roughly made limestone core-blocks in Zoser's pyramid, deliberately shaped like mud bricks, but proportionally larger than the normal mud brick dimensions of 23 × 12 × 7 cm up to 26 × 13 × 9 cm,[14] are still quite small when compared to the limestone core- and casing-blocks in Khufu's pyramid at Giza (Figures 7.5, 7.6). The average dimensions of the

FIGURE 7.5   Limestone core-blocks in Khufu's pyramid

Source: Image by D. Stocks

FIGURE 7.6 Close-up of the Great Pyramid's core-blocks

Source: Image by D. Stocks

core-blocks, and most of the casing-blocks already stripped from the pyramid, are 127 × 127 × 71 cm,[15] and they weigh an average of 2.75 tonnes each.[16] However, one of the base casing-blocks still in position on the northern side weighs about 16 tons[17] (16300 kg), six times the weight of the average core-or casing-block. The casing-blocks of Zoser's pyramid are somewhat larger in size than its core-blocks.[18] However, most of these were relatively easy to handle. When blocks were fitted together, in particular the rising joints, they could be tried in position, removed for adjustment, and refitted into place. The casing-blocks in the Great Pyramid, due to their weight, would have been extremely difficult to fit by these methods.

The main problem the mason encountered in fitting megalithic masonry was how to achieve parallelism between the end-faces forming the rising-joint between two adjacent blocks. It is clear that if an end-face of a block did not run backwards at precisely 90° from its front face nor rise truly vertically upwards from the horizontal bottom surface, then such blocks could not be fitted just anywhere; each block would have to be specially fitted to its neighbouring block. The rising joint surfaces of the remaining casing-blocks on the northern face of the Great Pyramid do run backwards from the front faces at 90° and rise vertically upwards from the horizontal bottom surfaces. In buildings, stone blocks often have obliquely fitted rising joints. The main reason why end-faces were unlikely to be at 90° to the front and bottom faces was due to quarrying; it was easier to fit oblique faces of blocks, if they were quarried that way, rather than make all the end-faces square to the front and bottom surfaces – a waste of time and stone. Whether the casing-blocks fitted elsewhere in the Great Pyramid had obliquely rising joints cannot now be known. However, such blocks fitted to each other must possess parallel end surfaces. If this condition can easily be met, the rising-joint does not become a problem. How could this have been achieved with megalithic casing-blocks?

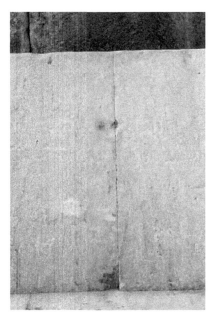

FIGURE 7.7   A rising joint between two large casing-blocks in the Great Pyramid

Source: Image by D. Stocks

Zoser's masons in the Third Dynasty did not fit the whole area of the rising-joint between two adjacent casing-blocks. Clarke and Engelbach noticed that the closely fitted front part of the joint only extended inward for, at most, 5 cm.[19] The joint then became wide and irregular, being filled with gypsum mortar.

Petrie took careful measurements of the rising joints of several of the remaining large casing-blocks in the Great Pyramid (Figures 7.7, 7.8). He found that the mean thickness of the 1.9 m vertical joints is 0.02 inches (0.5 mm), and that therefore the mean variation of the cutting of the stone from a straight line, and from an angle of 90° with a block's bottom surface, is but 0.01 inches (0.25 mm).[20] Petrie noted that the end-faces of these particular blocks (Figure 7.9) are some 35 square feet (3.3 m²) each in area, and were not only worked as finely as this, but cemented throughout.[21]

At Saqqara, in the early 1950s, M.Z. Goneim excavated a Third Dynasty wall, built by Sekhemkhet, made of dressed Tura limestone blocks. The wall, which is crenellated, still bore levelling-lines, made by stretching a cord dipped in red paint across the surface and 'flipping' it.[22] Goneim also noticed some red marks on the blocks. He ventured the opinion that their smoothness could be tested by using a facing-plate dipped in red paint, which left a mark on the high-spots.[23] Petrie also commented upon the use of facing-plates. He observed that the soft limestone casing-blocks were dressed by very fine picking or adzing, and that true planes, smeared with ochre, were used for testing the work to ensure its accuracy.[24]

FIGURE 7.8 Close-up of the rising joint shown in Figure 7.7

Source: Image by D. Stocks

FIGURE 7.9 The end surface of a casing-block on the northern side of the Great Pyramid

Source: Image by D. Stocks

R. Engelbach thought that the faces of the obelisks were dressed with dolerite balls until they were as flat as possible, tests being made by putting against them a portable flat plane smeared with red ochre and oil.[25] According to Petrie, a stone's surface was considered flat enough if the red ochre touched the stone at intervals of not more than an inch.[26]

Besides red ochre marks, there is no direct evidence to support the use of facing-plates for testing surface flatness in Ancient Egypt. No ancient facing-plates have been discovered and no known record has been left to illustrate their use. The modern facing-plate is usually made of cast iron, with ribs at the back to ensure rigidity. It must be larger than the area to be tested, to allow for the sliding movements made during the marking of the material's surface, and the plate's surface must be extremely flat and highly polished. The plate is used horizontally, and even a small one is heavy. In order to test if a machined metal surface is completely flat, a facing-plate is meagrely smeared with red ruddle, a mixture of red lead and oil, turned upside down, and rubbed several times over the metal's surface. The high spots are marked red, and these are scraped off with a flat scraper. This procedure can be repeated many times before a surface is deemed to be truly flat.

If it is assumed that a facing-plate was used to test the end-faces on the largest, or even the average-sized, casing-blocks in the Great Pyramid, then a facing-plate larger than the end-faces would have been required, otherwise the faces could end up curved. Such a facing-plate would need to be very rigid. What could it have been made from? Wood warps with differences in heat and humidity, and cannot be relied upon to retain its shape. Stone, perhaps? A stone facing-plate would be very heavy and extremely difficult to manage; the plate would need sliding over the surface being worked upon every few minutes. If facing-plates *are* to be rejected, how should the red ochre marks found on the flat stone surfaces be explained? This question will be examined in a later section.

The Kahun set of rods and string

In 1883, Petrie stated that the Egyptian method of dressing down large stone blocks to a true surface was to run saw cuts about half an inch (1.27 cm) in on all sides; the surface was then hammer dressed, nearly down to the plane of the cuts.[27] Petrie thought that the fine dressing of a block's surface was achieved by holding two rods of wood upright on the face, a string being stretched between the tops of the rods. Then a mason held a rod of equal length on any point of the stone, and the thickness of the rod standing above the string showed how much stone needed to be chiselled away.[28] Petrie had arrived at this conclusion after seeing a painting of the procedure in the tomb of Rekhmire at Thebes (Figure 7.10).[29] In this illustration, four rods are in use, two for stretching the string and two for testing the string's height from the stone; a third worker is dressing the surface. As in many other tomb scenes, the artist makes several operations concurrent, instead of consecutive. In reality, the surface testers would follow the masons to check their work, leaving marks of red ochre on the stone. Later, the masons would return to do more work, which would further be tested; many blocks would be at different stages of completion. During his excavations at the Twelfth Dynasty workers' town of Kahun,[30] Petrie found a set of three wooden rods, now MM 28, among the foundation blocks of a temple (see Figure 7.4). An Eighteenth Dynasty set of rods came from Hatshepsut's temple at Deir el-Bahri (MMA 23.3.169).

FIGURE 7.10 Checking surface flatness, using rods and string (left), and a diagonal check for flatness, employing a taut string only (right). From the tomb of Rekhmire at Thebes

Source: Drawing by D. Stocks after N. de G. Davies, *The Tomb of Rekh-mi-Rē' at Thebes*, New York, 1943, vol. II, pl. LXII. Courtesy of the Metropolitan Museum of Art

All of the Kahun wooden rods are flat at each end, two of them with holes for inserting and tying off the connecting string; a hole was drilled upwards at an angle from the rod's circumference, so that it exited in the centre of the rod's top end. The holes appear to have been made for 2 mm-diameter string. The third rod is plain. Petrie measured them and found their lengths to be 4.96 inches (12.6 cm), equal within two or three thousandths of an inch.[31] Petrie's measurements of the Kahun rods is a key piece of information in establishing this ancient tool's *modus operandi*. A set of Twelfth Dynasty rods, measuring 8.6 cm in length, has been found at Beni Hasan,[32] and an Eighteenth Dynasty set measuring 18.5 cm in length at Thebes; this set of three rods was still bound together with its string.[33] Because of the accuracy of the large blocks' surfaces at Giza, it is highly likely that this surface-testing tool was extensively employed during the Old Kingdom. Could the replica rods and string be used to test, and therefore direct, stone surfaces to the flatness measured by Petrie at Giza and, therefore, to indicate their presence in the Fourth Dynasty?

In order that this hypothesis could be examined, a set of three rods was manufactured from a suitable tree branch, which had previously been stripped of all its bark and allowed to season for two years (Figure 7.11).[34] All three rods were made to a similar length, and this was accomplished by setting two heavy stones into the ground, so that the minimum gap between two opposite projections became slightly less than the length of the shortest rod. This crude, yet effective, outside calliper ensured that the three rods, when each had been made precisely to fit between it, were indeed a *matched* set; the rods' lengths were finely adjusted by rubbing their ends on a sandstone block. Each rod's length was checked with a vernier calliper, and all were equal within a tolerance of plus or minus 0.005 cm (two thousandths of an inch). It does not matter that the actual lengths of the ancient rods were unknown to the mason: the rod sets in our possession do not conform to a standard measurement. Petrie's measurements indicate, and the experiments confirm, that ancient craftworkers were capable of making matched

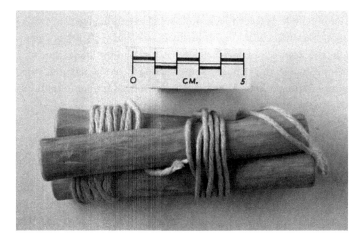

FIGURE 7.11 A replica set of rods, wound around with its string

Source: Image by J. Stocks

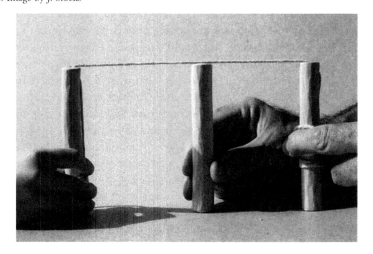

FIGURE 7.12 The rods and string ready for testing a surface for flatness

Source: Image by J. Stocks

sets of rods to these tolerances. Two rods were drilled and the string threaded and tied off in each rod (Figure 7.12).

Some ancient uses for rods and string

Martin Isler[35] has made some interesting observations with regard to the use of rods and string for testing the surfaces of obelisks. In his article on the Luxor granite obelisks, one of which is in Paris, France, the other still in the Luxor temple, he first refers to measurements of the Paris obelisk, which Henry Gorringe[36] made in 1882. Gorringe noted that the obelisk's north-west face, as it originally stood in the Luxor temple before its removal, was longitudinally convex, and that the opposite south-east face was longitudinally concave; the obelisk is 25 m long. Over this length, the convex north-west face has a maximum deflection of 2 cm from a straight line, while the concave south-east face has a maximum deflection of 1.27 cm from a straight line. The obelisk at Luxor has similar longitudinal convexity and concavity on two opposite faces.

Isler[37] proposed that, after the obelisk's shape was marked upon a suitable surface in the quarry, two troughs were cut at right angles to its longitudinal axis, one at each end. The troughs were levelled by testing their surfaces with an 'A' frame. A string was then tautly stretched between two rods, each rod standing upright in its levelled trough. The obelisk's top surface would be levelled with stone tools, its flatness being tested by using the third matched rod to check the space beneath the string along its whole length. Mathematical calculations[38] show that, over a length of 25 m, a tension of 14 kg force in a 2 mm–diameter string would allow it to sag 1.27 cm at its central point. This diameter string easily resists a pull of 14 kg. The obelisk's finished surface would follow the string's catenary curve and become concave.

Trenches were then pounded out around the obelisk's perimeter. If, as Isler suggests, direct measurements were taken from the finished top surface and transferred to the projected bottom surface, this would cause that surface to become convex. The two vertical sides would remain truly straight, as a string stretched between the rods held against a vertical surface would not sag toward it. A vertical testing frame could be used to check that the surfaces were truly vertical. Isler also suggested that a centre-line was made on one of the vertical surfaces with rods and string, and measurements taken from this line to obtain the bottom surface. Naturally, the stretched string would similarly curve downward and still cause the bottom surface to become convex. It is more difficult to hold the rods on a vertical surface than a horizontal one, and the string would be less taut. Calculations show that a tension of 9 kg force in the string would allow a sag of 2 cm. This may account for the bottom (north-west) face having a different curve to the top (south-east) face.

The present experiments[39] began by obtaining a horizontal surface, whose flatness was checked with a long straight-edge made of steel. The test rods were placed in position, with the string tensioned as much as possible. Measurements indicated that, over a length of 120 cm, the string sagged at its centre by approximately 0.25 mm (0.01 inch), the accuracy of the casing-blocks' end-surfaces measured by Petrie at Giza.

Earlier in this chapter, the suggested use of facing-plates, thinly smeared with red ochre, was discussed and rejected. The tomb of Rekhmire at Thebes contains the only scene depicting the use of rods and string in Ancient Egypt. In the left-hand block,[40] the masons are testing a vertical surface; as previously mentioned, the string's catenary curve does not influence the preparation of vertical surfaces. The masons may be moving the horizontal string downward to the bottom of the block, checking high spots as they did so. Naturally, they could test the surface for flatness by moving a vertical string *across* the block's face. Alternatively, they may be holding the left-hand rod stationary upon an already flattened edge (a datum

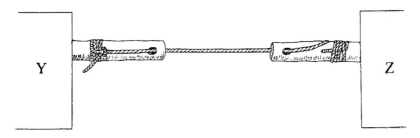

FIGURE 7.13 The rods and strings hypothetically acting as an inside calliper between two blocks, Y and Z

Source: Image by D. Stocks

or a reference point) and slowly swinging the taut string in an arc. Each corner of the block may be treated in a similar fashion. In fact, all methods may have been in use, and these would have ensured that the surface did not curve in any direction. Finally, as depicted on the right-hand block, a worker, or an overseer, checked the result by laying a taut string flat onto the surface in a diagonal position (see Figure 7.10). A check of this type would soon show up even the slightest spaces beneath the string.

The workers testing surface flatness could easily have dabbed the high spots with a fingertip coated in red ochre, where the test rods indicated these positions. Subsequently, other masons dressed these points down, at first with chisels or adzes, but later, sandstone rubbers were probably used for the final finishing procedures. As the work became closer to a flat surface, the spacing between the red ochre finger marks would decrease. At the end of all the procedures, the third rod should just touch the underside of the string along its length. However, on a horizontal surface the string's catenary curve deceived the mason into making it slightly concave.

In what other manner could ancient rods and string have been used? The string exits from a hole at the top of each rod. If the rods and string are stretched out in a straight line, the tool may now be utilized as an inside calliper. In this way, parallelism between the rising-joint surfaces of adjacent stone blocks could be tested before fitting them into a building (Figure 7.13).

In order to summarize the experimental evidence, and to suggest a method of fitting two large blocks of limestone together, the casing-blocks of the Great Pyramid have been chosen for illustrative purposes, even though no direct proof exists that the rods and string tool was in use during the Fourth Dynasty. These particular blocks were minutely measured and recorded by Petrie, and they serve a useful purpose in this respect.

Fitting two megalithic blocks together: a proposal

At Giza, between 1880 and 1882, Petrie formed the opinion that the Great Pyramid's casing, and some of the core-masonry, was planned. He noticed that lines were drawn on the casing- and adjacent core-blocks, showing that the blocks were probably first fitted together on the ground below.[41]

I.E.S. Edwards agreed with Petrie that adjacent casing-blocks' oblique rising-joint surfaces, those not at right-angles to the bedding joint, or not parallel to the central axis of the pyramid, together with the backing joints, were fitted together on the ground before laying them in their final positions on the face of the pyramid.[42]

If the previously given hypothesis is assumed, then two casing-blocks at a time needed to have been fitted on an already prepared, flattened and smoothed 'trial and assembly' surface. The use of the rods and string, and an 'A' frame, would have ensured flatness and true level. With regard to the bottom surfaces, Edwards also pointed out that the first stones to be hauled up to the platform would be core-blocks from the local quarries; their sides and top surfaces would be left rough, but the bottom surfaces – the so-called bedding joints – would already be flat and smooth.

The top surfaces of the casing-blocks in the Great Pyramid have been commented upon by Clarke and Engelbach. They noticed that the tops of the blocks were dressed *after* they had been laid, and that this procedure sometimes involved part of the core-block lying immediately behind the casing-block.[43]

It will further be assumed that the masons fitted casing-blocks along the face of the pyramid left to right; there would be no objection if the blocks were fitted right to left. Individual blocks, when arriving from the Tura limestone quarries, were selected because their lengths were suitable for laying with regard to the rising joints of the blocks below. These blocks would be marked with lines, drawn on their horizontal surfaces. It must be stressed that each casing-block in the Great Pyramid had to be fitted to the previously prepared block now ready for placing into position in the row of blocks on the pyramid's face (Figure 7.14).

FIGURE 7.14 Large stone blocks were made to fit adjacent blocks

Source: Image by D. Stocks

A proposed way to fit two megalithic blocks together can be summarized by using Figure 7.13. The left-hand block Y would already have had its bottom bedding joint flattened and smoothed and its left-hand rising-joint surface fitted to the preceding block's right-hand rising-joint surface. This last block would, by now, have been bedded into position along the line of casing-stones already fitted together into the pyramid. The right-hand rising-joint face of block Y would also have been flattened and smoothed with the help of the rods and string. This equipment would now be employed for testing the flatness of the bottom face of block Z.

Block Z would now be turned over so that both blocks, Y and Z, would be in position on the 'trial and assembly' surface. The left-hand rising-joint surface of block Z must now be flattened and smoothed and, at the same time, made precisely parallel to the right-hand rising-joint surface of block Y. In order to achieve this result, it is proposed that the rods and string were used as an inside calliper in conjunction with the normal use of another set of rods and string.[44] These operations must have been carried out by skilled masons, assisted by workers who manoeuvred the heavy blocks for them.

After a satisfactory result was obtained in aligning this rising-joint, the left-hand block Y, having had its front face roughly dressed to the pyramid angle, would now be bedded into position into the pyramid. So that levers and ropes could be used to assist in manoeuvring the block into position, masons left projections, called bosses, on the outer face of each casing-block: cut-outs for levers were sometimes made at the base of a block. After fitting, its top surface could be flattened and made truly horizontal with the aid of rods and string and an 'A' frame. This system ensured that any block's top and bottom surfaces became parallel, essential for making each complete layer of blocks horizontal throughout the pyramid.

The right-hand block Z now required its right-hand rising-joint to be flattened and smoothed; it would then become the new left-hand block and occupy the position Y on the 'trial and assembly' surface. A new block Z now needed to be placed to the right of block Y: thus, the fitting procedure, outlined previously, could be repeated. In this way, the casing would advance, row by row (Figure 7.15).

In summary, the key requirement for building with megalithic stone blocks is that each block must be fitted to its neighbour, and the Egyptian mason developed three surface-testing tools for just such a purpose. In particular, the rods and string tool could have directed the accurate surface flattening of large core- and casing-blocks. Therefore, the tool's presence at Giza may be suggested with considerable confidence.

Friction and force: physics to the rescue

The Egyptian craftworker was always fighting gravity and friction when moving large stone blocks (Figure 7.16). Let us consider how much force was needed to slide the casing-blocks across each other in the Great Pyramid. C.A. Coulomb[45] conducted a large number of experiments appertaining to the question of friction

FIGURE 7.15   Precisely fitted casing-blocks at the top of Khafre's pyramid at Giza

Source: Image by D. Stocks

FIGURE 7.16   Large stone blocks accurately fitted to their supporting pillars in the Osireion at the rear of the temple of Abydos

Source: Image by D. Stocks

between clean, dry surfaces. Coulomb's results are the basis for the laws of friction, and S. Timoshenko and D.H. Young[46] have summarized them as follows:

1   The total friction that can be developed is independent of the magnitude of the area in contact.
2   The total friction that can be developed is proportional to the Normal force. (The Normal force is that force acting upon two surfaces being pressed together.)
3   For low velocities of sliding the total friction that can be developed is practically independent of the velocity, although experiments show that the force F necessary to *start* sliding is greater than that necessary to *maintain* sliding.

   The formula $F = \mu N$ expresses these laws of friction, where μ (mu) is called the coefficient of friction and N is the Normal force – expressed in Newtons. (A Normal force of 1 kg pressing two surfaces together is equal to 9.8 Newtons at sea level.) If F is taken as the force necessary to *start* sliding, μ is called the coefficient of static friction. If F is taken as the somewhat smaller force necessary to *maintain* sliding, μ is called the coefficient of kinetic friction. In this study, only the greater force necessary to begin sliding will be considered.

   Sliding tests required a surface on each of two small blocks of soft limestone to be flattened and smoothed to a tolerance of 0.25 mm (Figure 7.17). The prepared blocks' dry flat surfaces were placed in contact, one block above the other, the bottom block being slowly tilted until the top block just began to slide across its surface. Several tests revealed an average angle of tilt to be 36°.[47] The tangent of this angle gives a coefficient of static friction of 0.73.

FIGURE 7.17   Two small limestone blocks, each with a surface flattened to a tolerance of 0.25 mm

Source: Image by J. Stocks

FIGURE 7.18   The lubricated sliding test using the prepared limestone blocks

Source: Image by J. Stocks

Several sliding tests were repeated with liquid mortar applied to the bottom block's top surface. The upper block now commenced sliding at an average angle of 8°, giving a coefficient of static friction of 0.14 (Figure 7.18). Other experiments revealed that a wooden sledge runner on liquid mud produced a similar coefficient of static friction.

One of the existing casing-blocks on the northern side of the Great Pyramid weighs approximately 16,300 kg. To find the force, F, to start this block to slide dry on a flat and smoothed stone surface, its weight must first be converted to the Normal force, N, in Newtons, i.e. 16,300 × 9.8 = 159,740 Newtons. The sliding force, F, can now be calculated by multiplying the coefficient of static friction of 0.73 by the Normal force, N. F = 116,610 Newtons. To find the force, F, starting the same block sliding on a surface lubricated with liquid mortar, the coefficient of static friction of 0.14 must be used. F = 22,363 Newtons.

These results show that over *five* times less force is needed to start a lubricated block moving than that of a dry block. This reduction factor of five applies to all blocks, no matter what their weight and area of surface contact.

In the Twelfth Dynasty tomb of Djehutihotep, at el-Bersheh,[48] Upper Egypt, there is an illustration of an alabaster statue of him, thought to weigh about 60 tonnes; 172 men are hauling it along a level surface on a sledge. A man is pouring some liquid, probably water, in front of the sledge's runners to maintain a muddy

FIGURE 7.19   Remains of a mud brick ramp in the Karnak temple, Luxor

Source: Image by D. Stocks

track. Calculations show that each worker needed to pull with a force of 478 Newtons (about 49 kg) in order to start the statue moving from rest.

The Djehutihotep illustration suggests that one worker was capable of initiating and maintaining a pulling force of about 500 Newtons (about 50 kg). Therefore, about 45 workers could have started a lubricated 16,300 kg block moving on a horizontal surface. Once started, the force required to keep the block moving would drop, allowing it to be pulled forward at a constant rate. A smaller, lubricated Great Pyramid casing-block of about 2,750 kg, this weight calculated from the average size of the core- and casing-blocks, required the initial force to be 3,770 Newtons (about 385 kg). Eight workers could easily start a block of this weight moving on a level surface.

The experiment with the mud-lubricated sledge runner explains why the angle of slope for some ancient ramps (Figure 7.19) was less than 8°. For example, a Nineteenth Dynasty papyrus in the British Museum[49] gives some measurements for a hypothetical ramp. A scribe, Hori, asks another scribe, Amenemope, how many bricks are needed to make a ramp of 730 cubits (383.25 m) in length, 55 cubits (28.9 m) in width and a height of 60 cubits (31.5 m). Calculations indicate that the ramp's gradient is 1 in 12, or nearly 5°. The gradient of the ramp left in the unfinished Fourth Dynasty mortuary temple of Menkaure is about 1 in 8, or just over 7°.[50] Also, two stone-built loading ramps, excavated at the southern end of the Gebel el-Asr region, Lower Nubia,[51] where gneiss was extracted from the quarries there, both measured approximately 9 m in length and 1.2 m high at the front, again giving a gradient of 7°.

Sliding laws state that *twice* the force for pulling a block along a level surface is required to pull a block up an incline at an angle equal to the angle at which it is about to slide backwards[52] – nearly 8° on a mud-lubricated ramp and nearly 36° on a dry ramp surface. An ideal lubricated ramp's gradient is 1 in 8. However, a ramp of 1 in 12 is quite adequate, completely eliminating the risk of an unattended block sliding backwards. Ramps sloping upwards at 8°, and higher, are likely to have been used dry, it being both counter-productive and dangerous to lubricate such a ramp.

I.E.S. Edwards[53] favoured a single supply ramp, constructed at 90° to a pyramid's side, for hauling the blocks up.[54] Calculations show that if a 7° (1 in 8) ramp was constructed in ancient times, it needed to be a maximum 1,100 m in length. This is about three times longer than the hypothetical ramp in the British Museum papyrus. However, by changing the ramp's direction through several turns it didn't need to extend 1,100 m in a straight line from the face of the pyramid while maintaining a similar inclination along its whole length.

Petrie estimated that the skilled masons employed permanently at Giza for the building of the Great Pyramid numbered between 3,400 and 4,000.[55] Herodotus stated that he was informed that the number of workers employed for transporting the stones in the inundation was 100,000, the pyramid being built in 20 years.[56] However, recent excavations carried out at a Fourth Dynasty industrial site at Giza by Zahi Hawass and Mark Lehner,[57] and subsequent assessments of the archaeological and scientific evidence, indicate that a maximum 20,000 skilled Egyptian masons and labourers were employed for 20 years to build the Great Pyramid.

The experiments with the three replica surface-testing tools indicate their presence at Giza in the Fourth Dynasty: they, alone, could have enabled craftworkers accurately to prepare the limestone blocks fitted into the Great Pyramid of Giza. The sliding experiments revealed significant advantages in moving stone blocks, and loaded sledges, along mortar- and mud-lubricated horizontal and ramp surfaces.

Notes

1 H. Junker, *Giza*, Vienna and Leipzig: Hinrichs, vol. I, 1929, pp. 96–9; D. Arnold, *Building in Egypt: Pharaonic Stone Masonry*, New York: Oxford University Press, 1991, Fig. 1.13.

2 W.M.F. Petrie, *Tools and Weapons*, London: British School of Archaeology in Egypt, 1917, p. 42, pl. XLVIII, B64, 65.

3 Ibid., B66.

4 Ibid., B64–89.

5 I.E.S. Edwards, *The Pyramids of Egypt*, Harmondsworth: Viking, 1986, pp. 265–7, Figs 54–6. For the *merkhet* and *bay* see L. Borchardt, 'Ein altägyptisches astronomisches Instrument', *ZÄS* 37, 1899, pp. 10–17.

6 CM JE27258 ('A' frame) and JE27260 (vertical frame). For illustrations, see Petrie, *Tools and Weapons*, pl. XLVII, B57, 59.

7 D.A. Stocks, 'Industrial technology at Kahun and Gurob: Experimental manufacture and test of replica and reconstructed tools with indicated uses and effects upon artefact production', unpublished thesis, University of Manchester, 1988, vol. II, p. 368.

8 Ibid., p. 369.

9 N. de G. Davies, *The Tomb of Rekh-mi-Rēʿ at Thebes*, New York: Metropolitan Museum of Art, 1943, vol. II, pl. LV.

10 W.M.F. Petrie, *Kahun, Gurob and Hawara*, London: Kegan Paul, Trench, Trübner, and Co., 1890, p. 27, pl. IX, 13.

11 Edwards, *Pyramids of Egypt*, p. 284.

12 S. Clarke and R. Engelbach, *Ancient Egyptian Masonry*, Oxford: Oxford University Press, 1930, pp. 78–80.

13 Ibid., pp. 78–9.

14 W.B. Emery, *Archaic Egypt*, Harmondsworth: Penguin Books, 1984, p. 181.

15 W.M.F. Petrie, *The Temples and Pyramids of Gizeh*, London: Field and Tuer, 1883, p. 210, bottom note. Petrie's measurements of 50 × 50 × 28 inches have been converted into centimetres.

16 Where limestone's specific gravity is 2.4 g/cm^3. Petrie used the British ton (2,240 pounds = 1018 kg) for his weight calculations.

17 Petrie, *Pyramids*, p. 44.

18 J.-P. Lauer, *Histoire Monumentale des Pyramides d'Égypte*, Cairo: Imprimerie de l'Institut Française d'Archéologie Orientale, 1962, vol. I, pl. V.

19 Clarke and Engelbach, *AEM*, p. 97, Figs 92, 94.

20 Petrie, *Pyramids*, p. 44; W.M.F. Petrie, 'The building of a pyramid', *AE*, 1930, vol. II, p. 34.

21 Petrie, *Pyramids*, p. 44.

22 M.Z. Goneim, *The Buried Pyramid*, London: Longmans, Green and Company, 1956, p. 40.

23 Ibid., p. 42.

24 Petrie, *Pyramids*, p. 213.

25 R. Engelbach, *The Problem of the Obelisks*, London: T. Fisher Unwin, 1923, p. 80.

26 W.M.F. Petrie, *The Arts and Crafts of Ancient Egypt*, Edinburgh and London: T.N. Foulis, 1909, p. 72.

27 Petrie, *Tools and Weapons*, p. 42.

28 Ibid.

29 Davies, *Rekhmire*, II, pl. LXII.

30 Petrie, *Kahun*, p. 27.

31 Ibid.

32 Petrie, *Tools and Weapons*, p. 42, pl. XLIX, B49.

33 Clarke and Engelbach, *AEM*, Fig. 265.

34 D.A. Stocks, 'Experimental stone block fitting techniques: Proposed use of a replica Ancient Egyptian tool', *The Manchester Archaeological Bulletin* 2, 1987, p. 46, Fig. 24; Stocks, 'Industrial technology', vol. II, pp. 274–92, 369, pl. XXVII, a, b.

35 M. Isler, 'The curious Luxor obelisks', *JEA* 73, 1987, pp. 137–47.

36 H.H. Gorringe, *Egyptian Obelisks*, London: J.C. Nimmo, 1885, p. 83.

37 Isler, 'The curious Luxor obelisks', p. 139, Fig. 5.

38 S. Timoshenko and D.H. Young, *Engineering Mechanics*, Tokyo: McGraw-Hill Kogakusha Ltd, 1956, pp. 162–7.

39 Stocks, 'Industrial technology', vol. II, pp. 274–92.

40 Davies, *Rekhmire*, vol. II, pl. LXII.

41 Petrie, *Pyramids*, p. 212.

42 Edwards, *Pyramids of Egypt*, p. 284.

43 Clarke and Engelbach, *AEM*, p. 100.

44 Stocks, 'Industrial technology', vol. II, Fig. 62.

45 C.A. Coulomb, *Théorie des machines simples*, Paris: Bachelier, 1821.

46 Timoshenko and Young, *Engineering Mechanics*, p. 50.

47 In dry sliding tests, using chalk blocks, the average angle at which sliding commenced was 37° (D.C. Cawsey and N.S. Farrar, 'A simple sliding apparatus for the measurement of rock joint friction', *Géotechnique*, June 1976, vol. XXVI, pp. 382–6).

48 P.E. Newberry, *El-Bersheh*, London: Egypt Exploration Fund, 1895, vol. I, pl. XV.

49 Papyrus Anastasi I (BM 10247).

50 Edwards, *Pyramids of Egypt*, p. 280.

51 I. Shaw, E. Bloxam, J. Bunbury, R. Lee, A. Graham and D. Darnell, 'Survey and excavation at the Gebel el-Asr gneiss and quartz quarries in Lower Nubia (1997–2000)', *Antiquity* 75, 2001, pp. 33–4.

52 Timoshenko and Young, *Engineering Mechanics*, pp. 162–7.
53 Edwards, *Pyramids of Egypt*, pp. 282–3.
54 For a comprehensive summary of the possible designs of pyramid ramps, see Arnold, *Building in Egypt*, pp. 98–101, Fig. 3.53.
55 Petrie, *Pyramids*, p. 211.
56 Herodotus, *The Histories Book II*, Harmondsworth: Penguin Books, 1961, vol. VIII, p. 124.
57 M. Lehner, 'Lost city of the pyramids', *Egypt Revealed*, Fall 2000, pp. 42–57.

PART III

Industrial revolution in Ancient Egypt

8

THEBAN MASS-PRODUCTION TOOLS

Early bead-making techniques

Bead-making began in the Epi-palaeolithic period (ca. 10,000–5500 BCE).[1] At first, craftworkers utilized natural objects, such as pebbles, shells and teeth. In the Pre-dynastic period, beads were made from copper, gold, silver, greenish-blue glazed quartz and steatite, glazed faience cores and stones; these included agate, calcite, carnelian, diorite, garnet, limestone and serpentine.[2] The Egyptians' most favoured bead shapes were rings, barrels, cylinders, convex bicones and spheroids, but amulets and pendants were also threaded into strings. A comprehensive classification and nomenclature of bead shapes has been assembled by Horace Beck.[3]

Glass beads were made from the Fifth Dynasty onward by winding a thin thread of drawn-out glass around a copper wire;[4] or by making beads from a glass rod or cane (tube); or by folding the glass and cutting it.[5] Horace Beck examined examples of Eighteenth Dynasty tubular glass beads from a glass factory at Tell el-Amarna.[6] Faience beads commonly were made around a thread,[7] which burnt away during the firing, but the tubular-shaped, barrel-shaped and the ring- and disc-beads were formed on a thicker rod. Some beads were dipped in a liquid glaze solution before firing, but see Chapter 9 for other glazing methods. Metal beads could be shaped by hammering, but hard-stone beads were first formed by breaking up pebbles, then roughly shaping the pieces by chipping with flint tools, followed by grinding on harsh and smoother grades of sandstone. Final polishing was achieved by rubbing along grooves carved into a wooden or stone bench, which sloped away from the polisher, the grooves being filled with a runny, finely ground polishing abrasive; this technique is displayed in the Eighteenth Dynasty tomb of Sebekhotep at Thebes.[8]

Threading perforations in stone beads were drilled with tools which changed in form and materials over thousands of years. The earliest material in use for drilling

DOI: 10.4324/9781003269922-12

stone beads was flint, but eventually copper and bronze drills were used in conjunction with a fine abrasive material. Small, hand-held pointed flints were twisted, and reverse twisted, under pressure. This action is being demonstrated by a craftworker drilling a cylinder seal in the Fifth Dynasty tomb of Ti at Saqqara.[9] The driller grips the tool's wooden handle in the clenched right hand, with the seal held close to the body in the left hand. In this position, only twists of the right forearm can turn the tool. Although the artisan is holding a wooden handle, it is not clear whether a flint or a copper tool is force-fitted into it.

Many bead-holes were produced by making conical holes on opposite sides of a bead, which met in the middle; the pointed, arrowhead-shaped flint tool used for this purpose may have been mounted into a wooden handle, or directly used by the hand. A good example of this technique is a carnelian bead in The Manchester Museum (5699). Gwinnett and Gorelick's[10] experiments with an arrowhead-shaped flint tool, twisted clockwise and anticlockwise by the hand into marble, demonstrated that incomplete rotation of the tool produced a misshapen, conical-shaped drill-hole. It is likely that early Egyptian bead drillers employed arrowhead-shaped flint tools in a similar manner for soft and hard stones. However, it is possible for a worker to produce a regular cone by occasionally moving the bead's position relative to the drill. This is similar to the way a figure-of-eight-shaped stone borer's position is changed within a vessel.

The tests with small arrowhead-shaped flints on amethyst and calcite have determined that the flint points are damaged during the twist/reverse twist process. The surface of a conical-shaped hole, made with pointed flints in amethyst, displayed a pitted, frosted surface, whereas similar holes in calcite had minute, irregular grooves, not dissimilar, if scaled up, to those made with flint crescentic borers in gypsum.

At Chanhu-daro, Sind, a city occupied by the people of the Harappa culture between ca. 3000 and 2500 BCE, Ernest Mackay[11] found chert drills during excavations conducted in 1935–1936. Mackay suggested that these drills were driven with a bow, and concentric marks were found in the slight depressions made into their drilling ends, which Mackay thought were deliberately created to hold an abrasive substance in place. Mackay assumed that the concentric marks were caused either by emery or crushed quartz; the drills' ends were circular, having been ground from rod-shaped chert blanks. After a period of drilling, the centre of the drilling end caused a dimple to be formed in the drill-hole, which was seen in broken, unfinished beads of agate and carnelian. This dimple was the result of the drill's perimeter grinding away more stone due to its greater rotational speed. C.H. Desch, the director of the National Physical Laboratory during the late 1930s, showed that by using emery, water and an Archimedean brace, these drills could penetrate 1 mm into carnelian in 20 minutes. Flat-ended chert, or indeed flint, drills must be used with a finely ground runny abrasive, if they are to perform any useful drilling; an initial depression was required to stop a drill 'wandering' around the bead's surface. There is no evidence, at present, that Egyptian bead makers used similarly shaped chert or flint drills in this manner. The present tests (Table 8.1) show that copper

TABLE 8.1 Specimen perforation results

A. Drilling times, ratios of bronze drill to stone wear rates and drilling rates

bead material	diameter of hole (mm)	depth of hole (mm)	drilling time (minutes)	drill-rod length lost (mm)	ratios bronze: stone	cutting rates (mm³/hour)
calcite	2	5	30	>0.05	1:>100	30
serpentine	2	1.5	15	0.3	1:5	18
quartz	1	0.5	12	0.2	1:2.5	2
amethyst	1	0.5	15	0.2	1:2.5	2

B. Indicated mass-production perforation rates (three drill-rods)

bead material	diameter of hole (mm)	depth of hole (mm)	single rate (minutes)	mass-production rate (minutes) one bead produced per:
calcite	2	10	60	20
serpentine	2	10	100	33
quartz	1	10	240	80
amethyst	1	10	300	100

and bronze bead drills penetrate more or less at the rate achieved by Desch's experiments with the Chandhu-daro chert drills.

At Hierakonpolis, J.E. Quibell and F.W. Green[12] discovered pointed flint implements, which they called bead drills. They were found in association with roughly chipped carnelian, amethyst and other types of stone, one or two of which showed signs of the commencement of the drilling operation, although Quibell and Green were uncertain of the methods employed. At Abydos, a Late Gerzean hamlet, T. Eric Peet[13] found over 300 tiny flint microblades. Michael Hoffman[14] thought they may have been bead drills. However, no microscopic examination of possible wear patterns was undertaken, and their true use has not firmly been established.

After the introduction of copper in the Predynastic period, small, bow-driven drills were probably made of this metal for bead perforation. Long, narrow perforations are much easier to make with metal drills and an abrasive paste. G.A. Reisner[15] found several bronze bead drills at Kerma in the Sudan. Some drills date to ca. 1970–1935 BCE, but two drills fitted with wooden handles were excavated from tumuli dated by Reisner to the Second Intermediate Period (ca. 1795–1650 BCE); at this time, a native culture employing Egyptian techniques flourished at Kerma. A particularly fine drill was force-fitted into a waisted wooden handle, which engaged with a bow-string. Reisner measured the drill's total length, without the handle, to be 5.4 cm, of which the top 1.4 cm was 2 mm square. The bottom 4 cm was circular in section, tapering from the squared section to a point. The cylindrical handle measured 2 cm in length and 8 mm in diameter, the waisted part being 5 mm in diameter. A replica of this drill was made from a bronze casting

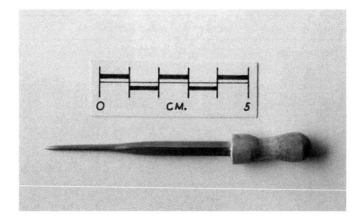

FIGURE 8.1   A replica Kerma-type bronze bead drill force-fitted into a waisted wooden handle

Source: Image by J. Stocks

FIGURE 8.2   A small bow rotating the replica bead drill

Source: Image by J. Stocks

containing 10 per cent tin.[16] After shaping and polishing, it was force-fitted into a replica wooden handle (Figure 8.1). A small bow rotated the drill, after a single turn of the string had been made upon the waisted part of the handle (Figures 8.2, 8.3). A comfortable stroke rate and length was 200 per minute and 15 cm respectively. The waist diameter of the replica handle, slightly larger at 7 mm, caused it to rotate at 1,400 revolutions/minute.[17] The Kerma drill, under similar conditions, would have rotated at 1,900 revolutions/minute. The replica drill made a small hole in a piece of calcite (Figure 8.4).

Reisner noticed that some of the stone beads were drilled from one side, but that others were drilled from two opposite sides, both perforations meeting in the

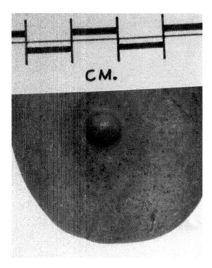

FIGURE 8.3   The capstone for placing pressure on the rotating replica bead drill

Source: Image by J. Stocks

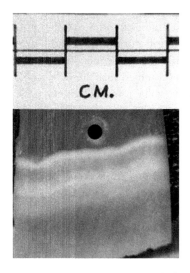

FIGURE 8.4   A 2 mm–diameter hole in calcite, made with the replica bronze bead drill

Source: Image by J. Stocks

middle.[18] In opaque stone, the string exits normally at each end. However, in polished amethyst, which is quite transparent, the string may be seen sharply to deviate from a straight line, where the two holes join in the centre (Figure 8.5).[19] Drilling from both ends of a long bead ensured that the string entered or exited a bead's surfaces at the correct positions, and enabled relatively short drills successfully to penetrate long beads. Drilling a long bead in a single operation would rarely have produced an accurate exit point for the hole.

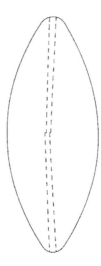

FIGURE 8.5 A cross-section of a long convex bicone bead shape, showing how holes drilled from each end often met at an angle in the centre

Source: Image by D. Stocks

Drilling was undertaken after smoothing the beads to shape, but before the final polishing operation. The drill-point usually had a diameter of 1–2 mm; a bead-hole narrows from its surface to the centre, caused by the wobbling of the drill and its tapered shape. Reisner assumed that the holes could be drilled with a copper drill, or a hard vegetable stalk, using *wet* emery powder.[20] However, tests with the reed tubes and a wet, finely ground sand abrasive demonstrated that the hard stem softened; likewise, a slim vegetable stalk, utilized with a wet abrasive, would be ineffective for the same reason. Middle Kingdom jewellery was discovered at Lahun: a particularly good example is a string of spherical carnelian beads (MM 207),[21] which came from a foundation deposit of Senusret II. The biggest bead is 6 mm in diameter, the smallest being 4.5 mm in diameter.

Six New Kingdom tombs in the Theban necropolis

At Thebes, Upper Egypt, six private tombs dating to the Eighteenth and Nineteenth Dynasties, and containing illustrations showing craftworkers drilling stone beads, indicate that the single bead-drill, probably in use for about two millennia before, evolved into a multiple bead-drilling apparatus. In the representations, each driller is simultaneously perforating at least two beads, but sometimes three, four or even five beads are being drilled at the same time. These changes not only required fundamental modifications to the drills, but also to the manner in which they were used. The equipment has not survived to the present day; only by testing anciently used bead materials with reconstructed drill-rods, and their driving bow, could the tomb illustrations be brought to life. In this way, the drilling tool's impact upon ancient stone bead production could be assessed. But first, we need closely to examine the tomb illustrations and glean every last bit of information from them.

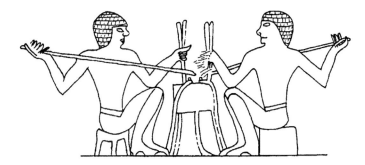

FIGURE 8.6   Two craftworkers drilling two stone beads each. From the tomb of Puyemre at Thebes.

Source: Drawing by D. Stocks after N. de G. Davies, *The Tomb of Puyemrê at Thebes*, New York, 1922, vol. I, pl. XXIII. Courtesy of the Metropolitan Museum of Art

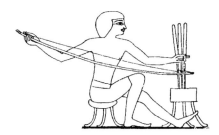

FIGURE 8.7   A single craftworker drilling three stone beads. From the tomb of Rekhmire at Thebes

Source: Drawing by D. Stocks after N. de G. Davies, *The Tomb of Rekh-mi-Rē' at Thebes*, New York, 1943, vol. II, pl. LIV. Courtesy of the Metropolitan Museum of Art

The first five tombs were constructed during a period of approximately 100 years (ca. 1475–1375 BCE), and all date to the Eighteenth Dynasty. The sixth tomb, that of the Nineteenth Dynasty Treasury Scribe of the Estate of Amun, Neferrenpet, was constructed about 85 years later than the last tomb of the Eighteenth Dynasty. The tomb illustrations are discussed in chronological order.

The tomb of Puyemre (ca. 1475 BCE, Th 39, reign of Tuthmose III)[22] shows two drillers facing each other seated upon low stools (Figure 8.6). They both use the same drilling table. Each craftworker simultaneously operates two drills. In the tomb of the Vizier Rekhmire (ca. 1471–1448 BCE, Th 100, reigns of Tuthmose III and Amenhotep II)[23] a worker is depicted using three drills at the same moment (Figure 8.7) and, similarly, a worker in the tomb of Amenhotpe-si-se (ca. 1415 BCE, Th 75, reign of Tuthmose IV)[24] also operates three drills (Figure 8.8).

The tomb of Sebekhotep (ca. 1415 BCE, Th 63, reign of Tuthmose IV)[25] is of crucial importance. An illustration, removed from the tomb in the nine_ teenth century, and now BM 920, shows two workers, each with four drills,

FIGURE 8.8 A single craftworker at the drilling table. From the tomb of Amenhotpe-si-se at Thebes.

Source: Drawing by D. Stocks after N. de G. Davies, *The Tombs of Two Officials of Tuthmosis IV at Thebes*, London: Egypt Exploration Society, 1923, vol. II, pl. X

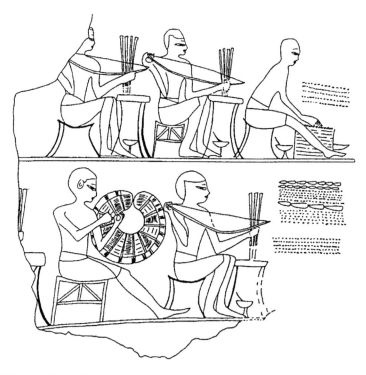

FIGURE 8.9 A New Kingdom bead-making workshop at Thebes, Upper Egypt. Two of the craftworkers are each using four drill-rods. From the tomb of Sebekhotep at Thebes (BM 920)

Source: Image by D. Stocks from the British Museum

and one artisan with three drills. A fragment of a fourth driller is on the left-hand edge of the scene. Another jeweller is polishing beads on a sloping bench, and yet another is threading beads into a collar (Figure 8.9). In the

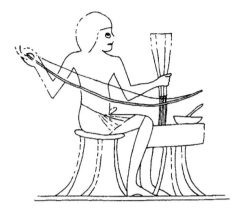

FIGURE 8.10   A worker using three drills simultaneously. From the tomb of Nebamun
and Ipuky at Thebes

Source: Drawing by D. Stocks after N. de G. Davies, *The Tomb of Two Sculptors at Thebes*, New York,
1925, pl. XI. Courtesy of the Metropolitan Museum of Art

tomb of the Two Sculptors, Nebamun and Ipuky (ca. 1375 BCE, Th 181, reigns
of Amenhotep III and IV),[26] a single craftworker simultaneously operates three
drills (Figure 8.10). The tomb of Neferrenpet (ca. 1290 BCE, Th 178, reign of
Ramesses II)[27] shows two workers, one spinning five drills, the other spinning
four drills.

Interpretation of the illustrations

The length of the bow is estimated to be 1.2 m; this is considerably longer than a
bow depicted in the Eighteenth Dynasty tomb of Rekhmire for drilling holes into
wood.[28] The bow-shaft thickness appears to be 1.5 cm. Also, the multiple bead-
drilling bow's arc-shape differs from the usual shape of a woodworker's bow. All of
the operators are shown holding the extreme ends of the bows, with their thumbs
or fingers intertwined with the bow-strings. The best depiction of multiple bead-
drilling technology occurs in the tomb of Rekhmire. However, the experiments
with the reconstructions indicate that the tomb artist may mistakenly have drawn
the bow-string in front of the operator's thumb, instead of behind it. Also, the artist
has depicted the driller's left hand holding the three wooden shafts in an impossible
position. The hand should have all the fingers behind the shafts, and the thumb in
front of them.

All of the operators are seated upon three-legged stools, except for the right-
hand man in the tomb of Puyemre, who is seated upon a block of some description. An Eighteenth Dynasty stool from Thebes (Figure 8.11) may be seen in
the British Museum (2481); the top of each leg is squared and force-fitted into a
similarly sized square hole in the curved seat. The drilling tables also possess three

FIGURE 8.11 An Eighteenth Dynasty three-legged stool from Thebes (BM 2481)

Source: Image by J. Stocks. © The British Museum

legs, which were probably fitted into the table-tops in a similar way to this stool's legs. Three-legged tables and stools are stable on uneven floors, and this was found to be essential for the multiple bead-drilling tests. The tomb representations of the table-tops do not show how beads were held in place. In some tomb illustrations, the table-top has a considerable thickness. This may be an edge board, fixed around each side. The inside of these table-tops, therefore, may have been hollow; this will be discussed later on.

Every operator drives the bow with the right hand – even the worker to the right of the scene in the tomb of Puyemre. The right arm is always outstretched, except for the artisan to the right of the painting in the tomb of Neferrenpet and the drillers depicted in the tomb of Sebekhotep. The operators' left hands hold the thicker, upper parts of the drilling equipment. In every case, except for the tomb of Sebekhotep, the bow-string is depicted around the thinner, lower parts of the drilling equipment. In particular, the representation in Rekhmire's tomb shows the bow-string looped around each of the drill-rods. In the Sebekhotep illustration, the artist has poorly presented the whole scene. It appears hurriedly executed, and the bow-strings are shown passing around the thicker, upper parts of the drilling apparatus, which the tests indicated to be incorrect.

Three out of the six paintings, the tombs of Sebekhotep, Nebamun and Ipuky and Neferrenpet, have bowls, with an implement projecting from them.

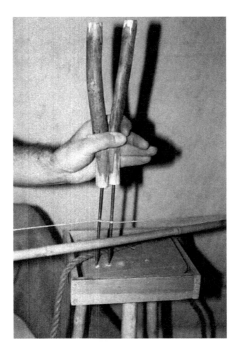

FIGURE 8.12   Holding a reconstructed drilling table steady with a rope. After an illustration from the tomb of Puyemre at Thebes

Source: Image by J. Stocks

Amenhotpe-si-se has the bowl, but no implement. The bowls are either shown upon, above or under the drilling tables. The bowls probably held the grinding medium, a thin, runny paste made, possibly, from the waste powders obtained from the drilling and sawing of stone with sand abrasive; the addition of muddy water made the test paste perfect for drilling beads. (It may be remembered that the finely ground, quartz-based powders are cohesive and do not 'flow' like dry coarse sand does.) The implements shown in Sebekhotep, Nebamun and Ipuky and Nefer-renpet are likely to have been spoon-shaped, for depositing small amounts of the grinding paste onto the drills' points. In the tomb of Sebekhotep, the bead polisher also has a bowl and implement within easy reach of his right hand.

The tomb of Puyemre depicts what is probably a rope passing over the table. The two projections on the rope may be large knots. Each operator has a foot over one end of the rope, which keeps it taut. This rope seems to be holding the table steady, while the two drillers operate their bows (Figure 8.12); Walter Wreszinski[29] also suggests this is the rope's purpose. If the two projections are indeed knots, then these would bring pressure to bear upon the table, *and anything within it.* The Rekhmire driller's outstretched left leg and foot appears to be holding the table's leg down. The craftworker in Nebamun and Ipuky's tomb could be holding the table steady between the knees. Therefore, in three separate tombs, and in three distinctive ways, the drillers kept their tables from rocking to and fro due to the motion created by the drilling action.

Norman de Garis Davies commented upon the multiple drilling scene in the tomb of Rekhmire.[30] He noted that the bow-string loops around each of the three yellow-coloured drills in turn, which revolve in the thicker red shafts. From this, it must be assumed that the drill-rods were made of bronze. They were estimated to be 5 mm in diameter and between 20 and 30 cm in length, and the string to be 2 mm in diameter, if compared with the diameter of the bronze drill-rods. The handles are all closely held together by the driller's left hand. Each drill-rod must, therefore, be rotating in a hole bored into the lower end of a handle. The lower ends of the rods rotate in the holes being drilled into the stone beads. This means that each drill-rod was spinning rapidly, clockwise and anticlockwise, each end supported in a bearing-hole.

A tomb representation of drilling with a bow-driven metal wood drill shows it forced into a wooden handle; a separate capstone acts as the top bearing.[31] The simultaneous multiple bead-drilling displayed in the Theban tombs takes this technique one stage further. Instead of the bow-string acting upon the waisted wooden handle, the string was now made to act upon the drill-rod itself. If this technology is accepted, then the length and the construction of the bow now become apparent. The handles are similar in length, about 30–40 cm, and taper from the top to the bottom. Their average diameter appears to be about 1.5 cm, at the lower ends. The experiments showed that this diameter allows up to five handles to be gripped in a line with one hand.

Manufacture of the reconstructed tools[32]

The bow-shaft could have been made from a slim, seasoned, arc-shaped branch or a common reed cane. Although the tomb representations of the bow-shaft do not show leaf joints,[33] reed blowpipes are depicted in the tomb of Pepionkh at Meir, without the leaf joints.[34] Possibly, the artists who painted the illustrations at Thebes were showing arc-shaped reeds.

The reconstructed bow-shaft was manufactured from a 1.5 cm-diameter cane, 120 cm long (Figure 8.13). The cane was bent into an arc, and left bent in this position for several hours; although the cane relaxed a little after release, it substantially retained its new shape. Tests were also conducted with a 1.5 cm-diameter arc-shaped branch. Both types of bow-shaft possessed similar controlled resistance to bending, which placed a reasonable amount of tension upon the string.

The three bronze drill-rods (Figure 8.14) were cast into vertical, open moulds in sand, made by a 5 mm-diameter rod of wood. The average length equalled 15.5 cm. The melted bronze consisted of 95 per cent copper and 5 per cent tin, by weight. These rods were cast without difficulty, but an occasional blow-hole, a small bubble of gas trapped in the casting, did occur. These small blow-holes did not affect the use of the rods. The drilling ends were finished by grinding them on a piece of sandstone. The points measured 2 mm in diameter, tapering slightly

FIGURE 8.13   The reconstructed arc-shaped bow, together with the three-legged hollow drilling table

Source: Image by J. Stocks

FIGURE 8.14   Three reconstructed Theban-type bronze drill-rods

Source: Image by J. Stocks

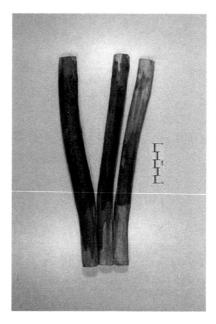

FIGURE 8.15   The set of three reconstructed wooden handles

Source: Image by J. Stocks

for a length of 3 mm; this dimension applied for the drilling tests on calcite and serpentine. Later, for the tests upon the quartz and the amethyst specimens, one point was ground to a diameter of 1 mm. The top ends of the rods were already rounded, due to the contraction of the bronze into a meniscus. This rounded contour was given a final polish, acting as a perfect bearing within the hole in the wooden handle. Two additional rods of steel were manufactured, in order to test drive five drill-rods simultaneously.

A set of three handles (Figure 8.15) and a set of five handles (Figure 8.16) were made from suitably seasoned tree branches. One of the drill-rod's upper ends was heated to a red colour, and made to burn a hole into each handle. The holes were burnt out to a depth of 10 mm; this technique ensured that they were slightly larger in diameter than the drill-rods, for clearance. The rounded end of the drill-rod created a similarly shaped bearing surface in the hole, and the carbonized layer facilitated the drill-rods freely to spin within their bearing holes, without additional lubrication.

As previously mentioned, the ancient artists have provided no clues regarding the manner with which the beads were fastened to the tables; each representation shows the drilling table in side elevation. There is no sign of any beads projecting up from the tops of the tables: they could have been similar to the reconstruction depicted in Figure 8.13. The reconstructed table is shown with a hollow top, which could have been filled with mud (Figure 8.17), similar to the manner in which mud bricks were made in a wooden frame.

FIGURE 8.16   The set of five reconstructed wooden handles

Source: Image by J. Stocks

FIGURE 8.17   One of the test mud blocks, with trial stone pieces held firmly within it

Source: Image by J. Stocks

Experiments with beads set into mud, which was then allowed to harden, demonstrated that they may conveniently be set in a line and spaced apart to match the distance between each drill-rod (see Figure 8.17). Also, any bead size or shape can be coped with in this manner, and may be placed at whatever angle is required for each perforation. After drilling, beads may easily be broken out of the dried mud in an undamaged state. Further, all long beads can be broken out after drilling halfway, and reset into a new mud block for the second half of the drilling operation. The experimental wet drilling abrasive did not soften the mud block's hold upon the beads. Other methods may have been in use during ancient times. For example, large and small beads could have been forced into holes drilled into the top of the wooden table. However, as the craftworker was aware of mud brick manufacture, the technology could have been adapted for multiple bead-drilling. The experimental mud block shrank as it dried within the reconstructed 20 cm-square hollow table-top, opening up a gap of 10 mm on all sides. The Puyemre rope, with its two knots, may have been made to secure such a block, in addition to keeping the table steady.

Experimental bead-drilling

The reconstructed multiple drilling equipment, using three drills simultaneously, followed the scene in the tomb of Rekhmire (Figure 8.18), while the testing of five drills followed the illustration in the tomb of Neferrenpet (Figure 8.19). The drilling rates, and the drill-rod wear rates for each type of stone tested, were recorded (see Table 8.1). Three pieces of calcite were carved into spherical beads, and a pointed flint tool was used to bore a small depression into each of their surfaces for

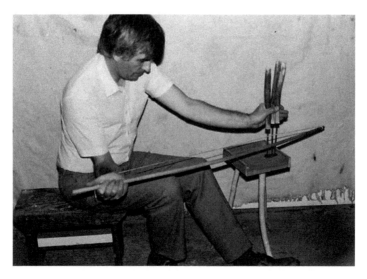

FIGURE 8.18   The reconstructed set of three drill-rods in operation

Source: Image by J. Stocks

FIGURE 8.19   The reconstructed set of five drill-rods is being revolved

Source: Image by J. Stocks

centralizing the drills' points. The beads were then set into a stiff mud mixture in a line, approximately 1.5 cm apart. After drying, each bead was immovably set into the mud block.

In ancient times, a bow-string was securely fastened to one end of the bow-shaft, the end furthest away from the operator, but the other end of the bow-string probably needed a loop, or a noose, which loosely fastened around the bow-shaft where the artisan's right hand held it. Sliding the loop toward the centre of the shaft would slacken the bow-string. This loop technique was adopted for the experiments; with the string considerably loosened, enough slack is made to allow one turn around each of the drill-rods. The turns are all in the same direction (Figure 8.20). The loop is now moved toward the end of the shaft, placing tension upon the string. All of the rods are engaged into the depressions in the beads' surfaces and each handle located onto the top end of a drill-rod, runny paste then being spooned onto the beads' points (Figure 8.21). The left hand tightly grips the handles together, with the thumb in front and the fingers behind.

The right hand now clasps the end of the bow-shaft, the string passing behind the thumb (Figure 8.22). The tension induced by pulling the thumb backwards ensures that each drill-rod is gripped by the bow-string. An examination of the Rekhmire representation shows the operator with the right arm outstretched, with the drill-rods at the opposite end of the bow. This initial position was imitated at the commencement of the experiment.

Tests now determined that the right arm could drive the bow forward until the hand reached the mid-chest position, that is, with the elbow almost fully bent, a distance of approximately 60 cm. In order to keep the bow travelling in a straight line, the right wrist progressively bent backwards on the inward stroke and, conversely, forwards on the outward stroke. All of the drill-rods revolved simultaneously. At

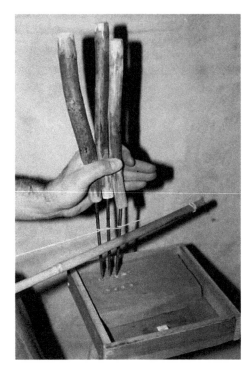

FIGURE 8.20 Close-up of the bow-string driving each drill-rod

Source: Image by J. Stocks

FIGURE 8.21 Determining a bronze drill-rod's cutting rate using the fine abrasive paste

Source: Image by J. Stocks

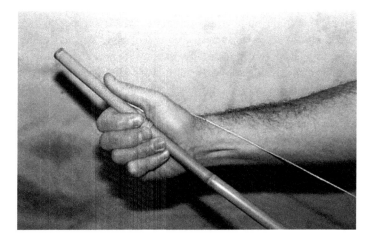

FIGURE 8.22   The thumb placed between the bow-string and the bow-shaft, which automatically adjusts the string's tension during drilling

Source: Image by J. Stocks

the end of the return stroke, the arm became almost fully straightened. The experiments determined that the tension imposed by the string on the drill-rods is critical. Should the tension be too great, the drill-rods would not turn. Conversely, if the tension was too weak, the string slipped around the drill-rods without turning them at all. It was quite noticeable that, whilst the bow was being driven to and fro, the right-hand thumb automatically adjusted the tension on the string.

Calculations based upon a stroke length of 60 cm, a rod diameter of 5 mm and a stroke rate of 40 per minute indicate that each rod revolves at 1,500 revolutions/minute. This, of course, takes no account of the extremely rapid acceleration and deceleration at the beginning and ending of each stroke. A stroke rate of 40 per minute was found to be the optimum frequency necessary to keep up high drill-rod rotations, and also to maintain the drilling action without instability or undue friction to the string. The actions necessary to maintain drilling are not too tiring. The weight the left arm naturally places upon the drill-rods is enough to make them cut into the stone. It is clear that each drill-rod needs its own handle, rather than one large handle containing all the bearing holes. In this scenario, any drill-rod changing its length over a period, due to excessive wear in relation to the other drill-rods in the same group, would rotate in its bearing hole, but no pressure could be exerted upon that rod. Consequently, no further penetration would take place. With independent handles, this difficulty is remedied by posture changes from time to time, which allows an individual handle to change its vertical position relative to the other handles.

Workers depicted in the tomb scenes are shown operating two rods (Puyemre), three rods (Rekhmire, Amenhotpe-si-se, Sebekhotep and Nebamun and Ipuky), four rods (Sebekhotep and Neferrenpet) and five rods (Neferrenpet). The use of five drill-rods in a line is not impossible. Tests with that number of rods demonstrated that the technique is just feasible. However, it is likely that the most skilled artisans were employed for driving five drills. It is instructive to note that the scenes show a progression in the numbers of drills in use, which is related to their chronological order; this indicates an increased confidence and skill in drilling multiple numbers of stone beads by a single craftworker over a period of nearly 200 years.

Experiments were conducted to establish if the ancient craftworker could have used smaller diameter rods. Five 2 mm-diameter copper rods, each hammered from a strip of copper, were manufactured for test. One rod was 26.2 cm long, two rods were 13.4 cm long, and two rods measured 6.8 cm in length. The longest rod bent when an attempt was made to rotate it, being also the fate of the 13.4 cm-long rods. The 6.8 cm-long rods could be rotated, but only with difficulty. It is clear that the turning moment imposed upon the drill-rods, by a similar diameter string, is too great for the rods to revolve with ease. Therefore, if it is accepted that the diameter of the ancient string in use for multiple bead-drilling bows was 2 mm, then the suggested diameter of 5 mm for the drill-rods may be near to the true ancient dimension. The ratio of string diameter to drill-rod diameter (2 mm to 5 mm) gave good rotational results, even with five rods. There can be no doubt that the New Kingdom craftworker possessed the ability to cast 5 mm-diameter drill-rods. The test drill-rods were used in a fully annealed state; this better allowed the tiny angular quartz fragments in the abrasive to embed themselves into the metal.

It was noticeable that the point of each test drill changed into a blunted, rounded shape (Figure 8.23), caused by the wobbling action of the drills. The drill-point and the perforation walls were striated by the tiny quartz fragments – mostly between 50 and 150 microns across – in the abrasive paste, but these striations are extremely fine in appearance. An examination of an 8 mm-diameter carnelian bead (Figure 8.24) in The Manchester Museum (63153) revealed similar striations. Flint tools produce quite different marks.

FIGURE 8.23   A close-up view of a bronze rod's drilling point

Source: Image by J. Stocks

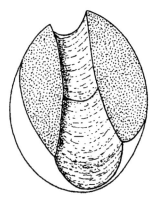

FIGURE 8.24   A section of an 8 mm-diameter carnelian bead (from MM 63153), revealing fine striations in the threading hole

Source: Image by D. Stocks from the Manchester Museum, The University of Manchester

Discussion of the experimental results

At the beginning of this chapter, single bead-drills were investigated. Clearly, the Kerma bronze drills, some with square-sectioned upper ends, were force-fitted into waisted wooden handles. The top bearing for such a drill was usually a capstone; the operator gripped the capstone, the handle being turned by the bowstring. The Theban illustrations show that two important inventive steps must have occurred prior to, or during, the New Kingdom period. First, the bronze drill-rod was lengthened and allowed to rotate in a lengthened wooden handle. This technological innovation meant that the original capstone bearing was dispensed with, and the bearing end reversed to the lower end of the longer handle. The handle was now used as a true handle, instead of being driven with a bow, and the bronze drill-rods were directly driven with the bow-string.

Second, the technique of driving several drill-rods was invented, the simultaneous multiple drilling technology being possible because several handles could be gripped by a single hand. The development of multiple bead-drilling technologies caused a lengthening of the bow, coupled with a change in the physiological approach to this type of drilling.

The results in Table 8.1 show that 10 mm-diameter calcite, serpentine, quartz and amethyst spherical beads could be drilled singly in 60, 100, 240 and 300 minutes respectively.[35] But the simultaneous use of three drill-rods increased the rate of production to three beads in a similar time period, or one bead per 20, 33, 80 and 100 minutes respectively.[36] In the tomb of Sebekhotep, the use of four drill-rods could have produced beads at the rate of one per 15, 25, 60 and 75 minutes respectively; and the use of five drill-rods could possibly have produced these beads at the rate of one per 12, 20, 48 and 60 minutes respectively.

The studies and the experimental work show that simultaneous multiple drilling of stone beads was feasible, and perforation must have been the most difficult part of the stone bead production process. All of the evidence examined – archaeological, pictorial and the experimental work – confirms that ancient craftworkers adapted earlier, single bead-drilling techniques into the multiple drilling technology of the Eighteenth and Nineteenth Dynasties. The implication from the representations, particularly from that of Sebekhotep's tomb illustration (see Figure 8.9), is that factory techniques for mass-producing stone beads were operating in the New Kingdom period at Thebes, and this must greatly have reduced the time, and the cost, for the manufacture of beads, amulets and pendants.

The Sebekhotep illustration is most revealing. It shows three out of the four jewellery-making steps involving stone beads – those of drilling, polishing and threading. The first step, that of shaping and smoothing the bead, is missing. However, it is clear that this small factory was making a complete jewellery product, and it is likely that jewellery factories existed in other workers' towns during this period. The availability of much larger numbers of stone beads, amulets and pendants, at a lower cost, must surely have meant that more people had access to jewellery products. The consequences of new industrial methods are felt today; lower production costs are transmitted downward to many parts of society. An example is the availability of motor vehicles at a relatively low cost, compared to their great complexity and large use of man-made and natural materials.

The evolution of the Theban multiple drilling technique is closely related to our own mass-production drilling capability – the driving of multiple drilling machines with electric motors under computer control. The Theban artisans must be viewed as the world's first known innovators of mass-production methods, an industrial process that didn't make its appearance in our civilization until the modern industrial revolution began in the eighteenth century.

Notes

1 A. Lucas and J.R. Harris, *Ancient Egyptian Materials and Industries*, London: Edward Arnold, 1962, p. 41.
2 Ibid.
3 H.C. Beck, 'Classification and nomenclature of beads and pendants', *Archaeologia* 77, 1927, p. 77, pls II, III.
4 W.M.F. Petrie, *The Arts and Crafts of Ancient Egypt*, Edinburgh and London: T.N. Foulis, 1909, pp. 121, 125.
5 Beck, 'Classification and nomenclature of beads and pendants', pp. 60–9.
6 Ibid.
7 Petrie, *Arts and Crafts*, p. 119; G.A. Reisner, *Excavations at Kerma*, Cambridge, MA: Peabody Museum of Harvard University, 1923, parts IV-V, pp. 91–2; Beck, 'Classification and nomenclature of beads and pendants', pp. 69–70.
8 See BM 920.
9 G. Goyon, 'Les instruments de forage sous l'ancien empire Égyptien', *Jaarbericht Ex Oriente Lux* VII, 1967, pl. XXII.
10 A.J. Gwinnett and L. Gorelick, 'An ancient repair on a Cycladic statuette analysed using scanning electron microscopy', *Journal of Field Archaeology* 10, 1983, pp. 378–84.

11 E. Mackay, 'Bead making in ancient Sind', *Journal of the American Oriental Society* 57, 1937, pp. 1–7, pls II, 5, III, 5, 8.

12 J.E. Quibell and F.W. Green, *Hierakonpolis II*, London: British School of Archaeology in Egypt, 1902, p. 11.

13 T.E. Peet, *The Cemeteries of Abydos, Part II, 1911–1912*, London: Egypt Exploration Society, 1914, p. 2.

14 M.A. Hoffman, *Egypt before the Pharaohs: The Prehistoric Foundations of Egyptian Civilization*, London and Henley: Routledge and Kegan Paul, 1980, p. 154.

15 Reisner, *Excavations at Kerma*, pp. 93–4.

16 D.A. Stocks, 'Industrial technology at Kahun and Gurob: Experimental manufacture and test of replica and reconstructed tools with indicated uses and effects upon artefact production', unpublished thesis, University of Manchester, 1988, vol. I, p. 216, vol. II, p. 351, pls XX, b, XXI, a.

17 Stocks, 'Industrial technology', vol. I, p. 217.

18 Reisner, *Excavations at Kerma*, pp. 93–4.

19 For example, G. Brunton, *Lahun I, The Treasure*, London: British School of Archaeology in Egypt, 1920, pl. I, showing an amethyst necklace and pectoral belonging to Senusret II and containing 141 spherical beads.

20 Reisner, *Excavations at Kerma*, pp. 93–4.

21 W.M.F. Petrie, *Kahun, Gurob and Hawara*, London: Kegan Paul, Trench, Trübner, and Co., 1890, p. 22, pl. XIV, 8.

22 W. Wreszinski, *Atlas zur altägyptischen Kulturgeschichte*, Leipzig: Hinrichs, 1923, vol. I, pl. 154; N. de G. Davies, *The Tomb of Puyemrê at Thebes*, New York: Metropolitan Museum of Art, 1922, vol. I, pl. XXIII.

23 P.E. Newberry, *The Life of Rekhmara*, London: Archibald Constable, 1900, pls XVII, XVIII; Wreszinski, *Atlas*, vol. II, pl. 313; N. de G. Davies, *The Tomb of Rekh-mi-Re at Thebes*, New York: Metropolitan Museum of Art, 1943, vol. II, pl. LIV.

24 Wreszinski, *Atlas*, vol. II, pl. 242; N. de G. Davies, *The Tombs of Two Officials of Tuthmosis IV at Thebes*, London: Egypt Exploration Society, 1923, vol. II, pl. X.

25 BM 920. The painting was removed from the wall of Tomb 63 at Thebes in 1869.

26 Wreszinski, *Atlas*, vol. II, pl. 360; N. de G. Davies, *The Tomb of Two Sculptors at Thebes*, New York: Metropolitan Museum of Art, 1925, pl. XI.

27 Wreszinski, *Atlas*, vol. I, pl. 73, a, b.

28 Davies, *Rekhmire*, vol. II, pls LII, LIII.

29 Wreszinski, *Atlas*, vol. I, pl. 154.

30 Davies, *Rekhmire*, vol. I, p. 49.

31 Ibid., vol. II, pls LII, LIII.

32 D.A. Stocks, 'Bead production in Ancient Egypt', *Popular Archaeology* 7 (5), 1986, pp. 2–7; Stocks, 'Industrial technology', vol. I, pp. 230–4; D.A. Stocks, 'Ancient factory mass-production techniques: Indications of large-scale stone bead manufacture during the Egyptian New Kingdom Period', *Antiquity* 63, 1989, pp. 526–31.

33 Compare Davies, *Rekhmire*, vol. II, pl. LIV (a bead driller's bow-shaft) with vol. II, pl. LIII (a jeweller's reed blowpipe).

34 A.M. Blackman and M.R. Apted, *The Rock Tombs of Meir*, London: Egypt Exploration Society, 1953, part V, pl. XVII.

35 Stocks, 'Ancient factory mass-production techniques: Indications of large-scale stone bead manufacture during the Egyptian New Kingdom Period', p. 530.

36 Ibid.

9

BY-PRODUCTS FROM A BYGONE AGE

Modern by-product materials

The technological success of modern society is dependent upon interaction between separate parts of industry. For example, one industry may produce a particular waste product, a consequence of its manufacturing process, which can be used in a totally different kind of industry. An instance of this practice is the manufacture of particle board from wood dust, a by-product of saw mills, which is mixed with adhesive and compressed to make a cheap, alternative material to timber. Another by-product is the fine ash produced by burning coal in power stations. This material is turned into building blocks, and is also used for motorway construction.

An enigma of Ancient Egyptian craftworking is the origin of the materials used for faience cores and glazes. Ancient Egyptian workers used copper tubular drills, with sand abrasive, to hollow stone artifacts;[1] the waste powders, rich in quartz, also contained copper from the drills. Did ancient craftworkers use these powders for making faience cores, blue and green glazes and, perhaps, blue frits and pigment?[2] To explore this possibility, the characteristics of ancient faience are compared with the microstructure and composition of experimentally made ceramics.

Ancient faience: a brief description

Faience was employed to make amulets, beads, scarabs, inlay for jewellery, statuettes, shawabti figures, vessels and tiles. Two particularly good examples of faience statuettes are to be found in The Metropolitan Museum of Art, New York: a Twelfth Dynasty blue glazed hippopotamus (MMA 17.9.1), from the tomb of Senbi at Meir, is decorated with open and closed lotus flowers, and an Eighteenth Dynasty glazed representation of Amenhotep III (MMA 1972.125), a deeper blue than the hippopotamus, is in the form of a sphinx. In Berlin is an Eighteenth Dynasty

DOI: 10.4324/9781003269922-13

9 cm-diameter blue faience bowl (Egyptian Museum, Berlin 4562), which is decorated with three fish depicted at 120° to one another. An equilateral triangle, at the bowl's centre, serves as the head for all three fish.[3] These superb examples represent art combined with technical brilliance. The production of faience was extensive during the whole of Egyptian history, with most glazes being blue or green. However, more rarely, violet, white, yellow, black and red types have been found.[4]

The first Ancient Egyptian glazed material, found by Guy Brunton and Gertrude Caton-Thompson[5] in grave deposits dated to the Badarian culture of Upper Egypt, consisted of carved and drilled steatite beads covered with a transparent and glossy glaze. It appears clear in cross-section, but in looking directly at the surface the optical effect is of translucency.[6] Glazes containing malachite (a copper ore) produced the greenish-blue colour, which imitated the rarer lapis lazuli and turquoise.[7]

About 4000 BCE, stone cores were replaced with ceramic ones,[8] made mainly from finely divided (ground) sand, but occasionally of comparatively coarser sand, which was modelled into shapes; these powders may have been obtained from the boring of stone vessels with hand-held stone borers using coarse sand as the abrasive. Cores also contain minor amounts of lime and either natron – a naturally occurring alkaline mixture of the sodium salts, carbonate, bicarbonate, chloride and sulphate – or plant ashes. Often very friable, they are frequently white, or practically white in colour, but can be tinted brown, grey, yellow, sometimes very slightly blue or green.[9] In the core, minute angular particles of quartz are bonded together by varying amounts of interstitial glass, and covered with an alkali-based glaze, typically coloured blue by copper.[10]

A summary by Pamela Vandiver[11] of a composite range of chemical analyses of the core material from a study of hundreds of faience objects contained in the Ashmolean Museum, Oxford and the Museum of Fine Arts, Boston, Massachusetts, shows 92–99 per cent SiO_2 (silicon dioxide), 1–5 per cent CaO (calcium oxide [lime]), 0.5–3 per cent Na_2O (sodium oxide), with small quantities of CuO (copper oxide), Al_2O_3 (aluminium oxide), TiO_2 (titanium dioxide), MgO (magnesium oxide) and K_2O (potassium oxide).

Most authorities accept kiln-firing temperatures for faience of 800–1,000°C.[12] A significant number of Ancient Egyptian faience cores[13] show that many particle sizes are less than 50 microns in diameter; even when coarser-grained quartz (100–200 microns in diameter) predominates, significant amounts of fine-grained quartz, less than 50 microns in diameter, are still present.[14] Dynastic cores, moulded, or modelled, from a stiff paste,[15] were glazed by efflorescence[16] (the firing of a core containing a glazing component, which partially rises to the surface during drying and fuses to become the glaze), or by cementation[17] (the firing of a dry core buried in a glazing powder), or by direct application of a glazing slurry to a dry core's surface before firing.[18]

Many thousands of pottery moulds for faience beads, pendants, scarabs and shawabtis have been found at Tell el-Amarna, Memphis, Thebes, Gurob, Qantir, Naukratis, Tell el-Yahudiyeh and other places by Flinders Petrie and others.[19] Petrie found the remains of siliceous paste still adhering to the moulds.[20] Moulds were open,[21] so separate ones were needed for the front and the back of an object, which were joined together with a moist paste before glazing took place. After naturally drying in the air, cores could be given greater detail by engraving them with flint points.[22] Some cores were made with a thick copper wire embedded within them, fired, and the wire removed to leave a stringing hole. An 8.1 cm-long copper wire used for this purpose, CM JE64523, was found by Mahmud Hamza at Qantir.

The glaze consists of a soda-lime-silica mixture,[23] generally 60–70 per cent silica, 16–20 per cent soda and 3–5 per cent lime.[24] Copper oxide content is variable. For example, Alfred Lucas's[25] analysis of a Nineteenth Dynasty tile's glaze showed 1.1 per cent CuO; analyses by Vandiver and W.D. Kingery[26] of faience glazes ranging from the Predynastic to the New Kingdom period found the lowest CuO content to be 1.5 per cent (an average of 5 pieces) and the highest to be 18.1 per cent (an average of 4 pieces). Analyses of the glazes of two New Kingdom faience rings (British Museum Research Laboratory specimens 16319 and 16321) by M.S. Tite show CuO content to be 9.7 per cent and 9.5 per cent respectively.

Experimental faience manufacture

In the Manchester drilling tests with a copper tube and sand abrasive, the powdered product contained, on average, by weight for granite, 97.7 per cent sand, 1.1 per cent stone and 1.2 per cent copper; for hard limestone, 94.46 per cent, 4.93 per cent and 0.61 per cent; for calcite 94.1 per cent, 5.43 per cent and 0.46 per cent. The usual amounts of sand consumed to grind away 1 cm^3 of granite, hard limestone and calcite were 200–250, 50 and 45 g respectively, and the times for grinding away 1 cm^3 of these stones were 40, 5 and 2 minutes respectively. The Aswan time for grinding away 1 cm^3 of the rose granite, with a three-worker drilling team, was 11 minutes, with a two-worker sawing team, 5 minutes. (See Tables 4.2, 4.3, 4.6, 4.7.)

If any quantity of sand is ground until a roughly homogeneous powder is produced, then most particles are 50–150 microns in diameter, with some of approximately 200 microns in diameter; a further short grinding period rapidly reduces most particle sizes to 50–80 microns. It could be distinguished, by listening to the sounds of grinding, and noticing the feel of the drilling action, whether the powder was ground to these fine dimensions.

After some unsuccessful experiments, a stiff paste, made from a mixture of 99 per cent of the powder obtained from drilling the hard limestone (Figure 9.1), or from 99 per cent of the calcite derived powder, and 1 per cent NaHCO$_3$ (sodium bicarbonate), produced a practically white, friable core (Figure 9.2).[27] After drying, each core was fired at a temperature of 850°C, and allowed to cool without a soak time; there were the minutest specks of blue in the core material. Using a scanning electron microscope to analyse the core (Figure 9.3) made from the hard limestone-derived powder (Table 9.1) found it similar to ancient faience in microstructure, especially in quartz angularity and particle size. The bulk composition is similar, with slightly lower silica and higher lime.[28]

FIGURE 9.1   The whitish, waste product powder obtained from drilling hard limestone with a copper tube and sand

Source: Image by J. Stocks

FIGURE 9.2   A test core, made from hard limestone–derived powder

Source: Image by J. Stocks

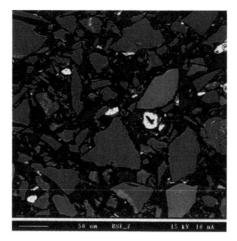

FIGURE 9.3   Scanning electron micrograph of a core, made from the hard limestone-derived powder. Scale bar = 50 microns

Source: Courtesy of M.S. Tite and the Research Laboratory for Archaeology and the History of Art, Oxford University

TABLE 9.1 Analyses of the experimental core and glaze

	Calculated composition (%)			Mean bulk analyses (%)	
	core	glaze		core	glaze
SiO_2	93.56	73.8	SiO_2	90.25	74.55
Al_2O_3		0.11	TiO_2	0.01	0.05
Na_2O	0.37	9.23	Al_2O_3	3.47	0.08
Cu	0.59	0.9	FeO	0	0.42
CaO	2.72		MnO	0	0.35
			MgO	0.2	0
			CaO	4.35	12.04
			Na_2O	0.95	11.1
			K_2O	0.52	0.86
			P_2O_5		0
			SO_3		0.01
			CuO	0.24	0.54

An experimental runny glaze, made with 75 per cent granite-derived powder and 25 per cent $NaHCO_3$ (see Table 9.1), was directly applied to an unfired core. This glaze was manufactured from a drilling powder, containing copper, produced several years before and including some quartz particles up to 200 microns in diameter. When the sample was fired at 950°C, without a soak time, a deep blue

FIGURE 9.4   A glaze sample, made from the granite-derived powder

Source: Image by J. Stocks

vitreous glaze was created (Figure 9.4).[29] A further short grinding period would soon have reduced the quartz and copper to smaller particles, improving the glaze's appearance by a more uniform dispersal and dissolution of the copper.

Discussion

The experimental faience manufacture indicates that the powders derived from drilling hard limestone and calcite are ideal for making cores, and that the hard stone–derived powders (more copper particles) are suitable for blue glazes. The powders are satisfactorily ground to the particle sizes and angularity seen in ancient faience cores, and the composition of the experimental core is similar to ancient faience.

Frit is distinguishable from faience in that it is all coloured and is not covered in a glaze. Frits may or may not contain a pigment for colour; they are heated high enough to fuse, but not high enough to flow as a glass. Egyptian blue is the most common frit of that colour; it is a sintered, polycrystalline material. Since both faience and Egyptian blue frit are made essentially from the same raw materials,[30] it could be that the frits were manufactured from the waste drilling powders containing more lime, that is, from the sand and the drilled stone. An increased copper content would give a suitable frit powder; differences in the details of the frit's microstructure, mineralogy, texture, hardness and colour would depend on the relative amounts of SiO_2, CaO, CuO and alkali, on the particle size of the powder and on the temperature (between 900 and 1,000°C) and the length of the firing time (up to 24 hours).[31] If the CuO content exceeds the CaO content, then Egyptian blue crystals, i.e. calcium-copper tetrasilicate ($CaO \cdot CuO \cdot (SiO_2)_4$, are formed, and the frit exhibits an intense blue colour.[32] Conversely, if the CaO content exceeds the CuO content, the copper oxide remains dissolved in the glass phase to produce a pale blue colour.[33]

Calculated composition and bulk composition analyses of the experimental faience core and glaze. They were made from powders derived from the drilling of hard limestone and granite with a copper tube and sand abrasive. The hard limestone powder contained 94.5 – SiO_2 (quartz), 4.9 – $CaCO_3$ (limestone) and 0.6 – Cu (copper). The granite powder contained 97.7 – SiO_2 (quartz), 1.1 – granite and 1.2 – Cu. (Analysis of the glaze by Chris Doherty; analyses of the core and the glaze by courtesy of M.S. Tite and the Research Laboratory for Archaeology and the History of Art, Oxford University.)

M.S. Tite states[34] that a fine-textured, light Egyptian blue was created by grinding the coarse-textured product from a first firing into a fine powder which, after dampening and reshaping, was fired for a second time at a somewhat lower temperature (850–950°C). Small, fine-textured objects of Egyptian blue were made using this two-stage firing cycle. In addition, the coarse-textured material would have been crushed for use as a blue pigment, a range of blues from dark to light being obtained by grinding to increasingly fine particle size.[35]

After ca. 3600 BCE, craftworkers did not need to produce powders specially made for faience, nor for blue frits and pigment, because the powders required were available as a by-product from the drilling of stone with copper tubes and sand abrasive. The ability to model quartz-based powders into cores after ca. 4000 BCE probably initiated a change from carved steatite ones, and blue and green glazes, made from copper-contaminated drilling powders, possibly supplanted earlier methods of colouring them with malachite. The expansion of stone vessel-making in the Naqada II period may have stimulated a commensurate increase in faience production: although there was a decline in hard-stone vessel manufacture during the Early Dynastic period, the making of calcite vessels continued unabated. The construction of hard-stone sarcophagi from the Fourth Dynasty onward, and other hard-stone artifacts hollowed with copper drill-tubes and cut with saws using sand abrasive, continued to make powders heavily contaminated with copper particles available for blue and green faience glazes.

If indeed the waste powders from drilling stones were the basis for ancient faience, then the varying mineralogical content seen in these ceramics can be traced to differences in the drilled stones and the sand abrasive, particularly with regard to the lime content. Also, the metallurgical content of the coppers and bronzes used to make the tubular drills and saws, whether from newly smelted ores, or from the metal obtained from the melting and casting of worn tools, would be different for each tube and saw. There is some evidence to indicate a direct connection between the metallurgical and glazing industries. J. Riederer's[36] analyses of Late Period bronze artifacts in three regions of Egypt – Lower, Central and Upper – allowed Alexander Kaczmarczyk and R.E.M. Hedges[37] to compare the average tin concentration in the bronzes with the tin concentration in the faience artifacts found in each region. The results clearly showed that the tin content of blue and green faience mirrored the composition of contemporary bronzes coming from the same geographical region.

This finding supports a proposition that the reason for this correspondence is that the waste powders, containing bronze particles worn off the bronze stone-cutting tubular drills and saws in use with quartz sand abrasive, were employed for making faience objects in the same geographical area. It is possible, therefore, that a similar correlation existed throughout the Dynastic era, and the preceding Naqada II and Naqada III/Dynasty 0 periods.

Although at present the ancient use of these powders cannot *directly* be proved, the experiments indicate that they should be considered as a material employed for some ancient faience. If it is assumed that the hard-stone waste powders did form the basis for glazes, it may be that sometimes the faience worker added extra copper to the powder, or less sand was employed for the drilling, increasing the percentage content of the copper. Finally, a question needs to be asked. Why would craftworkers continue separately to produce the powders for faience when similar powders were already being created by widespread industrial practices whose origins commenced in the Predynastic period?

Further proof may be forthcoming. If field archaeologists can identify the waste powders from the drilling and sawing of stone and, through analyses, associate them with the production of faience, blue frit or blue pigment in the same location, a truly positive answer may yet be given to this question. A promising place where these correlations might be made is Tell el-Amarna, where production processes common to the manufacture of pottery, faience, frits, glass and pigment[38] occurred at this Eighteenth Dynasty site.

Notes

1 W.M.F. Petrie, *Tools and Weapons*, London: British School of Archaeology in Egypt, 1917, pp. 45–6; A. Lucas and J.R. Harris, *Ancient Egyptian Materials and Industries*, London: Edward Arnold, 1962, p. 74; G.A. Reisner, *Mycerinus, the Temples of the Third Pyramid at Giza*, Cambridge, MA: Harvard University Press, 1931, p. 180.

2 D.A. Stocks, 'Indications of Ancient Egyptian industrial interdependence: Preliminary statement', *The Manchester Archaeological Bulletin* 4, 1989, pp. 21–6.

3 B. Fay, *Egyptian Museum Berlin*, Berlin-Charlottenburg: Ägyptisches Museum, 1984, pp. 22–3.

4 Lucas and Harris, *AEMI*, pp. 160–4.

5 G. Brunton and G. Caton-Thompson, *Badarian Civilisation and Predynastic Remains near Badari*, London: British School of Archaeology in Egypt, 1928, pp. 27–8, 41.

6 P.B. Vandiver and W.D. Kingery, 'Egyptian faience: The first high-tech ceramic', in W.D. Kingery (ed.) *Ceramics and Civilization*, Westerville, OH: American Ceramic Society, 1986, vol. 3, p. 20, Figs 1, 3.

7 Ibid.

8 J.F.S. Stone and L.C. Thomas, 'The use and distribution of faience in the ancient East and prehistoric Europe', *Proceedings of the Prehistoric Society* 22, 1956, p. 37ff.

9 Lucas and Harris, *AEMI*, p. 157; A. Kaczmarczyk and R.E.M. Hedges, *Ancient Egyptian Faience*, Warminster: Aris and Phillips, 1983, p. 123; Vandiver and Kingery, 'Egyptian faience: The first high-tech ceramic', p. 20.

10 M.S. Tite, 'Egyptian blue, faience and related materials: Technological investigations', in R.E. Jones and H.W. Catling (eds) *Science in Archaeology*, London: British School at Athens, 1986, vol. 2, p. 39; M.S. Tite, 'Characterisation of early vitreous materials', *Archaeometry* 29, 1987, pp. 23–4.

11 P.B. Vandiver, 'Technological change in Egyptian faience', in J.S. Olin and A.D. Franklin (eds) *Archaeological Ceramics*, Washington, DC: Smithsonian Institution Press, 1982, p. 167.

12 P.B. Vandiver, 'Appendix A: The manufacture of faience', in A. Kaczmarczyk and R.E.M. Hedges (eds) *Ancient Egyptian Faience*, Warminster: Aris and Phillips, 1983, pp. A10–11, A26ff.

13 M.S. Tite and M. Bimson, 'Faience: An investigation of the microstructures associated with the different methods of glazing', *Archaeometry* 28, 1986, p. 69.

14 Ibid.

15 W.M.F. Petrie, *The Arts and Crafts of Ancient Egypt*, Edinburgh and London: T.N. Foulis, 1909, pp. 115–16, 118–19.

16 C.F. Binns, 'An experiment in Egyptian blue glaze', *Journal of the American Ceramic Society* 15, 1932, pp. 71–2; J.V. Noble, 'The technique of Egyptian faience', *American Journal of Archaeology* 73, 1969, pp. 435–9.

17 C. Kiefer and A. Allibert, 'Les céramiques bleues pharaoniques et leur procéde révolutionnaire d'émaillage', *Industrie Céramique*, May 1968, pp. 395–402.

18 Petrie, *Arts and Crafts*, pp. 107–19; H.C. Beck, 'Notes on glazed stones', *Ancient Egypt and the East*, June 1934, pp. 19–37; Lucas and Harris, *AEMI*, pp. 172–4; P.T. Nicholson and E.J. Peltenburg, 'Egyptian Faience', in P.T. Nicholson and I. Shaw (eds) *Ancient Egyptian Materials and Technology*, Cambridge: Cambridge University Press, 2000.

19 For example, W.M.F. Petrie brought nearly five thousand moulds from Tell el-Amarna, after rejecting large quantities of the commonest (W.M.F. Petrie, *Tell el-Amarna*, London: Methuen, 1894, p. 30).

20 Petrie, *Arts and Crafts*, pp. 118–19.

21 Lucas and Harris, *AEMI*, p. 159.

22 Petrie, *Arts and Crafts*, pp. 115–16.

23 Vandiver, 'Technological change in Egyptian faience', p. 167.

24 M.S. Tite, personal communication.

25 Lucas and Harris, *AEMI*, p. 475.

26 Vandiver and Kingery, 'Egyptian faience: The first high-tech ceramic', p. 29, table II.

27 D.A. Stocks, 'Derivation of Ancient Egyptian faience core and glaze materials', *Antiquity* 71, 1997, p. 180.

28 M.S. Tite, personal communication; Stocks, 'Derivation of Ancient Egyptian faience core and glaze materials', Fig. 1.

29 Stocks, 'Derivation of Ancient Egyptian faience core and glaze materials', p. 181, Fig. 2.

30 Tite, 'Characterisation of early vitreous materials', p. 30.

31 Ibid., p. 27.

32 Ibid.

33 Ibid., p. 33.

34 Tite, 'Egyptian blue, faience and related materials: Technological investigations', p. 41.

35 Ibid.

36 J. Riederer, 'Metal analysis of Egyptian bronzes', *RAS* 3, 1981, pp. 239–43.

37 Kaczmarczyk and Hedges, *Faience*, pp. 274–5.

38 Lucas and Harris, *AEMI*, pp. 340–4.

10

PREDYNASTIC TRANSITIONS AND CONVERGENCE

Evidence of Late Neolithic stone-drilling reed tubes in Egypt's western Delta

The concept of using a bow to rotate a drill for penetrating stones could have been stimulated by workers' experiments with the hollow common reed (*Phragmites communis*), and it is probable that the reed tube remained in use for hollowing out softer-stone artifacts, for example, limestone and calcite vessels, until the introduction of copper smelted from malachite ore (Naqada II period, ca. 3600–3200 BCE) at Maadi, northern Egypt,[1] and also from malachite ore at Gerza.[2] Copying the reed tube's shape in copper immediately facilitated the hollowing of hard-stone vessels in a systematic, faster and safer way by the chain-of-touching-holes method (see Chapter 6, Figure 6.5) than by the previously tedious and physically demanding grinding procedure for carving out hard stone vessels;[3] and the drilling of long, accurate hafting holes in Naqada II hard-stone pear-shaped maceheads.[4]

Several hundred years before the conversion of reed tubes into copper ones, archaeological evidence[5] excavated from the Late Neolithic north-western Egyptian site of Merimde Beni-salame (ca. 4750–4250 BCE) revealed that stoneworkers needed to make narrow, round hafting holes through the long axes of pear-shaped ceremonial maceheads, and across the diameters of spherical maceheads, after initially carving both macehead types with flint tools from slate (geological hardness scale Mohs 4–5), from hard limestone (Mohs 5), and from calcite (Mohs 3–4). See Chapter 1, Table 1.1 for other Mohs hardnesses.

Although flint chisels and punches, and stone grinders, are able easily to work slate, limestone and calcite to shape,[6] the experimental use of flint chisels and punches indicate that their use for cutting out a long, round, narrow hole for a macehead's haft to be fitted accurately, and tightly, into an imperfect perforation would have been too difficult, and inadequate. For fitting a shaft securely into a

DOI: 10.4324/9781003269922-14

smooth, circular straight hole, pierced completely through an already-shaped mac-ehead, the craftworker needed a long straight drill.

It is thought that bow drilling in Egypt originated from the use of the bow and arrow, later developing into the bow-driven fire drill.[7] However, the concept of using a bow to rotate a drilling tool for penetrating stone maceheads could have been discovered by workers using a bow to revolve a prepared, hollow common reed that operated upon sand abrasive for making these hafting holes.

The mature reed's straight, round, hollow and thick-walled woody stem attains a maximum diameter of up to several centimetres, but a craftworker could select a stem suitable for the diameter of the hole envisaged for fitting a strong wooden haft into it. Whilst leaf joints (*nodes*) grow at intervals up the stem, blocking a tube's internal structure at these points, they can be broken through with a sharp-ened, thinner reed. An experimental, flat-ended reed made a satisfactory drill-tube, when rotated by a bow, with raw sand acting as the abrasive.[8] Later in Egyptian history, ca. 3600 BCE, when the smelting of copper ore commenced, a longer reed served as an experimental reconstructed blowpipe, based on a tomb drawing of six long blowpipes in use during the Sixth Dynasty,[9] which allowed assessment of its air flow capability for ancient smelting and melting furnaces' operation.

A series of experimental reed drilling tests[10] were made upon the following stones: soft and hard limestone, calcite, slate, hard sandstone (coarse-grained), hard sandstone (fine-grained) and blue granite (close-grained): all of the tests were car-ried out in Manchester, UK except for the test upon the fine-grained hard sand-stone, which took place in Aswan, Upper Egypt.

Each drilling test utilized a different 1 cm-diameter reed tube, which possessed 2 mm-thick walls. Tubes were rounded at the top, for the capstone, and driven with a bow (see Chapter 4, Figure 4.3); a load of approximately 1 kg/cm^2 was applied upon a tube. The drill-tubes were tested with dry and wet sand abrasive. Overcutting of the holes, due to the lateral motion imposed by the bow, was allowed for when calculating the cutting rates for each drill-tube. Therefore, the *volumes* of the reed stem worn off it, and the stone drilled out, were used to obtain a ratio between the two materials, rather than measuring a tube's lost length and a hole's increased depth. The results are shown in Chapter 4, Table 4.1. Dry sand abrasive caused some splintering to the tube, and the stem spread slightly outward. However, the drill retained its tubular shape, utilizing dry, free-flowing desert sand as the abrasive material, effectively drilling the soft limestone, together with the hard limestone, slate and calcite, these three stones possessing similar wear rate ratios.

The reed drill-tube used with wet sand abrasive soon softened and spread outward and inward, thus completely filling the originally hollow interior with softened stem material. Despite this alteration to the tube's configuration, it per-formed useful work upon the soft limestone, but performed poorly upon the hard limestone, slate, and the calcite. However, because the drill had assumed the shape of a solid stalk, instead of a tube, penetration into the soft limestone was reduced, even though the volumetric rate of drilling remained similar to that of the tube in use with dry sand. The use of a reed tube upon coarse-grained hard sandstone, and upon granite, with wet or dry sand, badly damaged them so that no useful cutting could be achieved.

The drilling experiments with the bow-driven reed tube, using *dry* sand abrasive, proved that slate, limestone and calcite can effectively be drilled using this tube. It is probable that Merimden craftworkers carried out experiments with bow-driven reed tubes, using dry sand abrasive, discovering their capability to drill accurate holes completely through pear-shaped and spherical-shaped slate, limestone and calcite maceheads in a *single* operation, hence permitting the fitting of accurately prepared hafts. A confirmatory experiment to drill hard limestone completely through in a single operation with a bow-driven reed tube produced a straight hole, after the core automatically dropped out as the drill broke through the underneath of the test block, imitating the bottom of an ancient macehead being drilled this way.

The stonecutting copper tubular drill: a primary generator of Egypt's economic strength

The experimental copper tubular drilling of igneous stone employed dry sand abrasive: it is likely that ancient drillers continued to employ dry sand, as they were obliged to do for reed tubes (see Chapter 4). Wet, fluid sand can be used as an abrasive with copper drill-tubes. However, experiments revealed that there are difficulties surrounding the removal of used-up wet sand from a tubular-shaped hole, and further experiments with both dry and wet sand abrasive clearly demonstrated that dry, free-flowing sand is not only far more effective as an abrasive with copper drill-tubes, but can easily be withdrawn from tubular-shaped holes (see next). This finding is important when considering whether ancient drillers could save the dry, finely ground waste sand-based powders, containing copper particles worn off a drill-tube, for manufacturing faience cores and glazes.

Although no copper stone drilling tubes have ever been found in Ancient Egypt, there is archaeological evidence that the ancient stoneworker was aware of the copper tube in the Naqada II period, being confirmed by the finding of a copper tubular bead (Figure 10.1) in a cemetery excavated at Naqada, now at the Petrie Museum of Egyptian and Sudanese Archaeology, University College London (UC5066). Archaeological evidence for copper tubes using sand abrasive in the Naqada II period include a drilled hafting hole in a 55 mm-long, mid-Naqada II pear-shaped hard-stone macehead (Bristol Museum and Art Gallery H 1936).

The tubular drills of copper were a major advance in tool technology compared to the tools employed in the immediately preceding Naqada I period (ca. 4000–3600 BCE). The workers in this period were obliged to create disc-shaped hard-stone maceheads (e.g., Bristol Museum and Art Gallery H 1502), possessing considerably shorter hafting holes to those drilled into Merimden softer-stone pear- and spherical-shaped maceheads.

FIGURE 10.1 A copper tubular bead from a grave at Naqada, Petrie Museum UC5066

Source: Courtesy of the Petrie Museum of Egyptian and Sudanese Archaeology, University College London

Significantly, and with regard to the indicated ancient waste sand-based powders created by drilling stone artifacts with copper tubular drills, it is probable that these powders, containing huge numbers of minute copper particles, were used for making faience cores and glazes, which is substantiated by the finding of faience beads in Naqada II period graves at Gerza.[11] Nicholson states that:

> Glazed steatite and faience beads are known from Predynastic graves at Naqada, Badari, el-Amrah, Matmar, Harageh, Abadiyeh, el-Gerzeh and elsewhere. At these sites semi-precious stones such as turquoise and lapis lazuli, are also found and, although glazed steatite is the most common, faience is definitely established. The glaze is blue or blue-green, probably in imitation of these stones and, perhaps, of green feldspar. The glazing of stones is not to be confused with the making of faience since here glaze is applied to a solid natural object rather than to an artificial body. How the transition to faience was made must remain a matter of speculation, but it is likely that, once discovered, the faience technique was to be preferred, since the irregular core surface would help to give a brighter, more sparkling appearance to the glaze than would the flat surface of steatite or quartz pebbles.[12]

The drilling experiments with copper tubular drills revealed that the finely ground cohesive, copper-contaminated sand/stone powder is gradually forced up the narrow space between the interior wall of a tubular drill rubbing against the drill-core's circumference, this being actuated by the drill's continuous gyratory, or precessional, clockwise and anticlockwise rotations: the powder progressively occupies the inside of the drill-tube just above the top of the core, sticking together as a mass, even though perfectly dry, and eventually filling the whole space between the top of the core and the underneath of the wooden shaft partly driven into the tubular drill, it being rotated by a bow.[13] However, the directly hand-rotated Twist/Reverse Twist Drill (TRTD), fitted with a copper tubular drill, and operating without precessional movement, still causes the drilling powder to be pushed upwards past the core into the space above it. In both cases, packed-in drilling powders can be removed from a tube, after its withdrawal from the tubular-shaped hole, with a sharp blow and saved for future use. This phenomenon explains why workers were able to tubular drill deep holes into heavy igneous, and other hard-stone Dynastic sarcophagi, yet intermittently supply fresh, raw sand abrasive into an unclogged tubular hole in order to continue the drilling process.[14]

For the experimental drilling of each stone type, when required, a drill-tube was necessarily emptied of powder into a designated, identity-marked lidded receptacle: these powders, for each stone type, are uncontaminated with any other material between a drill's removal from a hole and emptying the powder into separate receptacles. Even if the ancient drilling location was subjected to outside weather conditions, such as wind, the powder within a tubular drill would always remain securely in the drill-tube until saved in a receptacle. It is highly likely that ancient drillers did save the drilling powders in this way for faience manufacture, knowing that the highly valuable copper was being ground away off their shortening tubular drills, and mixing with the ground-away stone powders from drilling an ever-deepening hole, together with the sand abrasive, also being ground-up into a powder.

No experimental drilling powders derived from different stones were ever mixed together to make test reconstructed faience cores and glazes (see Chapter 4, Figures 4.14–4.16, and Chapter 9, Figures 9.1–9.3). Only hard limestone— or calcite-derived powders were each separately used to make test reconstructed faience cores, and only granite-derived powders, or any other igneous stone powders, used to make test reconstructed faience glazes: no substance, other than sodium bicarbonate and a little water, was ever added to the waste powders before firing them. The large proportion of silica in the test faience cores and glazes comes mainly from the ground-down sand intimately mixed in the powders, collected intact for each drilling session from inside the drill-tubes. For data on the drilling experiments, see Chapter 4, Tables 4.6 and 4.7.

Transitions and convergence

The introduction of smelting copper from malachite ore (ca. 3600 BCE) required multiple numbers of long reed blowpipes in order to supply significant volumes of air to a smelting furnace, and also up to six blowpipes to enable other furnaces to melt sufficient copper in crucibles for casting tools, such as chisels, adzes and axe-heads, in addition to castings for manufacturing tubular drills (see Chapter 2).

The archaeological and experimental evidence concerning the process of copper tubular drilling of igneous stone varieties, and less hard stones, with sand abrasive, in addition to the experimental manufacture of faience cores and blue glazes, using the waste copper–contaminated powders resulting from operating the reconstructed drills, indicate that a crucial *first transition* of the reed tube into a copper tube now facilitated the drilling of all soft- and hard-stone artifacts, such as vessels, an indicated *convergence* concurrently occurring between the smelting of copper, the making of copper tubular drills, and the manufacture of faience cores and glazes from the waste, sand-rich drilling powders containing variable amounts of copper particles.

The experimental use of copper tubular drills on hard limestone, calcite and igneous stones created light, creamy-coloured cohesive powders from drilling limestone and calcite, and grey-coloured cohesive powders from drilling granite and other igneous stones, the grey colour varying in shade commensurate with the type of drilled stone: for example, basalt-derived powders are a darker grey than granite-derived powders.

Copper content of hard limestone— and calcite-derived powders is quite small, whereas there is an expected larger amount of copper particles within the granite-derived powders.[15] Ancient copper tubular drilling of vessels, made from a variety of stones, must have produced large quantities of finely ground waste sand powders, which contained varying amounts of copper particles, dependent upon the stone type being drilled.

Experimental, dried unfired cores made from the calcite- and limestone-derived powders, combined with small amounts of an alkali, sodium bicarbonate, were glazed by dipping them in a runny mixture manufactured from granite-derived powders, and a greater amount of alkali: firing these samples made blue faience glazes, visually matching ancient blue faience glazes.[16] It is likely that ancient faience workers prepared dried unfired cores by carving extra surface details into them, and then applying a runny glaze to them for firing, there being no need separately to fire a core before applying the glaze to it.

An experimental lozenge-shaped core sample (see Chapter 9, Figure 9.4), made from the hard limestone-derived powder, followed by glazing with granite-derived powder, was sent to Professor Michael Tite, Research Laboratory for Archaeology and the History of Art, Oxford University for analyses. For his comments on the calculated compositions and bulk composition analyses of core and glaze, see Chapter 9 and Table 9.1.

The first glazes known in Ancient Egypt were created in the Badarian period (ca. 4500–3800 BCE). Small carved objects of steatite (hardness Mohs 3), for example, beads, were coated with an alkaline glaze,[17] which is associated with the use of crushed malachite, a copper ore indigenous to Egypt; these Badarian glazes turned green or blue-green, after firing.

Naqada II workers, discussing the sand-based powders packed into copper tubular drills after periods of drilling different stone types, would have reasoned that, because already known ground-up malachite ore created fired green or blue-green glazes to be formed on the surfaces of carved, solid stone objects, then the use of copper, now recently *smelted* from malachite ore to manufacture vitally important copper tubular drills, and capable of hollowing all types of stone vessels with sand abrasive, created powders containing fragments of copper ground off the drills.

Additionally, and importantly, Naqada II stone drillers, noticing the distinctly different shortening times of similar diameter copper tubes for drilling limestone and calcite, and for drilling granite must soon have realized that considerably less copper was abraded from their copper tubes when drilling limestone and calcite, than was ground away when drilling granite.

Nicholson draws attention to:

> Recent analyses of material from Naqada show that the composition of the faience varies considerably even within one grave, suggesting that the copper used in the mixture came either from several sources or from one very variable source.[18]

The copper variations in the sand-based powders recorded in the experimental results for drilling softer and harder stones are similarly comparable to the copper variations seen in the analyses of early ancient faience.

No copper particles were large enough to see directly within the experimental powders. Similarly, ancient stone drillers and faience makers would not have been able see the minutely ground-off copper particles in their powders. The quartz particles, most of them a few microns in size, coat the copper particles, which now become invisible within the rest of the powder. However, immersing and soaking the experimental powder with water, then draining it away using a paper filter, revealed copper particles when examined under a light microscope.

Copper particles are rendered invisible for the following reason: a bow-driven tubular drill of copper is continuously rotated clockwise, and then anticlockwise, and the swirling powders, containing copper and quartz particles in the drilled tubular-shaped hole, rub against each other. If two different materials are put into contact, in this case copper and quartz particles, it is possible for electrons to be pulled from one of the materials to the other. As a result, one of the materials has gained some extra electrons, in this case the copper, which becomes negatively charged, while the other material, quartz, has lost some electrons, becoming positively charged. This process creates static electricity, which attracts the copper and quartz particles together.[19]

Naqada II faience workers, experimenting[20] with these copper tube–generated powders, would have revealed, as did the author's experiments with similarly generated powders, that they could achieve a vital *second transition* from glazing small, carved solid stone objects with crushed malachite powders, to forming, by hand or by using later moulds, cores with calcite-derived, or limestone-derived drilling powders, then glazing the cores with the more heavily, copper-contaminated igneous stone-derived drilling powders. The swirling action of a rotating, and counter-rotating, tubular drill ensures uniform dispersal of the myriad copper particles within the powder, guaranteeing a continuous surface of translucent, hard blue glaze after firing.[21]

In the Naqada II period, the waste powdered product could now become a frequently created *by-product* material available for making faience cores and glazes on a large scale, the copper being used a second time for manufacturing faience, and so avoiding the loss of some of this valuable and expensively produced metal, used first for drilling stone in the form of a tubular drill. And faience workers, for example those at Eighteenth Dynasty Amarna, must have collaborated with the stone vessel workers, who were able to supply relatively large amounts of ground powder ideal for making faience objects, especially the larger volumes of softer-stone powders to make cores, even for large faience artifacts, without the need to do anything else but add water and natron.

When experimentally forming or moulding the resulting thixotropic product, experiments revealed that such a material feels, at first, to be solid, but it begins to soften and flow as it is worked and shaped by the fingers. By comparison, the glazing of carved steatite beads, and other small objects in soft stone in the Badarian period only required miniscule amounts of malachite ore to be crushed and ground. Separately grinding stone, sand and copper, later to be mixed into powders suitable both for cores and glazes, would be slow, tiring and unsatisfactory for the relatively large ancient faience objects to be seen in museum collections, whereas the automatic milling action of a copper tube drilling stone with sand abrasive, whether rotated by a bow for large stone artifacts, or by a group of stone vessel drillers working in one location with TRTD-rotated copper tubes, would steadily produce large volumes of powders suitable for faience manufacture.

The malachite ore, now principally required for manufacturing a growing number of copper drill-tubes, and of other copper cutting tools, such as chisels, generated rising production of both softer- and harder-stone vessels, accompanied by a steady rise in copper consumption, which required continuous, major ore mining and smelting operations.

Later, commencing in the Third Dynasty,[22] the sawing of hard-stone sarcophagi with a long, flat-edged copper saw with sand abrasive, also employed for other large stone artifacts, significantly increased copper use, stimulating additional economic activity connected with faience manufacture, and as an abrasive for drilling stone beads, as well as a smoothing abrasive for surfaces of stone artifacts, including large masonry components.

The experiments strongly indicate, with other evidence contained in the following section, that the waste powders obtained from the drilling and sawing of different stone types with copper or bronze tubular drills and saws, utilizing abrasive desert sand, were the raw materials for manufacturing ancient faience cores and blue and green glazes; and it could be expected that modern scientific analyses[23] of small samples taken from ancient faience artifacts would all differ in mineralogical and metallurgical content (see Chapter 9).

Evidence in support of the considerable use of copper was acquired by Flinders Petrie[24] who measured a slag heap, the product of extensive copper-smelting operations at Wadi Nasb, Sinai: he found that the heap weighed about 100,000 tonnes, confirmed by Alfred Lucas.[25] T.A. Rickard[26] calculated that the slag heap resulted from the smelting of about 5,500 tonnes of copper, with a further one third of copper remaining in the slag. The grinding of very large amounts of copper from stone-drilling tubes and stonecutting saws, over millennia, probably accounts for the significant mining of copper ore at sites in the Sinai, and in Egypt's eastern desert.

Some economic consequences of manufacturing soft- and hard-stone vessels

Following on from the earlier indications of 5,500 tonnes of copper being smelted from its ore at Wadi Nasb, archaeological and experimental evidence assembled in this book now allow indications concerning the ancient effort of manufacturing two differently designed vessels, one from softer stone, the other from an igneous variety, realistically to be assessed.

The first vessel is a Naqada II, mottled black and white diorite lugged oblate spheroidal type (MM 1776, from Hierakonpolis, hardness Mohs 7: see Chapter 5, Figure 5.3). Its external diameter, height and wall thickness are 56 cm, 34 cm and 3 cm respectively: its mouth measures 25 cm in diameter. The second vessel is a translucent Twelfth Dynasty, calcite Duck Jar (MM 5341, from the Southern Pyramid, Mazghuneh, hardness Mohs 3–4). This vertically sawn-down vessel, when originally whole, measured 46 cm in height, 24 cm in diameter at its widest point, and 11.5 cm in diameter at its mouth (see Chapter 5, Figures 5.14, 5.15).

After shaping with flint chisels, punches and scrapers, both vessels needed initially to be drilled out with copper tubes and sand abrasive, either by using the previously discussed chain-of-touching-holes method, using essential copper tubular drills for both calcite and igneous stones, but this method is more suitable for the large-mouthed diorite vessel:[27] or by drilling several, ever larger diameter tubular-shaped holes on the vessels' vertical axes, but a technique more appropriate for the narrow-mouthed calcite vessel (see Chapter 5, Figures 5.28–5.32).

In Chapter 6, the experimentally calculated weight of copper worn from the 11 cm-diameter (six royal fingers) tubular drills, employed to hollow Khufu's rose granite sarcophagus, yielded an approximate total weight of 266 kg, or about an overall length of 18 metres ground off the copper drills during all of the drilling processes, the experimental results being based upon the drilling of granite by a bow-driven 8 cm-diameter copper tubular drill in March 1999 at a rose granite quarry just south of Aswan (see Chapter 4, Figures 4.20–4.26).

The experimental casting of a copper tubular drill in a vertical mould (see Chapter 4, Figure 4.4 and Chapter 5, Figure 5.18) indicates that a 30 cm-long,

11 cm–diameter tube, possessing a wall thickness of 5 mm, can be cast this way. This calculation suggests that about 60 lengths of 30 cm-long copper tubes would be worn away to drill out Khufu's sarcophagus, but, in practice more lengths are required to allow for a short, unusable piece of tube to be returned to the casters to join with newly smelted copper for manufacturing a replacement tubular drill. (See the copper tubular drill cutting ratios, rates and losses of copper for rose granite, diorite, hard sandstone, hard limestone and calcite in Chapter 4, Tables 4.2 and 4.3B).

Unlike the slow wear caused to other copper tools, such as chisels and adzes working on soft limestone, the operation of a copper tubular drill on hard stones, and indeed the Dynastic copper, flat-edged stonecutting saw, inflicted considerable damage to both tools by the sand crystals, making their unique and necessary employment an extremely expensive process. The tools, materials and procedures employed to manufacture softer- and harder-stone vessels are listed in the following sequence, with indicated numbers of workers required for separate manufacturing techniques:

(a) The mining and smelting of copper ores, dated to the early Chalcolithic at sites in southern Sinai,[28] and mined at other sites in the eastern desert, required a considerable number of workers to be equipped with mining picks, carrying baskets, furnace fuel, and blowpipes for supplying adequate air to the smelting furnaces, and also for providing air to the melting furnaces, possibly required to re-melt the copper for casting ingots in open sand moulds close to the smelting operations, thus facilitating the movement of copper to workshops along the Nile Valley.[29] The supply of food and water to a large body of workers in the dry conditions of southern Sinai must have required considerable organization and implementation for each day's work.

(b) In Naqada II Nile Valley workshops, the process of making copper tubular drills first began with the casting of copper into rectangular shaped sheets, about 5 mm in thickness, the least thickness that can be cast in horizontal, open sand moulds, beating the sheets into thinner ones, and finally rolling fully annealed sheets around straight, wooden rods of the correct diameter. These operations necessitated a growing number of skilled workers supplied with stone hammers, with stone anvils, and with furnaces to both melt the copper for casting, but also frequently to anneal it as the copper work-hardened under a hammering regime: hardened copper is likely to crack by further hammering in an already work-hardened state. Workers not only needed to make increasing numbers of copper tubes to generate manufacturing expansion, but also to supply replacement tubes for those worn down by the desert sand in use with them.

(c) Naqada II workers, specializing in carving out different designs and sizes in vessels of differing stone varieties, required large numbers of flint chisels, punches and scrapers for this purpose: all stones can be shaped by flint, which is the only tool material capable of effectively working calcite, and all harder stones.

The mostly finished solid stone vessels were now passed to workers specialized in drilling and boring them. After satisfactorily completing the hollowing stage, smoothing and polishing of a vessel's exterior surface, for hard stones like granite, was achieved with coarse and smoother sandstone blocks, followed by rubbing the stone's surface by finely ground sand, mixed with water to form a runny paste, and finally by polishing such a prepared surface with a wet clay/mud mixture. The duties in providing large volumes of these materials must have been the responsibility of a non-skilled class of workers being directed by a senior person in charge of stone vessel workshops.

(d) In Chapter 5, the technology of drilling stone vessels up to the hardness of Mohs 7 with the Twist/Reverse Twist Drill, fitted with a copper tubular drill to the lower end of its weighted central shaft, is displayed in Dynastic tomb drawings of this tool. It is always depicted with a single worker to operate it: many skilled vessel makers were concurrently required to maintain manufacturing output. But even during the Naqada II phase of using a copper tubular drill for hollowing most stone vessels, there probably existed an early form of the TRTD upon which it was fitted.

(e) The approximate amount of copper consumed to drill the calcite Duck Jar (MM 5341), and the diorite oblate spheroidal vessel (MM 1776), has been calculated using the experimental evidence set out in Chapters 4–6. The Duck Jar was probably drilled with two or three ever-larger diameter tubular drills, centred on the vessel's vertical axis (see Chapter 5, Figure 5.28), with the holes reaching the planned internal bottom of the vessel in order safely to weaken the stone, the largest diameter drill being big enough to define the finished diameter of the vessel's mouth. After the inner solid core and the single or two tubular cores were carefully removed, the vessel could now be bored with shorter and longer figure-of-eight-shaped borers, admitted through the mouth (see Chapter 5, Figures 5.35–5.37) to follow its already carved elongated bulbous exterior shape. The weight of copper ground off the ancient tubular drills to hollow the calcite Duck Jar is calculated to be in the region of one kilogram.

The already-shaped diorite, lugged, oblate spheroidal vessel will have been initially drilled out with a copper tube, whose diameter could equally be divided around the circumference of its 25 cm-diameter mouth, just like the unfinished porphyry vase's (CM JE18758) mouth, which displays seven chain-of-touching-holes around the mouth's perimeter, and one in the centre. Mathematical calculations, and a full-sized model of the vessel's top surface, indicated that a copper drill diameter of three royal fingers (5.6 cm) make nine chain-of-touching-holes around the mouth's perimeter, with a similar sized tenth hole drilled on the vessel's vertical axis to weaken the central mass of diorite and, possibly, a second, larger drill-tube used to ensure the safe removal of the central mass of stone. All holes needed to be drilled to the full depth of the vessel's projected average internal depth of approximately 31 cm (i.e., the vessel's height of 34 cm, minus the bottom thickness of 3 cm). The weight of copper ground off the ancient tubular drills used to hollow this vessel, before its boring procedures, was in the order of 20 kilograms, and this included the copper worn off the tubular drill for making the holes in each of the two lugs.

The employment of *three* royal finger–diameter copper tubes for hollowing the spheroidal diorite vessel in the Late Predynastic period, together with the evidence of using a *six* finger–diameter copper tube to hollow Khufu's granite sarcophagus in the Fourth Dynasty, and other granite sarcophagi postdating the Fourth Dynasty, suggest that the sizes of these two artifact types, the stone sarcophagus and the stone vessel, were partly dictated by the exact numbers of holes required for hollowing them with a continuous chain-of-touching-holes. Further, in both the sarcophagus and the spheroidal vessel, there are favourable ratios of the total stone drilled out by the different diameter drill-tubes to the total stone hollowed out of the sarcophagus, and out of the spheroidal vessel, after removal of cores, and the pointed cusps left after core removal. There are sufficient margins of safety to ensure the integrity of both artifacts during the completion of these two drilling operations.

Large numbers of vessels being manufactured at a single workshop not only required numerous workers, but also a full TRTD tool kit composing of the main shaft/handle, its weights, or one centrally placed weight, a copper tubular drill partially force-fitted to the end of the shaft, a forked branch for lashing onto the main shaft and many figure-of-eight-shaped stone borers of increasing lengths for bulbous vessels' internal shaping. A complete stone vessel TRTD, and its ancillary tools, except for the manufacture of the copper tubular drills, which required a different set of industrial skills, may have been manufactured by a dexterous vessel worker who actually used it, making it likely that a such a skilled worker in a tightly knit community of this type of craft specialization, and its attendant skills set, gradually taught stone vessel making to a member of the next generation of their own family.

During the Late Chalcolithic, the increase of craft industries in the various parts of Egypt, one of them being the stone vessel industry, required a commensurate expansion in smelting copper, and the casting of it, to manufacture numerous tubular drills of different diameters, the kind of circumstance encouraged by the elite who took an increasing interest in their success and economic viability.[30] This gave impetus to the stone vessel manufacturing industry, as well as to other industries, such as the specialized manufacture of ceramic vessels, matching the increasing numbers of both hard- and softer-stone vessels created in different designs, sizes and stone varieties.

Also in the Late Chalcolithic, the saving of powders from the copper tubular drilling of softer and harder stones, and its suggested subsequent provision to a close-by faience workshop, allowed the joining of the two industries together, in the sense that stone vessel manufacture generated the raw material for the faience core and glaze makers, creating a formidable, dual wealth-creation team of specialized, skilled craftworkers. Their twin products of stone vessels, and artifacts made from faience, became ever more available to the controlling, supporting elites for regional and interregional exchange networks and thus to prestige goods, which served their desire publicly to display their position and to validate their status.[31] Other industries, at this time, were being established or expanded: for example, specialized pottery in southern Egypt, and the working of copper at Maadi. Also, importantly for the manufacture of stone vessels, and other stone artifacts, huge quantities of flint tools for working hard-stone vessels into shape, made by large numbers of skilled flint workers, and assisted by less-skilled workers needed to dig out flint potstones from the limestone beds, became vital for working both soft and hard stones for many purposes. Clearly the Naqada II period developed a wide variety of craft industries that served to drive economic growth.

Discussion

After the introduction of copper smelting in Ancient Egypt, the reed's tubular shape could now be copied in copper, allowing workers to increase the manufacture of igneous stone vessels. For example, the igneous stone vessels from the Predynastic cemetery at Naqada II Gerza, and the drilled mid-Naqada II pear-shaped hard-stone macehead (Bristol Museum and Art Gallery H 1936), substantiate the introduction of the copper tubular drill soon after copper smelting became established, ca. 3600 BCE. Stone vessels were attractive artifacts, easily exchanged at regional and interregional levels and, later, used for long-distance trade.

Comparisons concerning the weight of copper worn off the drill-tubes between drilling the calcite Duck Jar (MM 5341), drilling the diorite spheroidal vessel (MM 1776), and drilling Khufu's granite sarcophagus, reveal the true hardness differences concerning Mohs 3–4 calcite (absolute hardness = 14) and Mohs 7 diorite and granite (absolute hardness = 100): diorite and granite are seven times harder than calcite.[32]

The experimentally produced faience cores and glazes from waste drilling powders suggest that ancient workers must have reasoned that the waste sand powders from drilling softer and harder stones, the copper tubes noticeably shortening differentially, contained dissimilar amounts of copper fragments mixed within the powders, and further established, using their own experiments, that faience cores could indeed be made from softer-stone powders, and that the glazes could be manufactured from the igneous stone powders, just as glazes were previously made from crushed, powdered malachite, this mineral now, though, being smelted, and later melted, in order to fabricate copper tubular drills, and other tools and artifacts.

The indicated manufacturing transformations outlined in this chapter suggest transitions and convergence of particular Predynastic tools and processes, which developed into established industries, stimulating a growing production of Naqada II igneous and softer-stone vessels, in addition to the making of faience objects by using waste drilling powders containing copper particles. The experimental and archaeological evidence imply fundamental changes to ancient working procedures, suggesting that a primary generator of Egypt's economic strength throughout the whole of Egyptian civilization, and commencing at the beginning of the Naqada II period, was the copper tubular drill. Additionally, my extensive experiments, carried out over several decades with replica and reconstructed tools, point to three naturally occurring materials without which the Ancient Egyptians could never have developed their intricately devised civilization. I have placed them in my perceived order of importance: flint, desert sand and copper ore. However, a fourth material, the by-product, copper-contaminated drilling powder, is an early *manufactured* raw material, a hugely critical factor in the Predynastic period's progress towards a developed culture.

Notes

1 M. Amer, 'Annual report of the Maadi excavations, 1930–32', in *Bulletin, Faculty of Arts,* Egyptian University, 1933, vol. I, pp. 322–4; M. Amer, 'Annual report of the Maadi excavations, 1935', in *Bulletin, Faculty of Arts,* Egyptian University, 1935, vol. II, pp. 176–8; M. Amer, 'Annual report of the Maadi excavations, 1935', in *Chronique d'Égypte,*1936, vol. XI, pp. 54–7; I. Rizkana and J. Seeher, *Maadi III: The Non-Lithic Small Finds and the Structural Remains of the Prehistoric Settlement,* Mainz: Phillip von Zabern, 1989, pp. 13–18; J. Seeher, *Gedanken zur Rolle Unterägyptens bei der Heraus- bildung des Pharaonenreiches,* Abteilung Kairo: Mitteilungen des Deutschen Archäologische Instituts, 47, 1991, pp. 313–18; C. Köhler, 'Theories of State Formation', in Willeke Wendrich (ed.) *Blackwell Studies in Global Archaeology: Egyptian Archaeology,* Chichester: Wiley-Blackwell, 2010, pp. 36–54.
2 W.M.F. Petrie, G.A. Wainwright and E. Mackay, *The Labyrinth Gerzeh and Mazghuneh,* London: Bernard Quaritch, 1912, p. 17.
3 D.A. Stocks, 'Industrial technology at Kahun and Gurob: Experimental manufacture and test of replica and reconstructed tools with indicated uses and effects upon artefact production', unpublished thesis, University of Manchester, 1988, vol. I, pp. 168–213.
4 For example, Bristol Museum and Art Gallery H 1936.
5 J. Eiwanger, 'Merimde Beni-salame', in Kathryn A. Bard (ed.) *Encyclopedia of the Archaeology of Ancient Egypt,* London and New York: Routledge, 1999, pp. 501–5.
6 Stocks, 'Industrial technology', vol. II, pp. 246–73.
7 W.M.F. Petrie, *Tools and Weapons,* London: British School of Archaeology in Egypt, 1917, p. 59.
8 D.A. Stocks, 'Technology and the reed', *The Manchester Archaeological Bulletin* 8, 1993, pp. 58–68.
9 A.M. Blackman and M.R. Apted, *The Rock Tombs of Meir,* London: Egypt Exploration Society, part V, 1953, pl. XVI.
10 Stocks, 'Industrial technology', vol. I, pp. 137–40, vol. II, p. 344; Stocks, 'Technology and the reed', pp. 58–68.
11 Petrie, Wainwright and Mackay, *The Labyrinth Gerzeh and Mazghuneh,* p. 22, pl. V; D.A. Stocks, 'Derivation of Ancient Egyptian faience core and glaze materials', *Antiquity* 71, 1997, pp. 179–82.
12 P.T. Nicholson, *Egyptian Faience and Glass,* Princes Risborough: Shire Publications Ltd, 1993, p. 18.
13 D.A. Stocks, 'Sticks and stones of Egyptian technology', *Popular Archaeology* 7 (3), 1986, p. 27; Stocks, 'Industrial technology', vol. I, p. 128; D.A. Stocks, 'Interrelationships between significant tools and technologies developed in Ancient Egypt: Indications of an adeptly organized, expanding industrial economy, which influenced the direction, pace and structure of social evolution', Doctor of Letters thesis, Faculty of Humanities, University of Manchester, UK, 2018, p. 25.
14 D.A. Stocks, 'Testing Ancient Egyptian granite-working methods in Aswan, Upper Egypt', *Antiquity* 75, 2001, pp. 89–94.
15 See Chapter 4, Table 4.7.

16 Stocks, 'Derivation of Ancient Egyptian faience core and glaze materials', pp. 180–1.
17 G. Brunton and G. Caton-Thompson, *Badarian Civilisation and Predynastic Remains near Badari*, London: British School of Archaeology in Egypt, 1928, pp. 27–8, 41.
18 Nicholson, *Egyptian Faience and Glass*, p. 18.
19 C. Woodford, 'Static electricity', 2012/2018. Retrieved from: www.explainthatstuff. com/how-static-electricity-works.html [Accessed November 2020].
20 Nicholson, *Egyptian Faience and Glass*, p. 18; P.T. Nicholson, 'Faience', in Donald B. Redford (ed.) *The Oxford Encyclopedia of Ancient Egypt*, Oxford: Oxford University Press, 2001, vol. I, p. 491.
21 Stocks, 'Derivation of Ancient Egyptian faience core and glaze materials', pp. 179–82.
22 D.A. Stocks, 'Stone sarcophagus manufacture in Ancient Egypt', *Antiquity* 73, 1999, pp. 918–22; D.A. Stocks, 'Auf den Spuren von Cheops' Handwerkern', *Sokar* 10, 2005, pp. 4–9.
23 M.S. Tite, P. Manti and A.J. Shortland, 'A technological study of ancient faience from Egypt', *Journal of Archaeological Science* 34 (10), 2007, pp. 1568–1583; M.S. Tite and A.J. Shortland, *Production Technology of Faience and Related Early Vitreous Materials*, Oxford: Oxford University School of Archaeology, 2008; G.D. Hatton, A.J. Shortland and M.S. Tite, 'The production technology of Egyptian blue and green frits from second millennium BCE Egypt and Mesopotamia', *Journal of Archaeological Science* 35 (6), 2008, pp. 1591–1604.
24 W.M.F. Petrie, *Researches in Sinai*, New York: E.P. Dutton, 1906, p. 27.
25 A. Lucas, *Ancient Egyptian Materials and Industries*, London: Edward Arnold, 1948, pp. 237–8.
26 T.A. Rickard, *Man and Metals*, New York: McGraw-Hill, 1932, vol. I, pp. 196–7.
27 See Chapter 4: CM JE18758 unfinished porphyry, wide-mouthed vase displaying seven tubular holes around the mouth's perimeter, and one in the centre, the cores being removed before the vase was abandoned.
28 B. Rothenberg, 'Excavations at Timna Site 39. A chalcolithic copper smelting site and furnace and its metallurgy', *Archaeo Metallurgy* Monograph Number 1, 1978, p. 11, Fig. 11; B. Rothenberg, 'Pharaonic copper mines in South Sinai', in *Institute for Archaeo-Metallurgical Studies,* London: Institute of Archaeology, University College London, 10/11 (June/December), 1987, p. 4.
29 C.L. Costin, 'Craft specialization: Issues in defining, documenting, and exploring the organization of production', in M. Schiffer (ed.) *Archaeological Method and Theory*, Tucson, AZ: University of Arizona Press, 1991, pp. 1–56; J. Golden, 'The origins of the metals trade in the Eastern Mediterranean: Social Organisation of production in the early copper industries', in T.E. Levy and E.C.M. van den Brink (eds) *Egypt and the Levant*, London and New York: Leicester University Press, 2002, pp. 225–38.
30 E.C. Köhler, 'Theories of state formation', in Willeke Wendrich (ed.) *Blackwell Studies in Global Archaeology: Egyptian Archaeology*, Chichester: Wiley- Blackwell, 2010, p. 39.
31 M.A. Hoffman, *Egypt before the Pharaohs: The Prehistoric Foundations of Egyptian Civilization*, London and Henley: Routledge and Kegan Paul, 1980, pp. 200–14; E.C. Köhler, 'Theories of state formation', in Willeke Wendrich (ed.) *Blackwell Studies in Global Archaeology: Egyptian Archaeology*, Chichester: Wiley- Blackwell, 2010, pp. 39–40.
32 'Mohs Scale of Mineral Hardness' in Wikipedia Foundation, Inc., Creative Commons Attribution – ShareAlike License, edited 19 May 2021.

11

ANCIENT TECHNICAL INTERRELATIONSHIPS

Interconnected tools and processes

The Predynastic Egyptian artisan inherited a long tradition of making tools from stone. Stone tools, particularly the ones made of flint, had evolved into different shapes and sizes, which reflected their use. Predynastic stone tools, such as hand-axes, borers, projectile points, knives, end- and side-scrapers, burins and serrated sickles, were used to work upon flesh, skins, wood, plants and stone before the introduction of cast copper tools, ca. 3600 BCE. It is likely that some of these stone tool designs were reproduced in copper at the beginning of the Naqada II period. Four important stone tools, the flint end-scraper, the denticulated flint sickle, the flint knife and the stone hand-axe were probably transformed into five copper tools, namely, the chisel, the adze, the saw, the knife and the axe: copper allowed improved performance and life, and some different uses for similar tool shapes. The copper chisel was driven into softer materials with a mallet or a stone hammer, a use possibly given to flint tools in certain circumstances, but the slim copper adze blade, similar to a chisel's shape, was hafted and swung against wood and soft limestone, causing it to remove thin shavings from these materials.

Two stone tools, the hand-axe and the flint knife, retained their basic shapes, purposes and names after being cast and beaten in copper, although the copper axe-head, used by Dynastic carpenters and boat builders, was fitted with a wooden handle to increase the force of a blow. The copper saw blade could be beaten thinly, then serrated, which saved sawing time and effort, an improvement upon the thicker, denticulated flint tools, initially in use for sawing woody plant stems, such as reeds.

In addition to being utilized for driving chisels, spherical and hemispherical stone hammers were also employed to beat copper and bronze to shape, and also stone artifacts; most stone hammers were directly wielded by the hand. The

DOI: 10.4324/9781003269922-15

craftworker must have possessed many different sizes and weights of stone hammers, and the supply and fitting of wooden handles to such a large number of them would not have been a feasible proposition. Some stone hammers, picks and axes were fitted with two sticks twisted around a waisted section, but these were used for quarrying and roughly dressing stone to shape.

The smelting and casting of copper enabled the craftworker to change manufacturing methods in an important way. The skills required to fashion a flint nodule into a usable tool are considerable. However, by making open moulds in sand, and later reusable open pottery moulds, it was a relatively simple matter to pour molten copper into them and make multiple copies of the same tool shape; this is a modern, mass-production manufacturing method. Moulds were also used for casting glass and for making faience cores from a siliceous paste. Beating a copper casting into its final hardened configuration, and sharpening it on a piece of sandstone, did not take as much time, or expertise, as the making of flint tools. But in times of metal shortages, the craftworker could revert to stone tools, like the stone adze, and this is evident at Twelfth Dynasty Kahun, where stone tools outnumbered the metallic ones.

It is clear that craftworkers were profoundly influenced by their environment. Although Ancient Egyptians utilized natural materials for many domestic purposes, they also adapted nature's architecture for the designs of tools, as well as for parts of buildings made in stone. The importance of the common reed as the original design shape for two crucial tools cannot be overemphasized. The reed blowpipe and the reed tubular drill, and its copy in copper, and later in bronze, fundamentally changed the direction of Ancient Egyptian technology. Without the blowpipe, which evolved into the New Kingdom foot-operated bellows, the smelting of significant amounts of copper from its ore, and the subsequent melting of sufficient copper for casting into useful tools and other artifacts, would have been more difficult to accomplish if funnelled wind solely had been used to sustain the heat of a furnace.

The copper flat-ended tubular drill, for making holes in all stones, stands above every other copper tool in its contribution to the production of Ancient Egyptian wealth. The copper, and later bronze, tubular drill, driven by a bow, or by the Twist/Reverse Twist Drill (TRTD) tool, became vital for the hollowing of softer- and harder-stone vessels (and for making suspension holes in their carved lugs); for drilling out hard-stone sarcophagi, and their lid lowering rope holes; for shrine statue recesses; for defining statuary eye sockets; for some of the hieroglyphs in monumental texts, such as circular ones, and the rounded corners of figural depictions carved into, for example, statuary, stelae and granite obelisks (Note: stonecutting saws could be used to define some straight lines); for door hinge sockets and, sometimes, for sarcophagi lid-fastening slots.

These drilling methods, using different-diameter drill-tubes, would have been employed accurately to incise small- and large-diameter circular hieroglyphs in both sedimentary and igneous stones. The core produced was then chipped downwards from its centre to the bottom of the circular groove, the resulting curved surface being smoothed and polished. Possibly, some of the larger diameter drill-cores were employed for making small vessels, saving most of the shaping operations needed before hollowing them out with appropriately sized diameter drill-tubes, and necessary stone borers for bulbous vessels.

The copper flat-edged Dynastic stonecutting saw is the second most important copper tool employed for cutting stones of hardnesses up to Mohs 7. As mentioned in Chapter 4, the reciprocating stonecutting saw blade may be thought of as a straightened-out tubular drill: the cutting actions on stone, with dry sand abrasive for both tools, is identical, each possessing a flat copper edge, which is reciprocated for a saw blade, but for a tubular drill requires continuous clockwise and anticlockwise rotation, simply achieved by a reciprocating bow-shaft fitted with a taut string or rope tightly wrapped around the drill-shaft, or by continuous hand and wrist movements.

Archaeological and experimental evidence, assembled in Chapters 4, 9 and 10, point towards the *convergence* of three industries at the commencement of the Naqada II period. First, the copper smelting industry commenced ca. 3600 BCE. Second, the new copper tubular drilling technology became established soon afterwards, achieved by copying the reed tube's shape, a *first transition*, which immediately increased the production of hard- and softer-stone vessels. Third, and consequent upon the first transition, a *second transition* of earlier, incomplete faience-making methods developed into a growing faience core and glaze manufacturing industry. This industry utilized the waste drilling powders, now a *by-product* material from drilling stones with the copper tube and sand abrasive, possibly being later supplemented with powders generated by the use of the Dynastic stonecutting saw.

The ability to cast copper sheets large enough to make stonecutting saws and tubes, and serrated woodcutting saws, allowed craftworkers to saw the hard stones into blocks for building and for sarcophagi, to hollow vessels and sarcophagi from the hardest stones, and to cut long planks from tree trunks. To assist this latter operation, a sawyer used a counterweighted wooden tourniquet rod rapidly to tighten or slacken a rope securing a vertical baulk of wood to a post driven into the ground. Modifying a forked tree branch supplied the design for the central shaft and handle of the Twist/Reverse Twist Drill, and its conversion into a boring tool by the roping of an inverted forked shaft to hold and twist stone borers inside a stone vessel. Forked branches, in addition to already naturally curved branches, were also adapted for the construction of woodworkers' bow-shafts, for making the Y-shaped supports used in shipbuilding, as well as for the three-legged anvil used to help beat metal vessels into shape.

The craftworker employed naturally occurring substances to establish manufacturing processes. In particular, dry sand was in use as an abrasive in conjunction with copper saws and tubes. Without those two tools, Ancient Egyptian craftworkers would indeed have been poorly equipped for some tasks, particularly for working the hard stones. The finely ground waste (by-product) powders, containing sand, stone and copper, were probably in use as a fine abrasive for polishing stone, for drilling the stone beads, for making the faience cores and blue and green glazes and, possibly, for creating the blue frits and pigment. The rates of copper losses from the saws and the tubes into the sand abrasive for a particular stone would have been known to craftworkers and their supervisors.

It is hard to believe that the faience manufacturers would have gone to all the trouble of specially making finely ground sand and copper particle powders for faience cores and glazes, when huge amounts of similar waste powders from the sawing and the drilling of stones were available. Indeed, the introduction and expansion of modelled and moulded faience cores in the Late Predynastic period, concomitant with the expansion of soft- and hard-stone vessel manufacture after ca. 3600 BCE, supports the idea that faience cores and glazes were manufactured from the waste powders obtained from the drilling of stones with copper tubes. Therefore, the need for copper tubes for hollowing Predynastic stone vessels, particularly those made from the harder stones, allowed a previously accidental discovery of how to glaze carved steatite objects with malachite to be expanded into a larger industrial undertaking. Even though a decline in the manufacture of hard-stone vessels took place in the Early Dynastic period, the introduction of igneous stone sarcophagi in the Fourth Dynasty continued to generate powders suitable for making faience glazes. The experiments with the flat-edged copper saws and the copper tubular drills indicated that acceptable ratios of the metal lost from the tools to the stone sawn or drilled were obtained in working stone artifacts, but that the loss of copper from these tools cost the Ancient Egyptians a large percentage of their total copper production.

The experiments with copper, leaded bronze and bronze chisels demonstrated that calcite marks a dividing line between the 'soft' and the 'hard' stones. The cutting of soft limestone, red sandstone, gypsum, steatite (all of hardness Mohs 3, or below) and all wood types is within the capability of copper and bronze chisels, and serrated copper and bronze saws. Calcite, and stones harder than Mohs 3, are best worked with flint and chert chisels and punches. The loss of copper, and indeed bronze, from the chisels is too great to be tolerated for cutting calcite. It is likely that flint and chert tools were developed for both hard- and soft stoneworking, and the experiments indicated that the implements for working the hardest stones were disposable, or 'throw-away' tools. However, the experimental cutting of hieroglyphs into coarse-grained rose granite suggests that only flint chisels and punches can work this particular stone: the hardness of chert critically falls below that of flint for this purpose. The experiments with the steel chisel and punch suggest that Late Egyptian iron tools, and Roman iron and steel tools, were able to cut stones harder than the copper or bronze tools could, but that the igneous stones caused considerable damage to the edges of all ferrous tools.

Calcite also marks a dividing line with regard to drilling. A gypsum vessel can be bored with flint crescents, but calcite, and stones harder than this, cannot. Calcite, and fine-grained stones up to, and including, hardness Mohs 5 can be drilled with reed tubes and dry sand abrasive. Copper tubes and stone borers, also operating with dry sand, rather than wet, were vital for drilling and boring the harder-stone vessels.

The bow was an important power transmission device. It drove five different types of tool, from the fire drill to the mass-production bead drills of the Eighteenth and Nineteenth Dynasties. One of the tools, the drill-stock, could be fitted with different bits at its operating end and was, therefore, an early example of an interchangeable tool system. The first interchangeable tool system, the Twist/ Reverse Twist Drill (TRTD), with its central shaft and associated weights, was probably handed down in a family, or a group, of craftworkers. The lashed-on forked shaft, for driving the stone borers, needed occasional replacement, as did a copper tube fitted to the central shaft. It is clear that the TRTD was a vital tool, a cornerstone of Ancient Egyptian wealth production. The experiments and the archaeological evidence for stone vessel manufacture in fourth millennium BCE Mesopotamia suggest that the stone vessel craftworker there also employed some form of the TRTD.

The stone bead-drilling experiments demonstrated the feasibility of mass-producing perforations in hard-stone beads and other stone artifacts. The archaeological and experimental evidence suggest that inventive steps occurred between the Second Intermediate Period and the Eighteenth Dynasty, converting the single bead drill into a mass-production tool. The simultaneous multiple bead drill gave the bead-maker the ability to increase the manufacturing rate of stone beads and, as a consequence, the cost of jewellery must surely have decreased and made jewellery products more accessible to a greater number of people. This multiple drilling technology, the workers shown sat in organized rows in a small New Kingdom factory situated in Thebes, Upper Egypt, preceded modern mass-production drilling systems by nearly 3,500 years.

The lengths of three wooden rods found by Petrie at Kahun, for testing the flatness of stone surfaces, were found to be equal in length within 0.005 cm. It has been demonstrated, by using a replica set of rods and string, that the ancient craftworker was capable of making accurately matched sets of three rods, or even the four-rod set seen in the tomb of Rekhmire; ancient workers were, therefore, capable of chiselling, pounding and grinding stone surfaces to an accuracy of 0.25 mm over a 1.25 m square. Without these rods, together with the 'A' frame and the vertical testing frame, the building of temples, pyramids and walls would have been extremely difficult. Additionally, a set of rods and string may have been used as an inside calliper, accurately testing the surface parallelism of two adjacent stone blocks prior to fitting them into a building.

Indicated craftworkers' health problems

The experimental working of stone with copper saws, drill-tubes and flint and chert tools indicates serious pollution of the immediate working environment at ancient building and artifact manufacturing sites. The sawing and the drilling of stones must have produced large amounts of waste sand/stone/copper powders, much of the associated micron-sized dust being blown about in the wind. The present experiments with the copper saws and the tubular drills in use with dry sand abrasive upon stone show that sawyers and drillers must have inhaled considerable quantities of this dust, which is composed largely of silica and stone particles; this work must eventually have caused the workers serious silicosis, shortening their lives. Other workers were probably affected by inhaling the windblown dust at manufacturing sites.

Worn-out copper, or bronze, saws and tubes, in addition to other metallic tools, such as chisels, adzes, axes and wood drills, were sent back to the foundry to be melted down with new copper for casting replacement tools. At large building sites, and at workshops continuously in use for making stone and metallic artifacts, there must have been established a foundry consisting of numerous furnaces clustered together. Large copper or bronze saws, drill-tubes and other artifacts required the coordinated pouring of multiple numbers of crucibles of molten metal to fill the moulds. The foundry would, logically, have been sited downwind, that is, to the south of a manufacturing site. Nevertheless, large volumes of smoke and fumes from the furnaces and the moulds would have affected the health of the workers. Today, the casting of metal is still a dangerous occupation, even with modern health and safety regulations in place; ancient casters also risked severe burns from the accidental spillage of molten metal. How much the ancient furnaceworker suffered from hyperventilation by blowing air through reed pipes cannot be known, but certain people have a predisposition toward this debilitating condition of dizziness and, in extreme cases, paralysis.

The shaping of hard- and soft-stone objects, and the cutting of reliefs and hieroglyphs, with flint and chert chisels, punches and scrapers caused stoneworkers to risk eye and skin injury from flying fragments of flint and stone. Quarry workers also suffered considerable risks to their health. For example, the workers employed to pound away the granite surrounding the Unfinished Obelisk at Aswan not only risked eye and skin injury, but breathed a choking granite dust in their confined working areas. To be 'sent to the granite' was indeed a harsh punishment. The use of hand-held pounders and stone hammers for the working of stone, and the beating of cast copper and bronze into sheet metal and into tools, probably caused repetitive strain injury to a worker's hand, wrist and lower arm over a period of years. Large building sites, and the workshops established for the manufacture of stone statuary, vessels, sarcophagi and many other artifacts, were places of daily discomfort and danger to the craftworker.

Final summary

All of the technical evidence described indicates the establishment of an innovative, complex, sophisticated and interrelated industrial society that became sufficiently developed in the Predynastic period to supply significant numbers of valuable artifacts, particularly stone vessels, for domestic use and foreign trade. The experimental sawing and drilling of stone indicates that large amounts of copper ore were mined and processed *just* to replace the many thousands of tonnes of copper worn off the saws and tubular drills over millennia, particularly for making the hard-stone sarcophagi, and that prodigious amounts of waste sand/stone/copper powders were created. This implies that an organization was developed to administer and implement the following pivotal industrial procedures: the mining and smelting of copper ores; the casting and transportation of copper ingots to work centres; the casting and beating of copper into saws, tubes and many other tools; the sawing and drilling of artifacts; the probable supply of the waste powders to the stone polishers, the bead drillers and the blue faience, frit and pigment manufacturers.

Several important inventive technical steps progressively increased the production of artifacts, making them accessible to wider groups of people; this slowly altered the structure of Egyptian society. The most notable advances were the transformation of specific flint tools into copper; the conversion of the reed tube into a blowpipe and a drill-tube, later copied in copper and driven with the bow and the Twist/Reverse Twist Drill; stonecutting saws; reusable pottery moulds; the interchangeable tool drill-stock; accurately made surface-testing rods; expendable flint tools; the counterweighted tourniquet lever; the adaptation of tree branches to make bows, Y-shaped woodworking supports, tripod anvils and TRTD main shafts, together with their associated forked shafts for driving stone borers; the New Kingdom multiple bead-drilling apparatus; the establishment of factory mass-production methods.

The gradual formation and development of interdependent industrial processes employed ever-increasing numbers of administrators, technical staff and clerks to control the workers and their tools, and consumed huge amounts of materials. This implies vigorous organizational abilities to meet each new technical demand. Expeditions to known quarries and mines were also complemented by exploration to locate and secure new resources. In particular, the gathering and transportation of desert sand and flint nodules became vital to the manufacturing processes of sawing, drilling, boring and stonecutting during the whole of Ancient Egyptian civilization.

It is clear that the rulers of Ancient Egypt, and increasingly their subordinates, progressively ordered more complicated and elegant artifacts *partly* because craft-workers could modify existing technology to make them, as well as to invent new tools, when required. This in turn created an expanding economy, serving to increase wealth, which drove economic, social and organizational changes throughout the Predynastic and Dynastic periods.

GLOSSARY OF TECHNICAL TERMS

angularity Many quartz crystals have angular shapes, causing them to embed into metal drills and saws operating under a load. See also *hammer hardening*.

annealing The process whereby copper alloy tools are softened after the metal becomes hammer-hardened. The metal is brought to a red heat, and allowed slowly to cool until completely cold. It is now malleable, and hammering can continue.

arc-shaped bow The shape of bows seen in Eighteenth and Nineteenth Dynasty tomb representations depicting multiple bead-drilling. See also *woodworker's bow*.

axe (stone) See *maul*.

bamboo-like reeds Two such reeds were endemic to Ancient Egypt: *Phragmites communis* and *Arundo donax*.

blind end of a striation A phenomenon arising when a quartz crystal has worn away after scoring a stone's surface, leaving a blind end to the striation.

boring The rotating of a stone borer against a stone's surface, either by hand or as an attachment to the Twist/Reverse Twist Drill. A sandstone borer did not require an abrasive: other stone borers used sand abrasive.

brittle fracture Excessive hammering of copper and bronze alloys causes these metals suddenly to fracture due to complex changes to their internal structure.

calcite See *Egyptian alabaster*.

capstone A stone bearing-weight, with a hemispherical hole for engaging with the top of a bow-driven wooden shaft.

casting The pouring of molten metal from a crucible into a mould.

catenary curve The natural curve given by gravity to a horizontal string or rope under a certain amount of tension. See also *rods and string*.

chiselling Sudden, controlled blows of a chisel into wood or stone to remove small pieces of the material.

circumferential wear   The erosion of a mason's wooden mallet around its circumference by striking it on metallic, and possibly stone, chisels.

cire perdue or lost wax process   Two similar methods of casting, which involve the melting of wax cores to leave a space for the molten metal. 1. By making a solid core of wax and then covering it with thick clay. The loss of the wax, and the subsequent casting of the metal into the mould, makes a solid object. 2. By manufacturing a solid core of clay, covering it with wax, and subsequently adding another layer of clay on top. The loss of the wax, and then the filling of the space with molten metal, makes a hollow object when the inner clay core is removed.

closed mould   A mould made in two parts which, when joined together, makes a closed shaped space for the pouring of molten metal.

cold hammering   The forcible shaping, with a stone hammer, of cold copper alloys into thin sheet, and into chisels, adzes, axes and other tools and artifacts.

conical stone borer   A tool driven by a forked shaft lashed to a Twist/Reverse Twist Drill. The fork engages in two slots cut opposite to one another into the flat top of the borer.

convergence   The joining together of three industries, convergence, near to the beginning of the Naqada II period. These were the smelting of copper from its ores; the ability to increase the production of softer- and harder-stone vessels, using copper tubes with sand abrasive to hollow them; the manufacture of faience cores from soft stone–derived drilling powders, and of green/blue glazes from hard stone–derived drilling powders. See also transitions.

crescent-shaped flint tool   This tool generally comes in three distinctive crescent shapes: quarter, half and three-quarter.

crosscut chisel   A chisel having its cutting edge at right angles to its maximum width dimension. See also *flat chisel*.

cutting rates   The observed volume of stone or wood removed in a given amount of time.

cutting ratios   The observed ratio between the metal worn from a tool and the amount of stone or wood removed by that tool.

density   Stone: granite and other igneous stones are 2.7 g/cm³; hard sandstone and limestone are 2.6 g/cm³; calcite is 2.5 g/cm³; soft limestone and gypsum are 2.4 g/cm³. Metal: copper is 8.94 g/cm³.

drilling   The penetration into wood with a copper, bronze or iron drill, and into stone with a copper or bronze bead drill or tubes of reed, copper or bronze.

drill–tube eccentricity   The interior wall of a tubular drill being offset to its exterior wall. An out-of-centre core in a tubular mould may have caused this in ancient times. The rotation of such a drill overcuts a hole in stone.

dry quartz sand   The use of quartz sand as an abrasive has been found to be more efficient in the completely dry condition. This ensures a smooth interchange of worn crystals with new ones. The removal of used sand powder is possible from deep holes drilled into very heavy objects in the fully dry condition.

Egyptian alabaster   Usually alabaster means calcium sulphate (gypsum, Mohs 2), but the material employed in Ancient Egypt for many types of artifact was calcite (calcium carbonate). Egyptian calcite is a compact white or yellowish/white calcium carbonate (Mohs hardness 3–4). It is considerably harder than gypsum, which is similar in appearance to calcite.

fabricated   Any metal tool not directly cast into shape.

faience core   A ceramic material consisting of ground quartz sand, which is held together by varying amounts of interstitial glass. It contains small amounts of lime and copper, and either natron or plant ashes. It is usually fired at a temperature of 850°C.

faience glaze   A hard ceramic glaze made from similar materials as the faience body, but possessing greater quantities of alkali (approximately 20 per cent) and copper, and fired at about 950°C.

figure–of–eight–shaped stone borer   A borer possessing two opposite constrictions with which to engage a forked shaft to rotate it. This type of borer was used to widen the interiors of stone vessels.

first level, second level, etc.   A proposed method of removing the interior stone of a sarcophagus in stages. Each level represents a maximum theoretical depth, supported by evidence from Khufu's sarcophagus, thought possible to drill into the stone with tubular drills in any one drilling operation. All of the cores and the columns of the adjacent stone have to be removed before drilling the next level of holes.

flat chisel   A chisel having its cutting edge along its maximum width dimension. See also *crosscut chisel*.

flat–edged saw   A copper, bronze or iron saw, with a flat edge for pressing onto dry, quartz sand abrasive. See also *serrated saw*.

flat–ended tubular drill   A copper, or bronze, tubular drill, with a flat end-face for pressing onto dry, quartz sand abrasive.

forked shaft   A shaft for driving stone borers: it was lashed onto a main Twist/Reverse Twist Drill-shaft.

foundry   A place where a cluster of furnaces can be operated simultaneously, allowing the melting of sufficient metal to cast large objects.

frit   A ceramic material made from ground sand that, unlike faience, is coloured throughout and has no glaze layer. Frit has less than 5 per cent alkali and higher than 10 per cent of both copper and calcium oxides.

grinding   The abrading of a material's surface with small crystals of quartz, either contained in sand or embedded within the matrix of a stone.

gypsum   A soft stone (Mohs 2), similar in appearance to calcite. See also *Egyptian alabaster*.

gyratory drill–tube movement   The observed phenomenon of tubular drill and drill-rod movements caused by the to-and-fro action of a bow, the main axis of gyration being along the line of the bow's movement. The top end of a tube or a drill-rod gyrates, which act about the point on the drill-tube shaft and the drill-rod where a bow-string, or a bow-rope, is turning them. This results in the rounding of a tubular drill's end-face and the tubular-shaped slot at the drilling face. Equally, a solid drill-rod is rounded at its point, together with the stone at the bottom of the drill-hole.

hammer hardening The process by which relatively soft copper alloys are gradually hardened by hammering them cold. For obtaining the hardest edge possible on a cutting tool, final hammering should take place after the preliminary alternate hammering and annealing processes have shaped the tool. See also *annealing*.

handle 1 The inclined and tapered top part of a Twist/Reverse Twist Drill-shaft.

handle 2 The wooden shaft in which a simultaneous multiple bead drill rotates.

hardness marks In order to determine the hardness of a specimen of metal, a known load for a known time is placed on an inverted pyramidal-shaped diamond (Vickers hardness test) or a hardened ball (Brinell hardness test). Careful measurements of the hardness marks form the basis for a number scale of hardness for metals.

hole elongation The push and pull of a bow-shaft driving a tubular drill causes elongation of the tubular slot being cut into softer stones. Sand crystals trapped between the exterior wall of the tube and the wall of the tubular hole cause this elongation.

hook-shaped stone borers 1. A theoretical hand-held flint tool especially knapped for scraping an undercut in the internal shoulder of a stone vessel. 2. A theoretical hand-held stone borer, also for undercutting purposes. This tool works in conjunction with dry sand abrasive, unless made from sandstone.

in a line The positioning of each simultaneous multiple bead drill in a line and separated by an approximately equal distance.

inside calliper A device for measuring the distance between two close objects – not necessarily in units of measurement.

kerf The cut or slot that a saw produces in a material. This slot is wider than the saw blade's thickness, so that the blade above the teeth does not jam as the cut is deepened. It is usually achieved in modern saws by bending alternate teeth to the left and to the right, but in an ancient saw, teeth were chopped into the blade, causing the metal to bulge sideways, thereby creating the kerf.

Kerma-type bead drills Single bronze bead drills found at Kerma, Nubia, and dated to the Second Intermediate Period.

lap A piece of leather used to press either a mixture of waste powdered sand and mud, followed by mud only, upon a hard stone's surface in order to polish it.

lashed-on shaft Any shaft, straight or forked, tied with a rope or a cord to a main shaft of a Twist/Reverse Twist Drill.

main shaft configuration The main wooden shaft, inclined handle and fastened stone weight(s) of a Twist/Reverse Twist Drill.

matched rod sets Three or four short wooden rods, with their lengths carefully adjusted to a similar dimension.

maul 1. A large dolerite tool, possibly fitted with a handle, and used either as a pile driver, for driving poles into the ground, or for swinging against stone to break it. 2. An elongated stone tool of basalt, chert, granite, quartzite or silicified limestone. Many mauls were pointed (picks), or rounded, and often shaped like an axe. Mauls were sometimes carved with a neck, so as to fit them with handles. Two sticks were lashed to the maul's neck by twisting them together with a leather thong. See also *pounder*.

microlith   A small stone tool, generally less than 3 cm long.

micron   A micrometre (μm), a millionth of a metre.

Mohs hardness   A scale applied to stones to determine relative hardnesses. See Table 1.1 for stones' Mohs hardness.

mortise   A deep slot, usually cut into wood, which allows a tenon to fit tightly into it, so forming a joint between two pieces of work. Dovetail-shaped slots were often cut into adjacent stone blocks for joining them with a wooden or bronze 'butterfly' cramp. Sometimes, large cracks in stone sculpture were strengthened with stone 'butterfly' cramps. See also *tenon*.

mould   See *closed mould* and *open mould*.

mud block or pack   A proposed filling of the simultaneous multiple bead-drilling table-top with mud for holding stone beads in a line ready for perforation.

multiple cores on a similar axis   The production of several cores, the central one being solid, the outer ones being tubular-shaped, on the same axis by different diameter tubular drills.

natron   A naturally occurring alkaline mixture of the sodium salts, carbonate, bicarbonate, chloride and sulphate.

nodule – flint and chert   Naturally formed silica-based stones laid down in convoluted shapes in the limestone bed of the shallow sea covering part of Egypt millions of years ago.

oblique rising joint   A joint between two stone blocks, whose end-faces either rise at an angle greater or smaller than 90° to their bottom faces, and/or rise at an angle greater or smaller than 90° to their front faces.

open mould   A horizontal mould in damp sand, stone or pottery, open at the top.

outside calliper   A device for measuring the length or diameter of an object, not necessarily in units of measurement.

pick (stone)   See *maul*.

polishing   The rounding of angular pits and striations in a stone's surface with a leather lap and a polishing agent, probably mud.

pounder   Usually a spherical, or a roughly spherical, hard-stone hammer made mainly from dolerite. Examples weigh from 4 kg to 7 kg and were held with both hands. Pounders generally were used to work the granite. Pounders were also used with a handle, and these tools had constrictions with which to bind a handle into position with a leather thong. See *maul*.

powdered sand   The waste by-product of the tubular drilling and the sawing of hard stones with copper alloy tubes and saws operating on sand abrasive.

pull-saw   A saw with the teeth set toward the operator.

punching   The driving of a sharp-pointed tool into a material's surface.

push-saw   A saw with the teeth set away from the operator.

reconstruction   A tool indicated by the archaeological evidence for it.

replica   A copy of an ancient tool.

rhyton-shaped crucible   A crucible shaped like those displayed in the Sixth Dynasty tomb of Mereruka at Saqqara. Two of these crucibles, shown back to back in this tomb, are thought to be the basis for the hieroglyphic sign for a red earthenware pot of Old Kingdom date. The Old Kingdom sign is round at the bottom, appearing in tomb reliefs depicting metalworking scenes, where it either indicates the use of copper, or identifies a person as a metalworker.

rods and string   Three or four rods, the two outer ones connected by a taut string. The unconnected rod(s) are for testing that the horizontal or vertical stone surface at any point under the string is similar to the height of the string at the two outer rods. See also *catenary curve*.

runny paste   A theoretical mixture of muddy water and finely ground powdered sand, the waste by-product of the tubular drilling and sawing of stone with quartz sand abrasive.

serrated saw   A copper alloy saw whose teeth were either chopped into the edge or filed with sharp-edged sandstone rubbers. See also flat-edged saw, pull-saw and push-saw.

simultaneous multiple bead drills   A drilling apparatus displayed in several Theban tomb scenes of Eighteenth and Nineteenth Dynasty date. The apparatus consists of two or more drills simultaneously driven with a long, arc-shaped bow.

specific gravity   See *density*.

striations   Score marks, or grooves, in stone made by quartz crystals. In tubular drill-holes, and on their cores, the striations are horizontal to the vertical axes. In saw slots they are longitudinal. The tools' working surfaces are also striated.

surface truth   An acceptably flat surface after checking it with an instrument in use for that purpose.

tang   The end of a saw, upon which was forced a wooden handle. In Early Dynastic times, the tang may have been held without a handle.

tenon   A regularly shaped tongue fitting tightly into a mortise, making a secure joint between two pieces of work. See also *mortise*.

tourniquet   A device for maintaining tension on a rope lashing. The mechanism consisted of a wooden rod, one end of which was inserted into the lashing, the other end being counterweighted.

transitions   Two transitions are likely to have taken place, ca. 3600 BCE. The first transition involved the conversion of the reed tubular drill's shape into copper, when copper smelting appeared around this date. The second transition concerned the change from glazing small, carved solid stone objects with crushed malachite powders, to forming, by hand or by using later moulds, cores with calcite-derived, or limestone-derived drilling powders, then glazing the cores with the more heavily copper-contaminated igneous stone-derived drilling powders. See also *convergence*.

trifacial flint tool A theoretical flint tool for grooving stone.

tripod anvil A device illustrated in the Eighteenth Dynasty tomb of Rekhmire, which assisted in the forming of metal vessels. The anvil consisted of an inverted forked stem, drilled with an upward slanting hole. An anvil rod was slid easily through the hole as far as a vessel's size demanded, thus making a tripod. The settling of the tripod's parts, and the weight of the vessel, 'locked' the tripod firmly into place. It may also have been used as a support for the finishing of stone vessels' exterior surfaces.

TRTD See *Twist/Reverse Twist Drill.*

Tubular-shaped cores Cores produced by the use of two or more tubular drills on the same axis. See also multiple cores on a similar axis.

tubular-shaped mould or slot The use of two dried mud cores could have enabled a tubular mould to have been made in damp sand. The larger-diameter core can be pushed vertically into the sand and withdrawn. The smaller-diameter core can then be pushed centrally into the bottom of the hole. Molten metal poured into the mould forms a tube.

tuyère The nozzle through which a continuous stream of air reaches the furnace.

Twist/Reverse Twist Drill A tool for drilling and boring stone vessels of many types of internal design.

twist/reverse twist mode of operation Both hands usually hold the Twist/Reverse Twist Drill, although it may be operated with one hand. Once the hands are comfortably gripping the shaft and the handle, both wrists are twisted in a clockwise direction. A twist of 90° may be accomplished. The tool is then twisted anticlockwise to its original position. The actions constantly are repeated.

VPN Vickers Pyramid Number. See also *hardness marks.*

waist(ed) 1. A term used to describe the twin opposite constrictions cut into a figure-of-eight-shaped stone borer.

2. The concave or constricted part of a wooden drill-shaft, around which the string or rope of a bow-shaft is engaged.

wandering To prevent this, an initial groove is required to centralize a tubular drill onto a stone's surface before drilling can commence. A bead drill needs a scraped depression.

withies Long, slim, green sticks for holding a crucible full of molten metal.

woodworker's bow Extant bows, and those depicted in tomb scenes, show the mostly straight bow-shaft bent, or curved, at one end, where the craftworker held it. See also *arc-shaped bow.*

'Y'-shaped support A device made from a sturdy forked branch, used in pairs, to support a shipbuilding timber while work was carried out upon it.

BIBLIOGRAPHY

Adams, B., *Predynastic Egypt*, Princes Risborough: Shire Publications, 1988.

Aldred, C., *Egypt to the End of the Old Kingdom*, London: Thames & Hudson, 1965.

Amer, M., 'Annual report of the Maadi excavations, 1930–32', *Bulletin of the Faculty of Arts, Egyptian University*, I, 1933, pp. 322–4.

———— 'Annual report of the Maadi excavations, 1935', *CdÉ* XI, 1936, pp. 54–7, 176–8.

Arnold, D., *The Temple of Mentuhotep at Deir el-Bahari: From the Notes of Herbert Winlock*, New York: Metropolitan Museum of Art, 1979.

———— *Building in Egypt: Pharaonic Stone Masonry*, New York: Oxford University Press, 1991.

Aston, B.G., *Ancient Egyptian Stone Vessels*, Heidelberg: Heidelberger Orientverlag, 1994.

Baumgartel, E.J., *The Cultures of Prehistoric Egypt*, Oxford: Oxford University Press, vol. I, 1955.

Beck, H.C., 'Classification and nomenclature of beads and pendants', *Archaeologia* 77, 1927, p. 77, pls II, III.

———— 'Notes on glazed stones', *Ancient Egypt and the East*, June 1934, pp. 19–37.

Binns, C.F., 'An experiment in Egyptian blue glaze', *Journal of the American Ceramic Society* 15, 1932, pp. 71–2.

Bisson de la Roque, F., 'Trésor de Tôd', in *Catalogue Général des Antiquités Égyptiennes du Musée du Caire*, Cairo: Imprimerie de l'Institut Française d'Archéologie Orientale, 1950.

Blackman, A.M., *The Rock Tombs of Meir*, London: Egypt Exploration Society, 1914.

Blackman, A.M. and Apted, M.R., *The Rock Tombs of Meir*, London: Egypt Exploration Society, part V, 1953.

Boessneck, J. and von den Driesch, A., *Die Tierknochenfunde aus der neolithischen Siedlung von Merimde-Benisalâme am westlichen Nildelta*, Munich: Staatliche Sammlung Ägyptischer Kunst, 1985.

Bomann, A., 'Wadi Abu Had/Wadi Dib', in K.A. Bard (ed.) *Encyclopedia of the Archaeology of Ancient Egypt*, London and New York: Routledge, 1999.

Bomann, A. and Young, R., 'Preliminary survey in the Wadi Abu Had, Eastern Desert, 1992', *JEA* 80, 1994, p. 237, Fig. 2.

Borchardt, L., 'Beiträge zu "GRIFFITH" Benihasan III', *ZÄS* XXXV, 1897, p. 107.

———— 'Ein altägyptisches astronomisches Instrument', *ZÄS* 37, 1899, pp. 10–17.

———— *Das Grabdenkmal des Königs Ne-User-Re*, Leipzig: Hinrichs, 1907.

———— *Das Grabdenkmal des Königs Śa3hu-re*, Leipzig: Hinrichs, vol. I, 1910.

Bovier-Lapierre, P., 'Une nouvelle station néolithique (El Omari) au nord d'Hélouan (Égypte)', *Compte rendu, Congrès International de Géographie* IV, 1926.

Breasted, J.H., *A History of Egypt*, New York: Smith, Elder and Co., 1906.

Bronowski, J., *The Ascent of Man*, London: British Broadcasting Corporation, 1973.

Brunton, G., *Lahun I, The Treasure*, London: British School of Archaeology in Egypt, 1920.

Brunton, G. and Caton-Thompson, G., *Badarian Civilisation and Predynastic Remains Near Badari*, London: British School of Archaeology in Egypt, 1928.

Carnarvon, G.E. and Carter, H., *Five Years' Explorations at Thebes*, London: Egypt Exploration Society, 1912.

Carter, H., 'Report on the tomb of Zeser-Ka-Ra Amenhetep I, discovered by the Earl of Carnarvon in 1914', *JEA* 3, 1916, p. 150.

———— *The Tomb of Tut-Ankh-Amen*, London: Cassell, vol. III, 1933.

Caton-Thompson, G., 'The Neolithic industry of the northern Fayum desert', *JRAI* LVI, 1926, pp. 309–23.

———— 'Recent excavations in the Fayum', *Man* XXVIII, 1928, pp. 109–13.

Caton-Thompson, G. and Gardner, E.W., *The Desert Fayum*, London: The Royal Anthropological Institute of Great Britain and Ireland, 1934.

Cawsey, D.C. and Farrar, N.S., 'A simple sliding apparatus for the measurement of rock joint friction', *Géotechnique* XXVI, June 1976, pp. 382–6.

Černý, J., 'Egypt: From the death of Ramesses III to the end of the Twenty-first Dynasty', in I.E.S. Edwards (ed.) *The Cambridge Ancient History*, Cambridge: Cambridge University Press, vol. II, no. 2, 1975.

Clarke, S. and Engelbach, R., *Ancient Egyptian Masonry*, Oxford: Oxford University Press, 1930.

Coghlan, H.H., *Notes on the Prehistoric Metallurgy of Copper and Bronze in the Old World*, Oxford: Oxford University Press, 1951.

Colson, M.A., 'Sur la fabrication de certains outils métalliques chez les Égyptiens', *ASAÉ* IV, 1903, pp. 190–2.

Costin, C.L., 'Craft specialization: Issues in defining, documenting, and exploring the organization of production', in M. Schiffer (ed.) *Archaeological Method and Theory*, Tucson, AZ: University of Arizona Press, 1991, pp. 1–56.

Coulomb, C.A., *Théorie Des Machines Simples*, Paris: Bachelier, 1821.

Cowell, M., 'The composition of Egyptian copper-based metalwork', in A.R. David (ed.) *Science in Egyptology*, Manchester: Manchester University Press, 1986.

Currelly, C.T., 'Stone implements', *Catalogue Général des Antiquités Égyptiennes du Musée du Caire*, Cairo: Imprimerie de l'Institut Française d'Archéologie Orientale, 1913.

Curry, A., Anfield, C. and Tapp, E., 'The use of the electron microscope in the study of palaeopathology', in A.R. David (ed.) *Science in Egyptology*, Manchester: Manchester University Press, 1986.

Davey, C.J., 'Crucibles in the Petrie Collection and hieroglyphic ideograms for metal', *JEA* 71, 1985, pp. 142–8.

Davies, N. de G., *The Rock Tombs of Deir el Gebrâwi*, London: Egypt Exploration Fund, vols I, II, 1902.

———— *The Tomb of Puyemrê at Thebes*, New York: Metropolitan Museum of Art, vol. I, 1922.

———— *The Tombs of Two Officials of Tuthmosis IV at Thebes*, London: Egypt Exploration Society, vols I, II, 1923.

———— *The Tomb of Two Sculptors at Thebes*, New York: Metropolitan Museum of Art, 1925.

———— *The Tomb of Rekh-mi-Rē' at Thebes*, New York: Metropolitan Museum of Art, vols I, II, 1943.

Debono, F., 'El Omari (près d'Hélouan), exposé sommaire sur les campagnes des fouilles 1943–1944 et 1948', *ASAÉ* 48, 1948, pp. 561–9.

Debono, F. and Mortensen, B., *El Omari: A Neolithic Settlement and Other Sites in the Vicinity of Wadi Hof, Helwan*, Mainz: Philipp von Zabern, 1990.

Duell, P. (ed.), *The Tomb of Mereruka*, Chicago, IL: The Oriental Institute, University of Chicago, vols I, II, 1938.

Edgar, C.C., 'Sculptors' studies and unfinished works', in *Catalogue Général des Antiquités Égyptiennes du Musée du Caire*, Cairo: Imprimerie de l'Institut Française d'Archéologie Orientale, 1906.

Edwards, I.E.S., *The Pyramids of Egypt*, Harmondsworth: Viking, 1986.

Eichholz, D.E., *Pliny Natural History*, London and Cambridge, MA: Harvard University Press, 1962.

Eiwanger, J., *Merimde-Benisalâme*, Mainz: Philipp von Zabern, vols I–III, 1984–1992.

———— 'Merimde Beni-salame', in K.A. Bard (ed.) *Encyclopedia of the Archaeology of Ancient Egypt*, London and New York: Routledge, 1999.

Emery, W.B., *Archaic Egypt*, Harmondsworth: Penguin Books, 1984.

Engelbach, R., *The Problem with the Obelisks*, London: T. Fisher Unwin, 1923.

———— 'Evidence for the use of a mason's pick in Ancient Egypt', *ASAÉ* XXIX, 1929, pp. 19–24.

Fay, B., *Egyptian Museum Berlin*, Berlin-Charlottenburg: Ägyptisches Museum, 1984.

Firth, C.M., Quibell, J.E. and Lauer, J.-P., *The Step Pyramid*, Cairo: Imprimerie de L'Institut Française d'Archéologie Orientale, vols I, II, 1935–1936.

Fisher, M.J. and Fisher, D.E., *Mysteries of Lost Empires*, London: Channel 4 Books, 2000.

Gardiner, A., *Egyptian Grammar*, Oxford: Griffith Institute, Ashmolean Museum, 1976.

Gilmore, G.R., 'The composition of the Kahun metals', in A.R. David (ed.) *Science in Egyptology*, Manchester: Manchester University Press, 1986.

Golden, J., 'The origins of the metals trade in the eastern Mediterranean: Social organisation of production in the early copper industries', in T.E. Levy and E.C.M. van den Brink (eds) *Egypt and the Levant*, London and New York: Leicester University Press, 2002, pp. 225–38.

Goneim, M.Z., *The Buried Pyramid*, London: Longmans, Green and Co., 1956.

Gorelick, L. and Gwinnett, A.J., 'Ancient Egyptian stone drilling: An experimental perspective on a scholarly disagreement', *Expedition* 25 (3), 1983, pp. 40–7.

———— 'Minoan versus Mesopotamian seals: Comparative methods of manufacture', *Iraq* LIV, 1992, p. 62.

Gorringe, H.H., *Egyptian Obelisks*, London: J.C. Nimmo, 1885.

Goyon, G., 'Les instruments de forage sous l'ancien empire Égyptien', *Jahresbericht Ex Oriente Lux* VII, 1967, pl. XXII.

Griffith, F.Ll., *Beni Hasan III*, London: Egypt Exploration Fund, 1896.

Gwinnett, A.J. and Gorelick, L., 'An ancient repair on a Cycladic statuette analysed using scanning electron microscopy', *Journal of Field Archaeology* 10, 1983, pp. 378–84.

Harrell, J.A. and Brown, V.M., *Topographical and Petrological Survey of Ancient Egyptian Quarries*, Toledo, OH: University of Toledo, 1995.

Hartenberg, R.S. and Schmidt, Jr., J., 'The Egyptian drill and the origin of the crank', *Technology and Culture* 10, 1969, pp. 155–65.

Hassan, S., *Excavations at Giza 1930–1931*, Cairo: Government Press, 1936.

Hatton, G.D., Shortland, A.J. and Tite, M.S., 'The production technology of Egyptian blue and green frits from second millennium BC Egypt and Mesopotamia', *Journal of Archaeological Science* 35 (6), 2008, pp. 1591–1604.

Hayes, W.C., *The Scepter of Egypt*, New York: Metropolitan Museum of Art, 1953.

Herodotus, *The Histories Book II*, Harmondsworth: Penguin Books, 1961.

Hill, J., *Theophrastus's 'History of Stones'*, London: J. Hill, 2 books, 1774.

Hoffman, M.A., *Egypt before the Pharaohs: The Prehistoric Foundations of Egyptian Civilization*, London and Henley: Routledge and Kegan Paul, 1980.

Isler, M., 'The curious Luxor obelisks', *JEA* 73, 1987, pp. 137–47.

James, T.G.H., *An Introduction to Ancient Egypt*, London: Book Club Associates, 1979.

Jenkins, N., *The Boat Beneath the Pyramid*, London: Thames & Hudson, 1980.

Junker, H., *Giza*, Vienna and Leipzig: Hinrichs, vol. I, 1929.

———— 'Vorläufiger Bericht über die Grabung der Akademie der Wissenschaften in Wien auf der neolithischen Siedlung von Merimde-Benisalame (Westdelta)', *Anzeiger der Akademie der Wissenschaften in Wien, Philosophische – historische Klasse* XVI–XXVIII, 1929, pp. 156–250; V–XIII, 1930, pp. 21–83; I–IV, 1932, pp. 36–97; XVI–XXVII, 1933, pp. 54–97; X, 1934, pp. 118–32; I–V, 1940, pp. 3–25.

Kaczmarczyk, A. and Hedges, R.E.M., *Ancient Egyptian Faience*, Warminster: Aris and Phillips, 1983.

Kiefer, C. and Allibert, A., 'Les céramiques bleues pharaoniques et leur procéde révolutionnaire d'émaillage', *Industrie Céramique*, May 1968, pp. 395–402.

Klemm D. and Klemm, R., *Die Steine der Pharaonen*, Munich: Staatliche Sammlung Ägyptischer Kunst, 1981.

Köhler, C., 'Theories of state formation', in W. Wendrich (ed.) *Blackwell Studies in Global Archaeology: Egyptian Archaeology*, Chichester: Wiley-Blackwell, 2010.

Lane, M., 'The pull-saw in Egypt', *Ancient Egypt and the East*, June 1935, p. 57.

Lauer, J.-P., *Histoire Monumentale des Pyramides d'Égypte*, Cairo: Imprimerie de l'Institut Française d'Archéologie Orientale, 1962, vol. I, pl. V.

Leek, F.F., 'Teeth and bread in Ancient Egypt', *JEA* 58, 1972, pp. 126–32.

———— 'The dental history of the Manchester mummies', in A.R. David (ed.) *Manchester Museum Mummy Project. Multi-disciplinary Research on Ancient Egyptian Mummified Remains*, Manchester: Manchester University Press, 1979.

Lehner, M., 'Lost city of the pyramids', *Egypt Revealed*, Fall 2000, pp. 42–57.

Lepsius, R., *Die alt-aegyptische Elle*, Berlin: Buchdruckerei der Königl. Akademie der Wissenschaften, 1865.

Lucas, A., *Ancient Egyptian Materials and Industries*, London: Edward Arnold, 1948.

Lucas, A. and Harris, J.R., *Ancient Egyptian Materials and Industries*, London: Edward Arnold, 1962.

Mace, A.C., *Early Dynastic Cemeteries of Naga ed-Dêr*, Los Angeles, CA: University of California Publications, vol. II, 1909.

Mackay, E., 'The cutting and preparation of tomb chapels in the Theban necropolis', *JEA* VII, 1921, pp. 163–4.

———— 'Bead making in ancient Sind', *Journal of the American Oriental Society* 57, 1937, pp. 1–7, pls II, 5, III, 5, 8.

Maddin, R., Stech, T., Muhly, J.D. and Brovarski, E., 'Old Kingdom models from the tomb of Impy: Metallurgical studies', *JEA* 70, 1984, pp. 33–41.

Maréchal, J.R., 'Les outils égyptiens en cuivre', *Métaux, Corrosion, Industries* XXXII, 1957, pp. 132–3.

Mond, R.L. and Myers, O.H., *The Cemeteries of Armant*, London: Egypt Exploration Society, 1937.

Moores, R.G., 'Evidence for use of a stone-cutting drag saw by the Fourth Dynasty Egyptians', *JARCE* 28, 1991, p. 143.

Moorey, P.R.S., *Materials and Manufacture in Ancient Mesopotamia: The Evidence of Archaeology and Art, Metals and Metalwork, Glazed Materials and Glass*, Oxford: British Archaeological Reports, International Series S237, 1985.

Murray, M.A., *Saqqara Mastabas*, London: British School of Archaeology in Egypt, vol. I, 1905.

Naville, E., 'Excavations at Henassieh (Hanes)', *Egypt Exploration Fund Special Extra Report*, 1891, pp. 8, 9.

―――― *Cemeteries of Abydos*, London: Egypt Exploration Society, vol. I, 1914.

Newberry, P.E., *El-Bersheh*, London: Egypt Exploration Fund, 1895.

―――― *The Life of Rekhmara*, London: Archibald Constable, 1900.

Nibbi, A., 'Some remarks on copper', *JARCE* XIV, 1977, pp. 59–66.

Nicholson, P.T., *Egyptian Faience and Glass*, Princes Risborough: Shire Publications Ltd, 1993.

―――― 'Faience', in Donald B. Redford (ed.) *The Oxford Encyclopedia of Ancient Egypt*, Oxford: Oxford University Press, 2001, vol. I.

Nicholson, P.T. and Peltenburg, E.J., 'Egyptian faience', in P.T. Nicholson and I. Shaw (eds) *Ancient Egyptian Materials and Technology*, Cambridge: Cambridge University Press, 2000.

Noble, J.V., 'The technique of Egyptian faience', *American Journal of Archaeology* 73, 1969, pp. 435–9.

Pearson, C.E. and Smythe, J.A., 'Examination of a Roman chisel from Chesterholm', *Proceedings of the University of Durham Philosophical Society* 9 (3), 1938, pp. 141–5.

Peet, T.E., *Cemeteries of Abydos, Part II, 1911–1912*, London: Egypt Exploration Society, 1914.

Petrie, W.M.F., *The Pyramids and Temples of Gizeh*, London: Field and Tuer, 1883.

―――― 'On the mechanical methods of the Ancient Egyptians', *JRAI* 13, 1884, p. 93.

―――― *Kahun, Gurob and Hawara*, London: Kegan Paul, Trench, Trübner, and Co., 1890.

―――― *Illahun, Kahun and Gurob*, London: David Nutt, 1891.

―――― *Tell el-Amarna*, London: Methuen, 1894.

―――― *Deshasheh*, London: Egypt Exploration Fund, 1898.

―――― *Royal Tombs of the Earliest Dynasties*, London: Egypt Exploration Fund, vols I, II, 1900–1901.

―――― *Researches in Sinai*, New York: E.P. Dutton, 1906.

―――― *The Arts and Crafts of Ancient Egypt*, Edinburgh and London: T.N. Foulis, 1909.

―――― *Tools and Weapons*, London: British School of Archaeology in Egypt, 1917.

―――― *Social Life in Ancient Egypt*, London: British School of Archaeology in Egypt, 1923.

―――― 'The building of a pyramid', *AE* II, 1930, p. 34.

―――― *The Funeral Furniture of Egypt [and] Stone and Metal Vases*, London: British School of Archaeology in Egypt, 1937.

―――― *Egyptian Architecture*, London: British School of Archaeology in Egypt, 1938.

Petrie, W.M.F., Brunton, G. and Murray, M.A., *Lahun II, The Pyramid*, London: British School of Archaeology in Egypt, 1923.

Petrie, W.M.F., Wainwright, G.A. and Mackay, E., *The Labyrinth Gerzeh and Mazghuneh*, London: Bernard Quaritch, 1912.

Quibell, J.E., 'Stone vessels from the step pyramid', *ASAÉ* 35, 1935.

Quibell, J.E. and Green, F.W., *Hierakonpolis II*, London: British School of Archaeology in Egypt, 1902.

Reisner, G.A., *Early Dynastic Cemeteries of Naga ed-Dêr*, Los Angeles, CA: University of California Publications, vol. I, 1908.

———— *Excavations at Kerma*, Cambridge, MA: Peabody Museum of Harvard University, 1923.

———— *Mycerinus, the Temples of the Third Pyramid at Giza*, Cambridge, MA: Harvard University Press, 1931.

Rickard, T.A., *Man and Metals*, New York: Arno Press, vol. I, 1932.

Riederer, J., 'Metal analysis of Egyptian bronzes', *RAS* 3, 1981, pp. 239–43.

Rizkana, I. and Seeher, J., *Maadi III: The Non-Lithic Small Finds and the Structural Remains of the Prehistoric Settlement*, Mainz: Phillip von Zabern, 1989.

Röder, J., 'Steinbruchgeschichte des Rosengranits von Assuan', *Archäologischer Anzeiger* 3, 1965, pp. 461–551.

Rothenberg, B., 'Excavations at Timna Site 39. A chalcolithic copper smelting site and furnace and its metallurgy', *Archaeo Metallurgy* Monograph Number 1, 1978, p. 11, Fig. 11.

———— 'Pharaonic copper mines in south Sinai', in *Institute for Archaeo-Metallurgical Studies*, London: Institute of Archaeology, University College London, 10/11 (June/December), 1987, p. 4.

Said, R., *The Geological Evolution of the River Nile*, New York: Springer-Verlag, 1981.

Sebilian, J., 'Early copper and its alloys', *AE*, March 1924, p. 8.

Seeher, J., *Gedanken zur Rolle Unterägyptens bei der Heraus-bildung des Pharaonenreiches*, Abteilung Kairo: Mitteilungen des Deutschen Archäologische Instituts, vol. 47, 1991.

Seton Karr, M.H.W., 'How the tomb galleries at Thebes were cut and the limestone quarried', *ASAÉ* VI, 1905, pp. 176–84.

Shaw, I., Bloxam, E., Bunbury, J., Lee, R., Graham, A. and Darnell, D., 'Survey and excavation at the Gebel el-Asr gneiss and quartz quarries in Lower Nubia (1997–2000)', *Antiquity* 75, 2001, pp. 33–4.

Shaw, J.W., 'Minoan architecture: Materials and techniques', *Annuario della Scuola Archeologica di Atene* 49, 1971, pp. 69–70, Figs 61–3.

Shepherd, W., *Flint: Its Origin, Properties and Uses*, London: Faber, 1972.

Simpson, W.K. (ed.), *The Literature of Ancient Egypt*, New Haven, CT and London: Yale University Press, 1972.

Snape, S.R. and Tyldesley, J.A., 'Two Egyptian flint knapping scenes', *Lithics* 4, 1983, pp. 46–7.

Spencer, A.J., *Death in Ancient Egypt*, Harmondsworth: Penguin Books, 1982.

Spurrell, F.C.J., 'The stone implements of Kahun', in W.M.F. Petrie (ed.) *Illahun, Kahun and Gurob*, London: David Nutt, 1891.

Steindorff, G., *Das Grab des Ti*, Leipzig: Hinrichs, 1913.

Stocks, D.A., 'The working of wood and stone in Ancient Egypt: The experimental manufacture and use of copper, bronze and stone tools', unpublished dissertation, University of Manchester, 1982.

———— 'Bead production in Ancient Egypt', *Popular Archaeology* 7 (5), 1986, pp. 2–7.

———— 'Sticks and stones of Egyptian technology', *Popular Archaeology* 7 (3), 1986, pp. 24–9.

———— 'Stone vessel manufacture', *Popular Archaeology* 7 (4), 1986, pp. 14–18.

———— 'Tools of the ancient craftsman', *Popular Archaeology* 7 (6), 1986, pp. 25–9.

———— 'Experimental stone block fitting techniques: Proposed use of a replica Ancient Egyptian tool', *The Manchester Archaeological Bulletin* 2, 1987, pp. 42–50.

———— 'Industrial technology at Kahun and Gurob: Experimental manufacture and test of replica and reconstructed tools with indicated uses and effects upon artefact production', unpublished thesis, University of Manchester, vols I, II, 1988.

———— 'Ancient factory mass-production techniques: Indications of large-scale stone bead manufacture during the Egyptian New Kingdom period', *Antiquity* 63, 1989, pp. 526–31.

———— 'Indications of Ancient Egyptian industrial interdependence: A preliminary statement', *The Manchester Archaeological Bulletin* 4, 1989, pp. 21–6.

———— 'Making stone vessels in ancient Mesopotamia and Egypt', *Antiquity* 67, 1993, pp. 596–603.

———— 'Technology and the reed', *The Manchester Archaeological Bulletin* 8, 1993, pp. 58–68.

———— 'Derivation of Ancient Egyptian faience core and glaze materials', *Antiquity* 71, 1997, pp. 179–82.

———— 'Stone sarcophagus manufacture in Ancient Egypt', *Antiquity* 73, 1999, pp. 918–22.

———— 'Roman stoneworking methods in the eastern desert of Egypt', in N.J. Higham (ed.) *The Archaeology of the Roman Empire: A Tribute to the Life and Works of Professor Barri Jones*, Oxford: Archaeopress, 2001.

———— 'Testing Ancient Egyptian granite-working methods in Aswan, Upper Egypt', *Antiquity* 75, 2001, pp. 89–94.

———— 'Technical and material interrelationships: Implications for social change in Ancient Egypt', in W. Wendrich and G. van der Kooij (eds) *Moving Matters: Ethnoarchaeology in the Near East. Proceedings of the International Seminar held at Cairo, 7–10 December 1998*, Leiden: Leiden University, 2002.

———— *Experiments in Egyptian Archaeology: Stoneworking Technology in Ancient Egypt*, London and New York: Routledge, 2003.

———— 'Immutable laws of friction: Preparing and fitting stone blocks into the Great Pyramid of Giza', *Antiquity* 77, 2003, pp. 572–8.

———— 'Auf den Spuren von Cheops Handwerkern', *Sokar* 10 (1), 2005, p. 49.

———— 'Technology innovators of Ancient Egypt. Part One: The wonders of Egypt grew from stone age roots', *Ancient Egypt* 7 (3), December 2006/January 2007, pp. 37–43.

———— 'Technology innovators of Ancient Egypt. Part Two: Over millennia, an organized army of skilled workers completed many difficult tasks for their pharaohs', *Ancient Egypt* 7 (5), April/May 2007, pp. 44–51.

———— 'Technology innovators of Ancient Egypt. Part Three: During the long Dynastic period, craftworkers developed intriguing strategies for increasing artifact production', *Ancient Egypt* 8 (1), August/September 2007, pp. 37–43.

———— 'Werkzeugkonstrukteure im Alten Ägypten', *Sokar* 15 (2), 2007, pp. 74–81.

———— 'Das Bewegen schwerer Steinobjekte im Alten Ägypten: Experimente in der Ebene und auf geneigten Flächen', *Sokar* 18 (1), 2009, pp. 38–43.

———— *Experiments in Egyptian Archaeology: Stoneworking Technology in Ancient Egypt*, London and New York: Routledge, 2010.

———— 'Stoneworking, pharaonic Egypt', in *Encyclopedia of Ancient History*, Oxford and New York: Blackwell Publishing Ltd, 2013.

———— 'Making Khufu's granite sarcophagus', *Ancient Egypt* 14 (2), 2013, pp. 26–32.

———— 'Some Experiments in Ancient Egyptian stone technology', in C. Graves-Brown (ed.) *Swansea Conference – Experiment and Experience: Ancient Egypt in the Present*, Swansea: Classical Press of Wales, 2015, pp. 173–99.

———— 'Scientific evaluation of experiments in Egyptian archaeology', in C. Price, *et al* (eds) *Mummies, Magic and Medicine in Ancient Egypt: Multidisciplinary Essays for Rosalie David*, Manchester: Manchester University Press, 2016.

———— 'Interrelationships between significant tools and technologies developed in Ancient Egypt: Indications of an adeptly organized, expanding industrial economy, which influenced the direction, pace and structure of social evolution', Doctor of Letters thesis, University of Manchester, 2018.

———— 'The materials, tools, and work of carving and painting', in D. Laboury and V. Davies (eds) *The Oxford Handbook of Egyptian Epigraphy and Palaeography*, Oxford: Oxford University Press, 2020.

Stone, J.F.S. and Thomas, L.C., 'The use and distribution of faience in the ancient East and prehistoric Europe', *Proceedings of the Prehistoric Society* 22, 1956, pp. 37ff.

Täckholm, V. and Täckholm, G., *Flora of Egypt*, Königstein: Otto Koeltz Antiquariat, vol. I, 1973.

Teeter, E., 'Techniques and terminology of rope-making in Ancient Egypt', *JEA* 73, 1987, pp. 71–7, pls VII, 3, VIII, 1, 2, IX.

Tillmann, A., 'Dynastic stone tools', in K.A. Bard (ed.) *Encyclopedia of the Archaeology of Ancient Egypt*, London and New York: Routledge, 1999.

Timoshenko, S. and Young, D.H., *Engineering Mechanics*, Tokyo: McGraw-Hill Kogakusha Ltd, 1956.

Tite, M.S., 'Egyptian blue, faience and related materials: Technological investigations', in R.E. Jones and H.W. Catling (eds) *Science in Archaeology*, London: British School at Athens, vol. 2, 1986.

———— 'Characterisation of early vitreous materials', *Archaeometry* 29, 1987, pp. 23–4.

Tite, M.S. and Bimson, M., 'Faience: An investigation of the microstructures associated with the different methods of glazing', *Archaeometry* 28, 1986, p. 69.

Tite, M.S., Manti, P. and Shortland, A.J., 'A technological study of ancient faience from Egypt', *Journal of Archaeological Science* 34 (10), 2007, pp. 1568–83.

Tite, M.S. and Shortland, A.J., *Production Technology of Faience and Related Early Vitreous Materials*, Oxford: Oxford University School of Archaeology, 2008.

Tylecote, R.F., *Metallurgy in Archaeology*, London: Edward Arnold, 1962.

Tylecote, R.F. and Boydell, P.J., 'Experiments on copper smelting based on early furnaces found at Timna', *Archaeo Metallurgy* Monograph Number 1, 1978, pp. 27–51.

Vandiver, P.B., 'Technological change in Egyptian faience', in J.S. Olin and A.D. Franklin (eds) *Archaeological Ceramics*, Washington, DC: Smithsonian Institution Press, 1982.

———— 'Appendix A: The manufacture of faience', in A. Kaczmarczyk and R.E.M. Hedges (eds) *Ancient Egyptian Faience*, Warminster: Aris and Phillips, 1983.

Vandiver, P.B. and Kingery, W.D., 'Egyptian faience: The first high-tech ceramic', in W.D. Kingery (ed.) *Ceramics and Civilization*, Westerville, OH: American Ceramic Society, vol. 3, 1986.

Vattenbyggnadsbyrån (VBB), *The Salvage of the Abu Simbel Temples, Concluding Report – December 1971*, Stockholm: Vattenbyggnadsbyrån, 1971.

Warren, P.M., *Minoan Stone Vases*, Cambridge: Cambridge University Press, 1969.

———— 'The unfinished red marble jar at Akroteri, Thera', *Thera and the Aegean World* I, 1978, p. 564.

Weinstein, J., 'A Fifth Dynasty reference to annealing', *JARCE* XI, 1974, pp. 23–5.

Wild, H., *Le Tombeau de Ti*, Cairo: Government Press, vol. III, 1953.

Woodford, C., 'Static electricity', 2012/2018. Retrieved from: www.explainthatstuff.com/how-static-electricity-works.html [Accessed November 2020].

Woolley, C.L., *Ur Excavations*, Oxford: The Trustees of the British Museum and the Museum of the University of Pennsylvania, Philadelphia, PA, vol. II, 1934.

———— *Ur Excavations*, Oxford: The Trustees of the British Museum and the Museum of the University of Pennsylvania, Philadelphia, PA, vol. IV, 1955.

Wreszinski, W., *Atlas zur altägyptischen Kulturgeschichte*, Leipzig: Hinrichs, vols I, II, 1923.

Zuber, A., 'Techniques du travail des pierres dures dans l'Ancienne Égypte', *Techniques et Civilisations* 30, 1956, pp. 195–215.

INDEX

Note: Page numbers in *italics* indicate a figure and page numbers in **bold** indicate a table on the corresponding page.

9781032217666